THEATRES

AN ILLUSTRATED HISTORY

Simon Tidworth

THEATRES

AN ILLUSTRATED HISTORY

Pall Mall Press

THE PALL MALL PRESS
5 CROMWELL PLACE, LONDON SW7

FIRST PUBLISHED 1973
© 1973 BY THE PALL MALL PRESS
ISBN 0 269 02833 1

PRINTED IN GREAT BRITAIN BY THE GARDEN CITY PRESS LIMITED

CONTENTS

We are told that Epimenides—the same that slept fifty-seven years in a cave—when the Athenians were building a place for public shows, reproved them, telling them: You know not how much mischief this place will occasion; if you did, you would pull it to pieces with your teeth.

Alberti, *Ten Books on Architecture*,
translated in 1726 by James Leoni.

I

GREEK DRAMA:
THE RITUAL ENTERTAINMENT

Architecture and drama are sister arts, but like most sisters they fail to bring out the best in each other. Indeed by the end of this book it might seem that they have been deliberately avoiding each other's company. The great formative minds of drama—the Greek playwrights, the authors of the Miracle Plays, Shakespeare, Lope de Vega, Molière, Corneille, Racine—were all happy enough with the barest necessities of performance. Ibsen and Chekhov asked for little more. Strindberg's preferred 'intimate theatre' was an ordinary room. And conversely, those theatres of most architectural interest—Greek theatres of 300–100 BC, Roman theatres from AD 100–300, the theatres of Renaissance Italy and of Europe and America between 1700 and 1875—all belong to periods when the art of drama was at a low ebb.

Are theatres, in fact, judged primarily in functional terms? The ways in which each successive architectural style has tackled the problem of seating a large number of people in comfort facing a stage are in themselves of considerable interest. Should we ask for anything more? What has the relationship been between the theatre as architecture and the living drama of its time? In a general way, of course, the form of drama has determined the form of theatre. But in any particular instance it is clear that the form of theatre has normally conditioned the form of drama. Only very occasionally have dramatists insisted on a change in theatre design in order that their works may be more efficiently performed. Wagner is the most obvious example. Far more often they have written, as a matter of course, to fit the performing conditions of their time. The two really revolutionary periods of change in the history of European theatres—in the Renaissance and now in the mid-twentieth century—have come, as far as one can judge, through the insistence of patrons, producers, theorists, actors, even architects. The cry for new theatres in which to perform a new drama has been raised before there was any new drama to perform.

The three 'beginnings' of European drama offer an intriguing series of parallels. In ancient Greece, in the early Middle Ages and in the Renaissance, one sees physical settings for drama being evolved simply so that large numbers of people can participate in the same event. In each case, these physical settings generated conventions which the audiences accepted but which in turn began to modify the event that they had come to witness. Imperceptibly they placed a gulf between the audience and the event, in the sense that the stage became increasingly a world of its own, governed by its own laws. When a new form of drama, with a different physical setting, took the place of the old, the relationship between audience and event was re-established in a new way. At present, the theatre finds itself in a strange half-way position, anxious to preserve the repertory of the past, searching for new conventions, trying to decide what kind of architecture, if any, is suited to its needs, hankering after the ritual of earlier periods but unable to break free from the demands of entertainment. What, indeed, is the ritual aspect of drama? How did it arise? Can it be recaptured?

The great festival of Dionysus at Athens (the City Dionysia) took place at the end of March and the beginning of April. The first two days were devoted to processions, sacrifices and hymns; the third to comedies; the fourth, fifth and sixth to tragedies (a trilogy plus a satyr play each day); and the festival ended on the seventh. Plays were chosen several months in advance. The successful authors were allocated a patron (a wealthy man who paid for the production), actors and chorus, and at the end of the festival a prize was awarded for the best comedy and the best tragedy. We have long lists of these prizewinning plays, but only a handful actually survive: seven by Aeschylus, seven by Sophocles, eighteen by Euripides and eleven by Aristophanes. Upon these few texts, the writings of commentators like Aristotle, Pollux and Plutarch, and the remains of the theatres themselves, our whole knowledge of Greek drama has to be based.

Drama had begun only a generation or so earlier. It had developed from ceremonies performed in honour of Dionysus, involving odes sung by a dancing chorus dressed as animals, maenads or satyrs. Gradually they took in more and more mythological material (stories about Dionysus himself were supplemented by stories about other heroes such as Theseus, Jason and Prometheus) and the chorus leader came to be the performer of semi-dramatic monologues in which he assumed the character of the hero.

As time went on the ritual features were given less prominence than the dialogue and mime which carried the story along, but they remained present until the very end. Most Greek tragedies centred round an altar; the chorus remained on stage throughout the action, singing invocations to the gods and commenting on the plot from a moral and religious point of view; and each trilogy of serious plays ended with a satyr play in which the origins of the drama in a rustic fertility celebration were easily recognizable.

Technically, the form inherited (and probably largely created) by Aeschylus was taken over without much change by his successors. It was analysed in his usual methodical way by Aristotle in the *Poetics*. In Aeschylus' time all stage conversations were literally dialogues—only two characters appeared on stage at the same time; Sophocles added a third (comedy was more liberal in this respect). The action represented was supposed to take only as long as the play itself and the place normally remained the same throughout, although here again, comedy was much freer. Violence and death always took place off-stage and were described to the audience by a messenger. Strangest of all to a modern playgoer would have been the convention by which all the characters were masked and wore false shoes to make them appear taller. Masks and costumes made it easy for the audience to tell what sort of character was being represented [Pl. 1]. Pollux, writing in the second century AD, describes forty-four comic masks and twenty-three tragic ones. Nothing like naturalistic acting was attempted. In the large open-air spaces of Greek theatres (which were built to hold practically the whole population of a city) this would have been impossible anyway. Masks, costume, movement and language were all stylized, giving the dramatic poet freedom only within quite narrow limits. Even so, the three playwrights whose work has survived were notably individual in their approach—Aeschylus (525–456 BC) used the dramatic form to examine the rules by which men should live with each other and with the gods; Sophocles (496–406 BC) found wisdom through suffering by the acceptance of an implacable destiny; while Euripides (485–406 BC) was more interested in psychological observation and the portrayal of ordinary human beings in situations of stress.

It must always be remembered that the surviving buildings are all later than the surviving plays. Aeschylus' own theatre was almost certainly of wood. The original acting and dancing area (the *orchēstra*) was simply a circle cut into the hillside, surrounded on three sides by tiers of seats. By the time of Sophocles and Euripides this circle was probably reserved for the chorus, while the actors stood behind it, possibly on a slightly raised platform (this point is still in dispute). There was no scenery, but there must have been a few props (tombs, altars, etc.) and some sort of

Pls. 1, 2. The great age of Greek drama was the fifth century BC, but of theatres and conditions of performance at that time almost no visual evidence survives. Our earliest clues belong to the following century. Left: a costumed actor holding his mask, from a painted vase. Right: another vase fragment showing part of a wooden skēnē *built behind the* orchēstra—*a far less substantial building than we see later, but lavishly decorated with entablature and acroteria. There would have been another pedimented porch* (paraskenios) *on the right.*

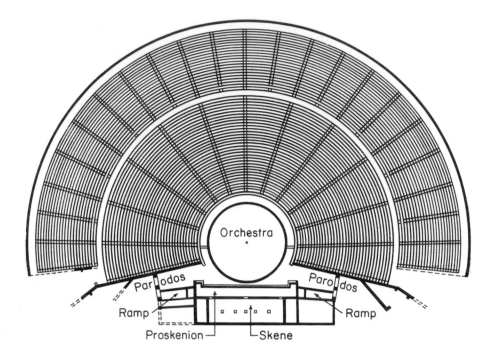

Orchestra

Par|odos   Paro|dos

Ramp   Ramp

Proskenion—   └Skene

Pls. 3, 4. The most complete Greek theatre, and the only one to preserve any real semblance of those used by Aeschylus, Sophocles and Euripides, is that of Epidauros, near Athens, built about 350 BC. The oldest feature is the orchēstra, the round dancing floor of the chorus. There was probably some form of skēnē, but the present remains do not enable us to reconstruct it. The plan (left) shows the theatre as it looked in the second century BC with a permanent skēnē, a stage (proskenion, i.e. in front of the skēnē) and ramps leading up to it.

mechanical devices for apparitions and furies. Somewhere at the back was a place for the actors to prepare—originally, it seems, a tent (the root meaning of the Greek *skēnē*), then a wooden hut and later—how much later we do not know—a stone building [Pl. 2]. The area between this changing room and the *orchēstra* (in front of the *skēnē*, *pro-skenion*) was what was to become the stage.

The only site to preserve these early arrangements in clearly recognizable form is Epidauros, in the Argolis, which, according to Pausanias (writing in the second century AD), was designed by the architect Polycleitus, and which would therefore date from the middle of the fourth century BC. 'The Epidaurians', he says, 'have within their sanctuary a theatre that in my opinion is specially worth seeing. Those of the Romans surpass all others in decoration, and that of the Arcadians at Megalopolis is of unequalled size; but what architect could rival Polycleitus as regards harmony and beauty? For it was Polycleitus who built both the theatre and the *tholos*.'

This dating may be accepted, although like most other dates in classical archaeology it is open to challenge. The sanctuary of Epidauros was one of the richest and grandest in Greece, and neither the scale nor the technical quality of the present remains were beyond the abilities of the period. It was remodelled in the second century, however, and the task of deciding which particular features belong to the original and which to the remodelled theatre is by no means simple.

The auditorium is certainly the original one [Pl. 4]. Nearly 400 feet in diameter, taking up slightly more than a half-circle, it climbs up the hillside in a total of fifty-five steps, each one a row of seats. Roughly half-way up it is divided by a horizontal aisle. The front half consists of twelve sections of thirty-four rows, while the back has twenty-two sections of twenty-one rows, with staircases between the sections. The slope gets steeper above the dividing aisle and the seats higher, so that those at the back had a clear view (at the front, each row is thirteen inches above its neighbour, at the back, seventeen inches). The whole theatre could accommodate 14,000 spectators.

The plan of the auditorium makes it clear that the whole focus is upon the *orchēstra*, the circular dancing space in the centre, rather than upon the stage behind it [Pl. 3]. It is almost a theatre-in-the-round, sixty-seven feet in diameter and outlined by a white limestone border. In the centre is a small stone which probably marks the site of an altar.

Behind this *orchēstra* was the back wall of the *skēnē* (the actors' room), whose original appearance has to be reconstructed from very scanty evidence. It was probably flanked by side rooms (*paraskenia*) built not exactly in line with it but turned slightly towards the audience. Behind the *skēnē* (and forming part of it) was a hall sixty-four feet long, resembling a *stoa*, or open-air meeting place, and this was in fact probably the equivalent of the present-day foyer. Like all Greek theatres, that of Epidauros stood in a sacred precinct. Its *stoa* formed a link between the parts of the precinct, rather like the cloister of a monastery.

The second-century reconstruction made radical changes, alterations which were invariable in all Greek theatres at this time and which were demanded by the changes in the conventions of drama. The back wall, from now on referred to in its own right as the *skēnē*, was gradually becoming more and more important until it constituted a permanent architectural set. It had three entries, those on the left and right conventionally standing for the city and the country and the central one for a palace or temple. Characters could stand on the top of the *skēnē* as watchmen on towers, or as people appearing at upper windows. There may also have been objects described by Vitruvius and Pollux as *periaktoi*. They were wooden posts, triangular in section, which could be revolved, presenting three different surfaces to the audience. These surfaces were painted to show the country, the sea-shore, the clouds, etc., and were clearly meant to indicate to the audience the setting of the play. No feature of the ancient theatre has given rise to so much dispute as these *periaktoi*. Where could they possibly have been placed? They seem totally pointless as scenery in the modern sense, since the three doors of the *skēnē* clearly remained visible throughout the play, and anyway the scene in classical plays nearly always remains the same. Professor Beare is surely right in his surmise that they stood next to the side entrances and served to tell the audience where these exits were supposed to lead—whether to the harbour, the forum, the countryside, etc. They may also have been used to herald the approach of gods on the stage, by showing pictures of the sky. The only traces of *periaktoi* that have been found are a few post-holes, and the mystery will probably never be finally solved.

During this period at Epidauros the stage (*proskenion*) was raised and a more elaborate architectural background built behind it. The old *paraskenia* disappeared under two ramps by which the actors ascended the new stage. At the end of the ramps two imposing gateways were built, each with twin openings—one leading to the *orchēstra* and the auditorium, the other to the stage [Pl. 5]. The old *orchēstra*, however, was allowed to remain, and the only other concession to the new style of performance seems to have been the removal of the seats of honour from the front row next to the *orchēstra* to the front row of the upper range, where presumably a better view could be gained of the higher stage.

The stage buildings, both original and remodelled, are in ruins, but much of the rest is excellently preserved, the only substantial modern restorations being to the two ends of the auditorium and the two gates. The theatre is as serviceable now as it was over 2,000 years ago. Regular performances of classical plays have been given there every summer since 1954.

Epidauros gives us today our most complete picture of the classical theatre, but of course it was neither the earliest nor the most important.

Pl. 5. Right: one of the restored gateways (paradoi) at Epidauros. The right hand opening led into the orchēstra, the left to the ramp leading to the proskenion.

Pl. 7. *The theatre at Syracuse, as at Athens, has been much altered since classical times. The* orchēstra *would originally have been a complete circle, as at Epidauros. Like nearly all Greek theatres, the auditorium is cut in a natural hollow in the rock.*

Pl. 6. *Left: the theatre of Dionysus at Athens. The semi-circle of seats, though enlarged at various periods, is the original one from which the first spectators watched the Oresteia. The stage area, however, (out of sight on the right) was altered beyond recognition in Hellenistic and Roman times. At the back rise the retaining walls of the Acropolis.*

The fountainhead was Athens. It was here, it seems, that the crucial decision was made to transfer the Dionysian dance from the *agora* (the market-place) to the hillside of the Acropolis, and to lay stone foundations [Pl. 6]. The date was just before 500 BC and the reason given by tradition was severely practical: the wooden stands built in the *agora* for one of the festivals had collapsed, and the neighbouring hillside offered a stable and convenient auditorium. The site was already sacred to Dionysus, a temple dedicated to him having existed there from at least the second half of the sixth century. This may fairly count as being the first theatre in the world. The benches were of wood and the rows of seats not nearly so tidily arranged as later theatres would suggest (excavations at another Greek town, Thoricus, on the east coast, of about the same date, have revealed a flattened semi-circle with irregular sides and an uneven slope). But it was here that the plays of Aeschylus were first produced and European drama began.

Probably towards the end of the fifth century it was replaced by a more elaborate structure in which all of the features noted in the first theatre of Epidauros were already present The *orchēstra* circle was moved about twenty feet closer to the hillside, the dug-out earth being piled at the top of the slope to provide more seats at the back. The rows were made semi-circular as far as possible (the back rows could never be complete because of the nature of the site). The *skēnē*, as at Epidauros, was formed by the back wall of a portico over 200 feet long which faced the precinct of Dionysus on the other side. What sort of raised platform there was, if any, between this wall and the *orchēstra*, and how much movable scenery could be fitted against it are questions that are still being debated.

Outside Greece, in Sicily, the theatre at Syracuse, dating in its present form from the third century BC, also preserves its auditorium intact, hollowed out of the gently rising rock [Pl. 7]. Syracuse was second only to Athens as a dramatic centre. It was while on a professional visit here that Aeschylus' unlucky death was caused when an eagle dropped a tortoise on his head.

It was probably comedy rather than tragedy that stimulated most of the developments in staging. Greek Old Comedy is in some ways easier for modern playgoers to take than tragedy. Easier because we are definitely in the world of ordinary men—the cynical, selfish, down-to-earth citizens of Athens—yet also harder because the form is more complex and the humour so topical.

Choruses with animal masks are known from vase-paintings of the sixth century and were, as we have seen, connected with the origins of drama [Pl. 8]. They play a main part in three plays by Aristophanes, the only comic writer whose works have survived. His plays seem like combinations of *opera buffa* and satirical review, with a dash of pantomime. The satire is mostly political (Aristophanes supported the peace party in Athens which was trying to end the war with Sparta) or literary; he was particularly addicted to making fun of Euripides. The setting is often fantastic—'Cloud-Cuckoo Land' or 'the road to Hades'; and even when confined to the real world his plays have the flavour of impossibility, as in the *Lysistrata*, where all the women of Athens refuse to sleep with their husbands until they have ended the war.

Two stage devices that were certainly in use by the time of Euripides and Aristophanes were the *eccyclema* and the 'flying machine'. The first was a means of pushing forward the props of an indoor scene from within the central doorway to a position in full view of the audience. Some such action is assumed, for instance, in *Hippolytus*, where Phaedra does not walk on to the stage but is 'discovered' lying on a bed. Flying machines were used for the ascent and descent of gods and goddesses, and by Euripides with notable effect for the final exit of Medea in a winged chariot. In Aristophanes' *The Peace*, a character is carried up to heaven on a beetle. Some sort of crane was obviously involved, but the exact method is impossible to reconstruct.

The deaths of Euripides and Sophocles in the same year (406 BC) mark a break in the history of drama. The old religious tragedy was dead, killed as

Pl. 8. Vases of the sixth century BC show scenes of dancing men dressed as birds. Nothing is known about these dances, nor how they could have evolved, by the middle of the fifth century, into the choruses of the Aristophanic Comedy. Yet such an evolution certainly took place.

Pl. 9. Some idea of how the New Comedy looked in performance can be gleaned from Pompeiian wall-paintings, which copied lost Greek paintings. Here, an old slave mocks two lovers.

much by the psychological preoccupations given to it by Euripides as by the laughter of parodists like Aristophanes. There are no more surviving Greek tragedies. They went on being written but, if one may guess from vase-paintings and descriptions, they tended more and more towards sensationalism. Comedy, too, suffered a transformation. Aristophanic satire stopped, partly for political reasons, and its place was taken by the innocuous 'New Comedy', whose only representative—with one complete play, a few more that can be patched together and a string of fragments—is Menander (c. 342–291).

New Comedy developed more from the lighter plays of Euripides (such as *Iphigenia in Tauris* or the lost *Antigone*) than from the Old Comedy. The chorus disappears altogether. So do the gods, mythology and contemporary politics. Athens, quietly subservient to Macedonian rulers, amused itself with sentimental romances about parted lovers, clever slaves, angry old men, misers and cuckolds [Pl. 9].

Between 340 and 326 BC, the theatre at Athens was rebuilt again to conform to the demands of the New Comedy. The auditorium was enlarged and a new single storey *skēnē* was built. The action was transferred from the space in front of the *skēnē* to the top of it, and a new upper *skēnē* was built as the background to the new stage. (During the reign of Nero, to finish this particular story, it underwent a further transformation, with a lower stage brought forward towards the auditorium, covering part of the old *orchēstra*. Finally, about AD 270, the stage buildings were rebuilt yet again, and much of the earlier decoration placed in new positions. The eventual height of the stage was a mere four and a half feet.)

By one of those frustrating accidents that often beset literary history, it is only now, when the stream of plays dries up, that we begin to be well informed about the theatres. Hellenistic theatres of the third and second centuries BC survive in quantity and in good preservation. There are also large numbers of scenes represented on vases, though that evidence requires careful interpretation. But no plays.

It is clear, however, that theatre architecture had lost most of its early religious connotations and had become completely secular. The acting area tended to be raised and isolated from the *orchēstra*, which diminished in importance and was already being invaded by seats. Old theatres no doubt continued to be used, though often with alterations, side by side with new ones, so that even in Menander's time plays were probably acted in one city in the *orchēstra*, in the old style, and in another on the high *proskenion*, in the new. On these new raised stages painted scenery was almost certainly used as a background.

Some of the theatres of the Greek colonies, in Asia Minor, the Aegean Islands and Sicily, provide evocative pictures of what Epidauros, Syracuse and Athens must have looked like in Hellenistic times. The theatre at Priene, originally one of the earlier type, was among the first to be

Pls. 10, 11.   The Hellenistic theatre of the second century BC presented a picture in many ways different from that of classical times. These illustrations show the theatre at Priene, a Greek colony in Asia Minor, as it now is and as it probably looked in its prime. Most of the action took place on the upper stage, though the orchēstra *could still be used when necessary. Bolt-holes in the row of columns in the front prove that wooden panels were fixed between them, and it has been plausibly suggested that these were sections of painted scenery.*

remodelled [Pl. 11]. At first the new high stage was of wood, but by about 200 BC this was made permanent by a stone structure, much of which remains [Pl. 10]. It consisted of a long building two storeys high; at the first floor level a platform, the *proskenion*, projected, supported on a row of columns. The actors could use either the ground level or the raised stage—probably both, depending on the type of play. The columns at ground level are actually demi-columns attached to square piers and in these piers have been found bolt-holes, as if for securing wooden panels. It has been plausibly suggested that these were painted and changed according to the setting of the play. At Delos, the *proskenion* colonnade was carried right round all four sides of the stage building, like a Greek temple without its pediments. The architectural treatment of these colonnades, and of the upper stage background, was getting steadily richer and more elaborate. At Pergamon, however, the steep site made it necessary for the stage to overlap a terrace leading to the temple of Dionysus (later rededicated to Caracalla) [Pl. 13]. It was therefore impossible to build a permanent *skēnē* and it seems that for every dramatic festival a temporary wooden structure was erected and then dismantled. Segesta, on the other hand, in the early first century BC, probably had a stone *skēnē* which was itself two-storeyed,

Pl. 12.   The theatre at Segesta, Sicily (reconstructed below), of about 100 BC, was a Greek theatre more than half-way to becoming Roman. The skēnē *retains its tripartite division but has grown into an elaborate palace façade. Gods appeared on the upper storey.*

Pl. 13.   *The site of the theatre at Pergamon made it impossible to construct either a fully semi-circular auditorium or permanent stage-buildings. Dating from the second century BC, it partly overlapped a terrace connecting the forum with the Temple of Dionysus.*

making it to all intents and purposes a Roman theatre, such as we shall be examining in the next chapter [Pl. 12].

Greek theatres remained in some ways curiously conservative to the very end, partly perhaps because the great plays of the classical period went on being admired and acted. As soon as the focus of interest had shifted from the *orchēstra* to the raised stage behind it, the logical plan for the auditorium was a semi-circle or less. Yet plans using more than a semi-circle went on being built. Anyone sitting at the edges saw the action taking place at an uncomfortably acute angle.

Two more aspects of Greek theatres remain to be noted: their high acoustic quality and the beauty of their settings. The first seems largely the result of accident. A semi-circle hollowed into the side of a hill and lined with marble happens to conduct sound in a particularly satisfactory way, and even in the largest Greek theatres the voice does not need to be unduly raised for it to be audible a hundred yards or so from the stage. Greek engineers had no way of understanding this. The science of acoustics is still fifty per cent guesswork, as some unhappy modern experiments are enough to prove.

Pl. 14. Delphi: the theatre with, beyond it, the Temple of Apollo. The high, rocky sanctuary of Delphi had been a Greek religious centre since early times, but the present theatre dates only from the second century BC.

Were the settings equally accidental? Probably. Love of natural scenery for its own sake is not a characteristic that emerges very clearly from Greek literature. It would anyway be difficult in Greece to find sites lacking in grandeur. Yet to stand in the theatres themselves is to find the question less easily dismissed. Delos with its view over the shining waters and islands, Segesta at the summit of its hill above the Sicilian countryside, Pergamon with its sweeping dive to the valley hundreds of feet below, and especially sacred Delphi perched among the cliffs and peaks of Parnassus [Pl. 14]—all these make it hard to dispel the idea that the sublime theme of man's union with nature was expressed not only in the dramas that the Greeks conceived in honour of Dionysus, but equally in the places where they chose to perform them.

II

THE ROMAN INHERITANCE

Hellenistic theatre leads without a break into Roman. As the Romans took over more and more of the Eastern Mediterranean they found themselves occupying countries with highly advanced theatrical techniques and these naturally percolated back to the mother country. In the two generations following Menander, Plautus and Terence successfully adapted the New Comedy to Latin taste. Plautus relies almost entirely on plot. Terence is interested in the way characters react to plot. Both rely absolutely on Greek plays, and both remain tied to the stock New Comedy situations. Young men fall in love with slave-girls only to discover, after complicated conspiracies to abduct them, that they are really free-born Athenians after all; clever servants weave webs of deception in which they only just avoid snaring themselves; fathers, mothers, uncles, aunts and guardians scold, bully and grumble but forgive everything in the end.

There must have been a theatrical tradition in Italy before Greek plays became fashionable, and indeed this seems to have continued side by side with them, but no examples survive. From literary sources and (with less certainty) vase-paintings, it is judged to have consisted of crude farces, and a good case can be made out for tracing Punch and Judy back through the *Commedia dell' Arte* and the popular entertainments of the Middle Ages to these very ancient Roman entertainments. They were called *togatae* because they were played in Roman costume, i.e. togas. Plays adapted from the Greek New Comedy were called *palliatae* ('cloaked') because the actors wore cloaks in the Greek style. There were also a few plays drawn from Roman history about which one would like to know more, because they must have been quite independent of the Greek models. One play attributed to Seneca, *Octavia*, may reflect this old type.

Acting conditions in the days of Plautus and Terence have to be reconstructed from literary evidence. Performances were no longer directly related to a religious cult, but they continued to coincide with religious festivals. As in Greece, they were public occasions, paid for by the state or by wealthy individuals anxious for prestige. One result of this was that plays normally formed only part of a more varied entertainment which included races, wild-beast fights and so on. It is in Rome that we first encounter the theatrical businessman, the impresario-producer who negotiated with the officials on the one hand and the dramatists on the other. The first step to success for any playwright was to gain the ear of one of these men. Actors were professionals, organized into companies.

Pl. 15.   Sabratha, Libya: junction of the auditorium and the stage. The upper rows of seats have not been rebuilt, but would have stretched back until they reached the height of the scaenae frons.

Early Roman theatres were made of wood, often without seats for the bulk of the audience, but they could nevertheless be extremely ornate. Pliny describes one built by Aemilius Scaurus in 58 BC which held 80,000 and had a stage background of marble, glass(!) and gilded wood. Audiences were rowdy, their attention spasmodic but (contrary to the custom in Greece) it was considered ill-bred to take refreshments into the theatre. Augustus once rebuked someone for this, saying: 'When I want a drink, I go home.' 'Yes', said the culprit, 'but the Emperor is not afraid of losing his place.'

The general layout was similar to that of a Hellenistic theatre, except that the *orchēstra* was smaller. The wooden stage was raised a few feet from the ground, and behind it was the *skēnē* (or in Latin, the *scaenae frons*), also of wood and probably painted, containing the three doors. Projecting side buildings, used as dressing-rooms, also had a door each, so that there were five doors altogether. Every play had a street setting. The three centre doors represented houses, as in the Hellenistic theatre, the two side ones standing for the different directions of the street.

By the end of the first century BC, the typical Roman theatre was of stone and had the following characteristics distinguishing it from the Hellenistic: it was built on level ground in the centre of a city, the seats being raised on arches rather than cut into a slope; the *scaenae frons* rose to the full height of the auditorium and joined it at the sides, so that the whole space was enclosed and cut off from the outside world in a way that the Greek theatre was not; the audience entered from the back instead of coming in at *orchēstra* level and walking up to their seats.

We are well informed about Roman theatres from about the beginning of the Christian era onwards. Not only do dozens of them survive in moderately good preservation all over the Empire, but we also have a lengthy description by Vitruvius which, while not always easy to reconcile with the remains on the ground, tells us a great deal which we might not otherwise suspect. Theatres, he says, should be built on solid foundations, on healthy sites, and designed so that everybody has a good view and is able to hear. To aid the acoustics he recommends that bronze jars should be set in niches between the seats to give resonance, according to the laws of harmony. In his rules for the layout of seats and stage Vitruvius is extremely precise and geometrical, obviously giving an ideal prescription rather than describing actual examples, but his account tallies in general with what was actually built.

The theatre occupied a place in Roman civic life hardly inferior to that of the temple, the forum, the public baths and the amphitheatre. One realizes this very clearly on the briefest visit to Pompeii or Ostia, or even better to one of the ruined cities of North Africa. Possibly the best preserved of all Roman theatres is that at Sabratha, in what is now Libya [Pls. 15, 16]. Built about AD 200, it is a late and completely developed example, carried through to a single design, and unhampered by previous buildings on the site. No luxury was spared, the reigning emperor, Septimius Severus, being a native of North Africa and keen to encourage its prosperity; it was never altered, has survived in good condition, and has been ideally restored by Italian archaeologists.

What makes Sabratha so immediately impressive is its great *scaenae frons*, which rises in three storeys, the height of the columns subtly diminishing as it goes up [Pl. 16]. In plan it consists of three large niches framing doors, and connected by groups of four columns sharing a continuous plinth. The niches contain coupled columns, so that across the façade one gets an alternating rhythm of four and two.

The columns themselves were once vividly distinct, though time and weather have blurred their original brilliance. Those on the lowest storey and the coupled columns of the two upper storeys are of a dark-bluish stone called *pavonezetto*; the other columns of the middle storey are of banded white marble, fluted vertically or spirally; and those of the top storey are of black granite. Between the columns at each stage must certainly have been statues, as we see them in Pompeiian wall-paintings. From the top, covering the stage, a wooden roof projected on brackets.

In the undulating wall of the *scaenae frons* are tiny rooms, probably used for keeping stage properties; at each end narrow staircases lead to the upper storeys upon which the actors—precariously—often had to appear. The two big areas of blank wall which now flank the stage were originally fairly large rooms, accessible from the portico behind the scene building and opening also on to the upper tiers of the auditorium. They were once articulated on the exterior by superimposed Corinthian columns, uniting them visually with the *scaenae frons*.

The stage itself is low, its front edge reproducing in miniature the indentations of the *scaenae frons* plan, three niches alternating with four square recesses. Like the Roman Theatre of Dionysus at Athens, it has sculptured reliefs, with theatrical and allegorical scenes.

The *orchēstra*, by now a mere semi-circle with a diameter less than half the width of the stage, was paved with white marble. Movable seats for special guests of honour were placed on the four wide steps that ran round its outer rim, and the space thus created was separated from the front row of seats by a marble screen ending in two dolphins.

The auditorium shows the Romans' talent for efficiency at its best [Pl. 15]. The seats rest on twenty-seven arches. Two of these (those at each end of the semi-circle) lead straight into the *orchēstra*. The other twenty-five lead into a continuous corridor which encircles the whole building at ground level. From this corridor six staircases lead to an upper corridor immediately above the first. Six more lead into an inner corridor at ground level, from which the front seats were reached (in three of these, the bases of what might have been turnstiles have been found). The remaining

Pl. 16. Right: the orchestra, stage ▶ *and* scaenae frons *at Sabratha. The central doorway has a projecting porch framed by a large niche. This is flanked by a straight colonnade of four columns on each side; then come subsidiary doors, also with porches in niches.*

Pls. 17–19. Three Roman theatres. Left: Lepcis Magna, Libya. In its original state this would have been very similar to Sabratha. Right: Aspendos, Asia Minor. This exterior view conveys the sense of enclosure which Roman theatre architects, unlike their Greek counterparts, wanted. On the left, on the back wall of the stage building, can still be seen the row of brackets where masts were fixed to hold the velarium *over the audience. Below: reconstructed* scaenae frons *of Ephesus, one of the most elaborate and inventive works of late Roman architecture.*

thirteen arches open into vaulted rooms which could have been cellars or refreshment rooms.

The seats themselves were divided into three tiers separated by two semi-circular ambulatories, which were reached by stairs from the corridors already mentioned (i.e. the top one from the upper corridor, the lower one from the inner ground floor corridor). The spectator, provided he knew exactly where he was sitting, could quickly find his place by going in at the appropriate entrance, emerging by the nearest staircase and then climbing up or down the short flight of steps between the wedge-shaped blocks of seats. Anyone who has attended a performance at the Royal Albert Hall in London can easily imagine the procedure.

The exterior of the auditorium was three-storeyed like the stage building, forming an architectural composition in itself, something for which there was no equivalent in the Greek theatre. Like the Colosseum or the Theatre of Marcellus in Rome, it was articulated by a small order (Tuscan), supporting round arches threading through a large order (Corinthian) which supported a flat entablature. What the top storey looked like is not entirely certain, but we may be sure that, as in other Roman theatres, it had brackets on which the sailcloth that gave shelter from the fierce sun was fixed. The maintenance and management of this was a complicated business and was the responsibility of the Roman navy.

The theatres of Dugga, Timgad and Lepcis Magna are so similar to Sabratha that they constitute almost a distinct North African school. Lepcis Magna, which was built originally in the time of Augustus, received substantial additions in the second century AD, including its new three-storeyed *scaenae frons* in polychrome marble [Pl. 17]. The subtle and varied ground-plans of these stages, with their curved and straight-sided niches and their intriguing views of spaces half-hidden behind columns, are characteristic of the late 'Baroque' phase of Roman architecture.

Every province of the Roman Empire, however, had its notable theatres. In areas where Greek influence was still strong (and where the audience and the architect were still probably Greek) they were often hollowed out of the hillside on sites commanding superb views, for example at Taormina in Sicily. This illustrates, too, the practice of finishing off the back of the auditorium with a curved colonnade (a feature that has vanished at Sabratha), corresponding to the top of the *scaenae frons*. The wooden roof over the stage, useful acoustically, also became standard.

In the Old World—Asia Minor, Egypt, the Near East—the Romans often adapted Greek theatres to their own more grandiose taste, as we have already seen them doing at Athens. The most complete idea of such a transformation can be seen at Aspendos, now in Turkey [Pl. 18]. Here, the auditorium is not raised on a substructure but is partly hollowed out of the slope in the Greek manner. The whole height of both the *scaenae frons* and the auditorium still remains, the latter crowned by a colonnade which meets the side buildings of the stage at each end. On the exterior can still be seen the brackets where masts were fixed to hold the sailcloth that covered the audience. The stage and its background are now shorn of ornament; but, complete with its superimposed columns (at least forty, Ionic and Corinthian), its statues in niches or above the pediments (probably over thirty), its sculptured friezes and painted decoration, it must have been of a slightly distracting grandeur to any playgoer. The whole area, indeed, is rich in ruins of the very highest architectural quality.

Pl. 20. A scene from Terence's Adelphi, *copied in the early Middle Ages from a late Roman manuscript. Aeschinus and Ctesiphon are the brothers of the title, Syrus is the inevitable clever slave, Sannio—on the right—a pimp.*

Pl. 21. *Tragic scene, from a Roman wall-painting. The play has not been identified, but the man on the left appears to be a judge, and the couple near the middle seem to be quarrelling over three children in a basket.*

As much thought went into the *scaenae frons* of Ephesus [Pl. 19], say, as into the Temple of Venus at Baalbek. Roman theatres offered much greater opportunities to the architect than did those of Greece and the best of them can rank among the highest achievements of Roman art.

It seems certain that, for some types of entertainment at least, a curtain was used—not lowered from above but raised on a line from the floor. Long recesses, or slots, running along the edges of some surviving stages (e.g. Vaison in France) are thought to have been to hold this curtain while the play or mime was in progress. At the end of it, the curtain would be raised again and, according to a passage in Ovid, the figures embroidered on it seemed to be standing on the edge of the stage. There was probably some mechanical device for doing this quickly. Some slightly later literary evidence also suggests that a curtain was introduced which worked in the opposite way (like a modern curtain), but this raises questions which archaeology cannot answer. It may conceivably have been connected with the roof over the stage.

Vitruvius implies that scenery of an elaborate kind was in use in his day: 'There are three types of scenery, one of which is called tragic, a second comic, the third satyric. Now the subjects of these differ severally from one another. The tragic ones are designed with columns, pediments and statues, and other royal surroundings, the comic have the appearance of private buildings and balconies and projections with windows made to imitate reality, after the fashion of ordinary buildings; the satyric settings are painted with trees, caves, mountains and other country features, designed to imitate landscape.' This is all very circumstantial, but has given rise to extreme perplexity. No trace of such scenery has survived and it is difficult—even more difficult than with Pollux's *periaktoi*—to see how it could have been used in the theatres as they have come down to us. As we shall see, this description by Vitruvius was to have important consequences in the Renaissance.

From Apuleius, writing a good deal later, we have a description of an even more elaborate set, 'a mountain of wood planted with shrubs and living trees', 'a stream', etc. But this was more of a pantomime spectacle than a play. We know that for special shows in the arena the Romans equalled Hollywood in expense and surpassed it in realism.

In Italy and the western parts of the Empire, theatres were at first an exotic importation. It is unlucky that no examples survive from Britain (the outline of a theatre in the earth at Verulamium, St. Albans, is poor consolation), but there are fine buildings in Spain (Merida) and France (Arles, Orange, Lyons).

In these western areas it was usual for the Romans to erect two buildings for public entertainment in every large town—the theatre for plays, recitations and recitals, and the amphitheatre for gladiatorial conflicts and animal fights. But in the formerly Greek colonies, popular enthusiasm for these latter spectacles was limited, so the two functions were often combined in the same building. It has been found in several theatres in Asia Minor that the front of the stage has small doors for animals to enter the *orchēstra*, which must therefore have been convertible into an arena (one is again reminded of the Royal Albert Hall, which can be converted into a boxing arena). This would also account for the stone screens which surround the *orchēstra* in many theatres and which would have served to protect the spectators. It seems likely also that gladiators sometimes fought on the stage itself.

This leads to one of the big problems of Roman drama. What plays were actually performed in these huge theatres whose ruins are so impressive? Plautus and Terence both lived at the dawn of Latin culture, before any stone theatre existed in Rome. Plautus was a success in his lifetime and managed to win audiences away from the clowns, acrobats and conjurors who competed for attention, but only just. Roman audiences, in fact, must have been pretty impossible. Terence puts this speech into the mouth of the producer of his play *The Mother-in-Law*: 'At the first performance, the fame of some boxers, as well as the rumour that a tight-rope walker would appear, the mob of their supporters' shouting and women's screaming forced me off the stage before the end. I put it on a second time. The first part was doing well when news arrived that there was to be a gladiators' show. Off rushed my audience, pushing, shouting, jostling for a place . . .'

Terence left Rome in disgust and probably died in an accident abroad. He was twenty-five. His plays [Pl. 20] and those of Plautus, for all we know to the contrary, continued to be acted as long as the Roman Empire lasted,

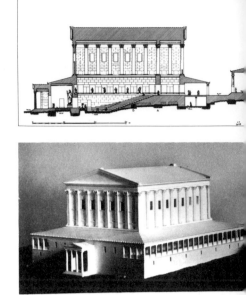

Pls. 22, 23. *The Romans also had in-door theatres* (odea), *though it is doubtful whether plays were acted in them or whether they were used only for music and recitation. The Odeum of Agrippa at Athens, reconstructed above, had a large hall with seating for about 1,000 and a wide but shallow stage.*

but the art of drama made no further progress. Other playwrights (the names of a few are known) relied just as heavily on Greek originals, except in the 'togata' comedies which made no great claim to dramatic merit. The only surviving tragedies, those of Seneca, were probably not meant to be acted in public theatres at all [Pl. 21]. Popular favour went to the farces and the mimes (which were not necessarily acted in theatres) and to the bloody spectacles of the arena. We read of performances in which men were actually killed on the stage. Seneca's plays, exercises on Greek themes in which physical horror stifles every other emotion, are symbolic of the predicament of the Roman playwright. It is as if the conventions necessary for stage representation had been crushed by a brutal and meaningless literalism.

Perhaps because of the bad reputation acquired by the public theatres, small, more exclusive indoor theatres seem to have enjoyed a certain popularity, and one would like to know more about them. How far they were used for real plays and how far for recitation or music only is an open question. The fact that some had a *scaenae frons*, which was apparently painted, points towards drama. One of the earliest of all surviving Roman theatres, the small theatre at Pompeii (*c.* 75 BC) was of this kind. It held about 1,500 spectators and was fitted into a rectangular plan in a way that anticipates Palladio. The prototype of such buildings was probably the Greek *odeum* or pillared hall, which goes back at least to the time of Pericles. Interesting examples are to be seen at Taormina and Athens—the Odeum of Agrippa [Pls. 22, 23].

Greek theatres had been integrated into complexes of temples and sacred precincts. Roman theatres were integrated into complexes of secular buildings and, in keeping with the Roman genius, this integration was more formal and systematic than the Greek had been. At Ostia (dating from the beginning of the Empire), the theatre forms one side of the forum.

Pl. 24. A Roman theatre normally formed part of a whole civic complex. At Orange, in France, the stage building backed on to a forum, while beyond it was a large stadium. (This sort of promixity explains why it was so easy for Terence's audience to desert him if something more exciting was happening elsewhere.)

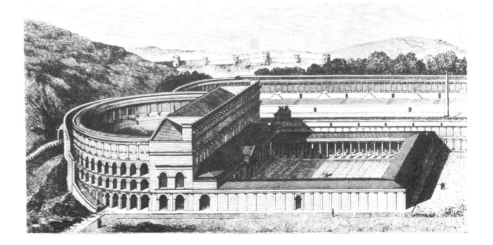

Pl. 25. The most recently discovered Roman theatre is that of Alexandria, built in the first century BC. Though fairly small in scale, it had an elaborate scaenae frons. Close by was a complex of bath buildings.

The theatre built by Pompey at Rome was planned as part of an extensive new civic centre, and the same is true at many sites elsewhere, for instance at Orange, where the theatre was joined at the back to a public forum and at one side to a race-course [Pl. 24].

It is impossible not to admire the logic and confidence of such planning, but, as often with Roman architecture, one feels that it pursues monumentality at the expense of the human scale. The theatre may be a ritual institution but it is not a monumental one. Roman theatres, expressive as they are of dignity and taste, still convey (or is this all imagination?) a feeling of spiritual emptiness. No playwrights demanded them, no producers experimented with them, no fresh ideas moulded their evolution. They represent not the perception of a living drama but the pride of an all-powerful state.

III
THE MIDDLE AGES:
THEATRE WITHOUT THEATRES

Roman drama, having died a natural death, was buried by Christianity. Tertullian, not without reason, counted plays among the works of the Devil, and although Augustine saw no harm in reading them, they had probably ceased to be acted by the fourth century AD. The great theatres stood empty, and either fell into ruin or were occupied and patched up as warrens of tiny houses, as one can see in the Theatre of Marcellus in Rome today. Throughout the Middle Ages Plautus and Terence went on being read and, if the works of Hroswitha, a tenth-century German nun are any indication, even imitated. But the tradition of performances died out entirely. The new drama that now arose represented a completely new start.

Some time in the tenth century, a part of the Mass for Easter Sunday was embellished by a question and answer sequence telling the story of the Three Maries at the Sepulchre [Pl. 26]: 'Whom do you seek in the Sepulchre, O followers of Christ?' asks one speaker representing the angel. 'Jesus of Nazareth, who was crucified', is the reply. 'He is risen, as he foretold; go and tell how he is risen from the tomb.'

As the years passed, other episodes from the Gospels were dramatized in the same simple way. The performers were priests and choristers, the language Latin, the setting the chancel of the parish church. But the dialogue was working itself free from the actual words of the Biblical text, a few stage properties were introduced and there was action of a sort. Subjects included the Nativity, the Journey to Emmaus, the Ascension and Pentecost. The staging was elaborated so that the whole church, including the nave, was used, with each bay of the arcade representing a particular place (Pilate's Palace, Gethsemane, etc.). Rich costumes were provided and the characters carried their traditional attributes. In spite of ecclesiastical controls, comedy kept breaking in and certain characters (for instance the man who sold spices to Mary Magdalene) became recognized comic types.

The breakthrough came when the vernacular replaced Latin and the plays emerged from the churches into the market squares. Drama, in fact, had proved too popular for the church to monopolize it. The plays were taken over by lay people—the craft guilds in England, special fraternities in France (like the famous Confrérie de la Passion, founded in 1402), municipal

Pl. 26. The beginnings of Christian drama: a twelfth-century manuscript of the Quem Quaeritis *trope, spoken on Easter Sunday. The Three Maries approach the empty tomb and are met by the angel who tells them that Christ is risen.*

authorities in Germany. And they expanded from the Gospel story to include, in a long series of scenes, the whole history of the world from the Creation to the Last Judgement.

Methods of staging differed in various parts of Europe. In some countries they continued to be acted in churches. In England they were performed on movable carts called 'pageants' which went through the streets in slow procession, stopping at certain points to act a scene and then moving on to make way for the next. The York Cycle, for instance, consists of forty-eight short plays. Each was the responsibility of a particular guild, often chosen because of some connection with the subject of the play—the story of the Ark, for example, was acted by the shipwrights, the visit of the Magi by the goldsmiths, and so on.

Most large cities seem to have had their own cycle of plays, written in simple stanzas of rhyming verse, and often accumulated over the years. The day of performance was Corpus Christi Day (which falls in the first week of June), when the day was longest.

The pageants were elaborate structures of two storeys—'a high place', runs one contemporary description, 'made like a house with two rooms, being open at the top; in the lower room they apparelled and dressed themselves and in the higher room they played.' There was a way down from the pageant to the street, and the action often spilled over in this way. 'Herod rages on the pageant and in the street also', says one stage direction. Some of the pageants were given special shapes; that for the Noah play, for instance, suggested a ship, Hell was a gaping mouth, etc. The scenes were acted with as much realism as possible, and some surprising effects were attempted, especially in the Hell scenes. The comic element was also allowed to grow. One of the most famous plays from the English cycles is the Shepherds' Play from the Towneley Cycle, in which the chief character is a thief called Mak, who steals a sheep and hides it in a cradle, pretending that it is his new-born child. The truth is discovered, Mak is tossed in a blanket, and only then does the Angel appear to announce the birth of the Christ Child.

Four complete cycles of Mystery or Miracle Plays exist in English, as well as fragments from others. They are the Chester Cycle (early fourteenth century), the York Cycle (1380), the Towneley Cycle, which probably really belonged to Wakefield (mid-fifteenth century), and the so-called *Ludus Coventriae*, which had in fact no connection with Coventry (late fifteenth century). From the theatrical point of view the last is especially interesting, for it was intended to be played not on movable pageants but on a series of stationary ones, with the audience assembled in front of them. The acting area is described in one of the stage directions as 'a place like a park'. The pageants, called 'scaffolds', stood for particular places, e.g. 'Herod's scaffold shall unclose, showing Herod in state with all the Jews kneeling'.

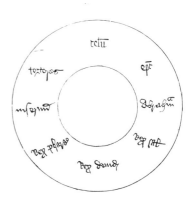

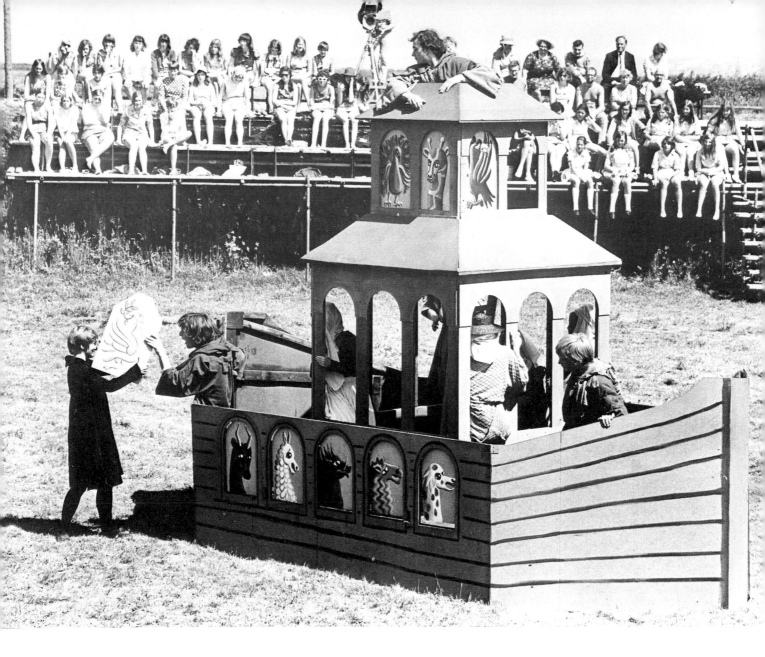

Pls. 27, 28. The Old Cornish Mystery plays were acted in circular arenas ('rounds') possibly adapted from much earlier, prehistoric structures. A manuscript of a play about the Creation of the World (left) indicates where the various scaffolds were located: in this one Hell is on the left, Heaven at the top. Above: in 1969 the play was revived at the Piran Round by students of Bristol University Drama Department. This scene shows Noah and the Ark.

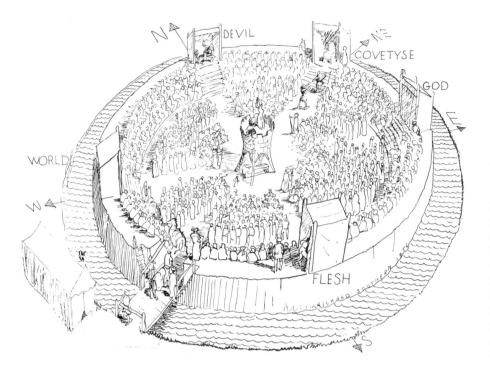

Pls. 29, 30. The Castle of Perseverance: *a drawing from the medieval
manuscript (right) and a reconstruction of
how it probably looked in performance
(left) by Dr. Richard Southern. No distinction was made between stage and
auditorium. The actors performed either
in front of the various scaffolds or in the
centre, under or on the castle. Men with
staves kept the way clear for them to
move from place to place.*

An interesting parallel to the *Ludus Coventriae* is provided by the Cornish
Mystery Plays [Pls. 27, 28]. Those that survive are late in date (sixteenth and
seventeenth century) but they clearly belong to a much earlier tradition,
with links, via Brittany, with Northern France. They were acted on open
circular stages, 'rounds', with scaffolds grouped in a ring. A few sites
survive: at St. Just the *Plan-an-Guare* ('place of the play') is 126 feet in
diameter and made of stone, but whether it is a medieval theatre or a
prehistoric fort is a debatable point. At Perranzabuloe it is even larger,
though of earth only. The following description by Richard Carew in 1602
tells us almost all we know about the staging of these Cornish plays: 'They
raise an earthen amphitheatre in some open field, having the diameter of his
enclosed plain some 30 or 40 feet. The country people flock from all sides,
many miles off, to hear and see it; for they have therein devils and devices
to delight the eye and the ear.' The dialogue of these Cornish plays is even
more homely than the English ones, and is full of local allusions—Solomon,
for instance, distributes villages round Lostwithiel to his supporters as a
reward. The actors did not learn their parts by heart but were accompanied
on stage by a prompter who whispered the lines to them.

During the fifteenth century the Miracle Cycles began to be supplemented by the so-called Morality Plays, allegories concerned with the
predicament of Man beset by temptations and sins, and saved by divine
grace, conscience and the virtues. Two of the best-known English
Moralities are *The Castle of Perseverance* (1440) and *Everyman* (1500). We are

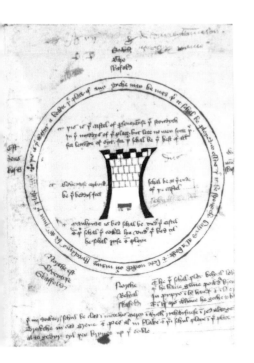

fortunate in possessing a sketch showing the staging of the former and doubly fortunate in having it interpreted in a most masterly way by Dr. Richard Southern [Pls. 29, 30]. The details must remain conjectural, but the general lines of his reconstruction are wholly convincing, and the parallels both with the Cornish 'rounds' and the *Ludus Coventriae* are too striking to be ignored. The play must have been acted by a travelling professional company. A circular ditch was made and the earth banked up inside the circle ('the place') to make a 'hill'. In the centre was erected a wooden tower, standing on legs so that one could see through it at ground level. This was the 'Castle' of the title. Round the edge of the circle, against or on top of the 'hill', were five scaffolds for God, the Devil, Covetousness, Flesh and the World. The audience stood inside the circle and on the surrounding 'hill'. Action moved swiftly from scaffold to scaffold, across the 'place' and around the 'castle'. What is so intriguing about this arrangement is the intimate contact between players and audience; the crowd would naturally move to get a better view of whatever happened to be going on at any particular moment, and actors would often have to walk right through it.

Other Morality plays like *Everyman* may well have been staged in a similar way. A late example, Sir David Lindsay's *Satire of the Three Estates* (or *Thre Estaitis*), also requires scaffolds grouped round a central space and has been staged successfully in modern times in an open hall.

If we turn from the British Isles to other European countries we find few parallels with the processional pageants but many with the static setting of scaffolds arranged round an acting area. In France vernacular plays go back to the twelfth century. The *Mystère d'Adam* was meant to be played in front of the church porch. *Résurrection* envisages an acting space with ten scaffolds (*mansiones*) in two lines, five on each side, the crucifixion taking place between them at one end—evidently referring back to a church with the two arcades of the nave and the altar in the chancel. The décor and acting were already fairly sophisticated. For the Paradise, for instance, 'curtains and silk cloth are to be hung about it at such a height that persons in Paradise are visible from the shoulders. Fragrant flowers and leaves are scattered there; in it are diverse trees with hanging fruit . . . Whoever names Paradise must look towards it and indicate it with his hand.' Hell, by contrast, was a place 'of a great smoke', with devils banging pots and kettles.

Later French cycles were monumental in scale. Pictorial evidence is scanty, since the illustrations usually show the scenes as they were imagined to have been, not as they were actually acted on a stage. A miniature by Jean Fouquet, however, shows an episode from a *Passion of St. Apollonia* in the conditions of stage performance [Pl. 32]. The saint herself (women did appear in plays in France but not in England) is being tortured in the foreground, but at the back a series of *mansiones* can clearly be seen

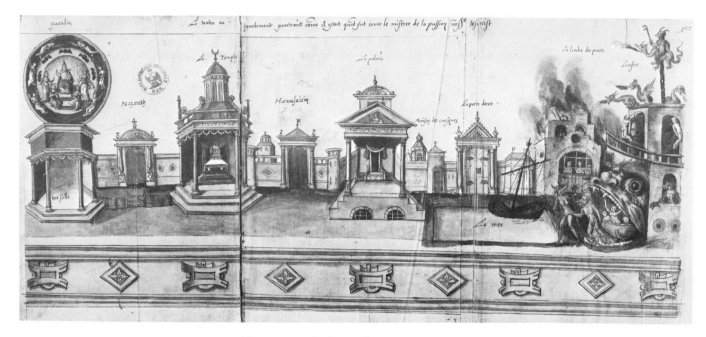

Le teatre ou ... fondement pourtrait come il estoit quad fut ioue le mistere de la passion ... Iesucrist

paradis

Le Temple

Nazareth

Hierusalem

Le palais

Maison des euesques

La porte doree

Le limbe des peres

Lenfer

La mer

une salle

Pl. 31. *Multiple set for the Valenciennes Passion Play, 1547. The* mansiones *were probably grouped round three sides of a courtyard. From left to right, they represent Heaven, Nazareth, the Temple, Jerusalem, Herod's Palace, 'Bishop's House' (i.e. the Sanhedrin), the Golden Gate, in front of which is the Sea (of Galilee) and finally, on the extreme right, Hell.*

arranged in a semi-circle, with Heaven on the extreme left and Hell on the right. (Hell was usually constructed like a mouth, 'a great gargoyle which opens and closes', in the words of a play acted at Rouen in 1474.) The actors evidently came down from these structures into the open space in front. The Emperor, who is supervising the torture, has obviously descended from the one with an empty throne. Note, too, the figure with staff and book—the producer or perhaps (remembering the Cornish plays) the prompter. A more schematic illustration, again late in date (1547), is one from the manuscript of the Valenciennes Passion, which shows the *mansiones* set up in the Duc d'Archot's palace courtyard very clearly [Pl. 31].

The most famous and popular of the French cycles was the *Passion d'Arras*, which covers the events of the New Testament from the infancy of Jesus to Pentecost. It is nearly 25,000 words long and took four days to perform. Its author, who died in 1440, was Eustache Mercadé, priest, theologian, and doctor of common law. Mercadé displays his learning at great length: God and Satan hold frequent theological arguments and there is a debate on the fate of man between Pity, Truth, Justice and Peace. Over a hundred characters take part; there are opportunities for comedy, such as the Shepherds and the scene in the Tavern at Emmaus, and the whole cycle shows the same growing sophistication and taste for

Pl. 32. *Right: Fouquet's miniature of ▶ the martyrdom of St. Apollonia (c. 1455) sets the scene as if it were a Miracle Play. Round the back is a semi-circle—no doubt in reality a full circle—of scaffolds, which can be identified as follows: first Heaven, with God and angels; then the musicians; then the Emperor's palace, with his empty throne (he has stepped down by the ladder and is supervising the torture of the saint); the next two seem to be occupied by spectators; and finally Hell.*

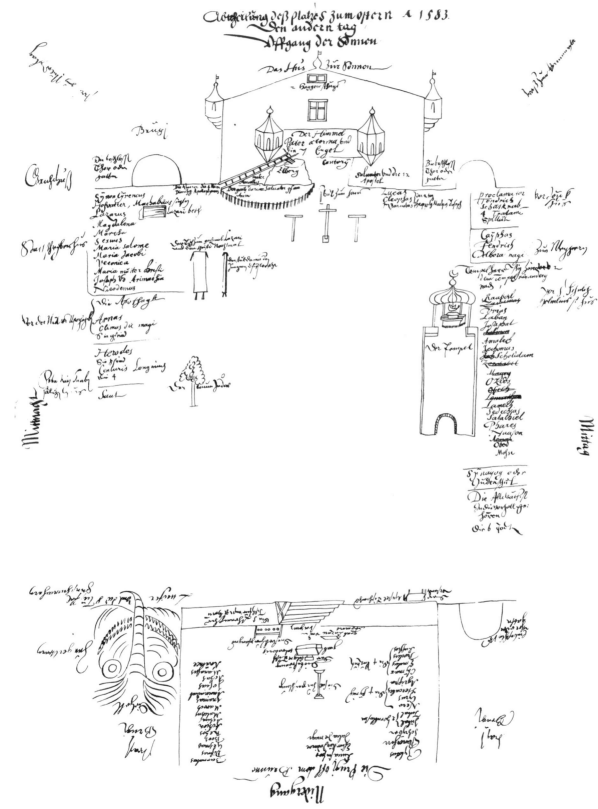

abstraction and allegory which we have noticed already in the English Morality Plays.

Fairly detailed records survive of a traditional Miracle Play acted at Mons in 1501. It took four days. Some of the records of expenses are amusing (e.g. 'live fishes for the aforesaid Creation' and 'fitting of serpents with pipes for throwing flames'), and it was evidently intended to be acted with a set like that for the *Castle of Perseverance* or the Fouquet play or that for Valenciennes, with characters passing from one scaffold to another, e.g. 'Joseph and Mary holding Jesus in her arms must pass before a temple and as they pass the idols fall to the ground'. It had sixty-seven *mansiones* but not all were used together.

The text of the Lucerne Passion Play (which may in fact have been acted in other places as well) exists in several fifteenth-century manuscripts, but the drawings which give it special interest in the present context relate to performances in 1583 and after [Pls. 33, 34]. These show how it was staged in the Weinmarkt, the principal public square of Lucerne. The square itself, which is still more or less as it was then, is lined with four- and five-storey houses, and divided into two by a fountain. Only the upper half was used for the play. The scaffolds were set up all round in front of the houses, with space behind for the actors. One street was left open for processional entrances. Behind the scaffolds, and high enough to see over them, were stands for the spectators, who also watched from the windows and even the roofs of the houses. The 'stage' was the open space in the centre. The scaffolds represented the places in the story—Heaven at one end, Hell at the other—and could 'double' at different times for other localities. The play took two days and the drawings show what changes were made.

Pls. 33, 34. Left: a contemporary manuscript sketch showing how the Weinmarkt of Lucerne was arranged for the performance of the Passion Play in 1583. At the top is a large house with decorative tourelles, the Haus zur Sonne, which was used for Heaven (reached by a ladder), and the three crosses of Calvary. At the bottom is the city fountain, on the right of which was Hell. The building with the cupola, centre right, is the Temple. Opposite is the tree on which Judas hangs himself. Right: a cut-away reconstruction gives an idea of how the market place probably looked.

Another German play of which graphic evidence survives is that of Donaueschingen in the Black Forest, dating in its present form from the second half of the sixteenth century [Pl. 35]. In this case the sketch is more difficult to interpret. The narrowness of the plan may be only accidental, and it probably represents a town square much in the same way as the Lucerne drawing. It is divided even more distinctly into Heaven, Earth and Hell, but it is impossible to decide where the audience was placed. Probably they watched from surrounding houses; they had to be able to see into the *mansiones* since much of the action takes place there.

The most famous of all Passion Plays, that of Oberammergau in Bavaria, is a comparative latecomer. It was compiled from earlier sources only in 1634, when the villagers vowed to perform it every ten years as an act of gratitude for surviving a plague epidemic. With a few lapses, they have kept their vow, and still keep it, though the text has been modernized several times and a simple though ugly auditorium was built in 1899 and enlarged during the present century.

Even when theatres were well on the way to their modern form, with the stage raised on trestles at one end of a hall, the multi-location set was not given up. We have one vivid view of such a stage constructed for a play about St. Laurence by Stefan Broelman, acted at Cologne in 1581 [Pl. 36].

The sixteenth century marks the second great turning point in the history of the European theatre. In Italy, the spur of the Renaissance, with its re-evaluation of classical literature, led to the ambition to revive Plautus, Terence and Seneca in conditions as close as possible to their original performance, and then to create new works worthy to stand beside them. But at the same time, in the north, the old Mystery and Morality Plays were still very much alive, and a whole range of dramatic forms, influenced at various removes by classical example, were springing up and flourishing: court entertainments—pageants, processions, masques; 'Chronicle' plays, glorifying national history; plays on Roman themes in Latin or the vernacular performed by the learned professions; and finally the wandering popular entertainers—singers, mimes and jesters—who earned their living at country fairs and left nothing to be remembered by in the history of literature. Out of all these were born the various national dramas that we know.

We might usefully pause at this point to ask how much continuity there was between medieval and Renaissance conditions of performance. It is customary to find the sources of modern theatre design entirely in Renaissance Italy (and beyond that in ancient Rome) but is this really the case? Let us recall a typical medieval theatrical situation: a series of scaffolds raised several feet off the ground arranged in a rough circle; the actors at first occupy these scaffolds but they can also descend to the ground, where the audience mostly stands. Here we already have a 'theatre' in embryo without needing to appeal to classical precedent. If we add that

Pl. 35. Medieval plan of the Donaueschingen Passion Play. It is divided into three sections, each entered by a door. In the lowest section, Hell is on the left, the Mount of Olives on the right. In the centre are the two pillars of the Flagellation and the Cock, and scaffolds for Annas, Caiaphas, Pilate and the Last Supper. In the upper section are the three crosses and the Sepulchre, with Heaven at the very top.

44

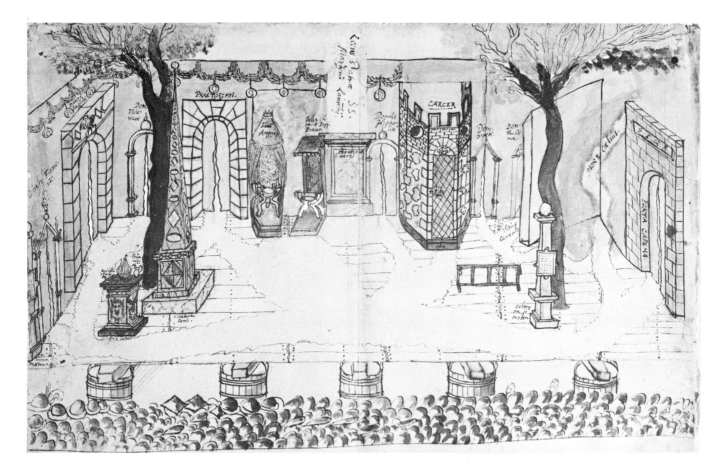

Pl. 36. A Cologne school production of a play about St. Laurence in 1588 still used the multiple set characteristic of medieval drama, but the whole collection is now crowded on to one platform. (The two trees were growing there before the stage was put up.) The rather baffling objects in the foreground are the backs of the audience's heads.

in many cases scaffolds were also used to accommodate sections of the audience, the likeness grows more pronounced. Two scaffolds in the Fouquet miniature do seem to be occupied by spectators [Pl. 32], and there are records of scaffolds for the audience for a number of medieval performances—at Metz in 1437, Angers in 1471, Amiens in 1494 (where money was charged, twice as much for the scaffolds as for the ground), Vienna in 1510 and Autun in 1516. The Vienna scaffolds had locks and keys. Is it too much to see here the origin of the box? The French terms to describe these scaffolds include both *estages* and *logeis*, which neatly summarizes, if it does not prove, the case. This is not to reduce the importance of the revived classical theatre, to which we are about to turn, but simply to suggest that another influence was also present.

45

IV

CLASSICAL THEATRE REBORN

The revival of interest in everything connected with ancient Rome which grew up in Italy in the late fourteenth and early fifteenth centuries and which marks the beginning of the Renaissance naturally included the theatre. Plautus, Terence and Seneca had never ceased being read. Now the desire arose to see them once again performed. All over Italy, rulers vied with each other in attracting humanist scholars who could adapt, stage and if required act in classical plays. One of the luminaries of the Papal court in the late fifteenth century, Tommaso Inghirami, became so celebrated for his playing of Seneca's heroine that he was nicknamed 'Phaedra'.

The places where these performances were staged were either the halls or the outdoor courtyards of noblemen's palaces, lavishly decorated for the occasion. Many of the best-known architects of the Renaissance tried their hand at this sort of thing, but it is probably misleading to describe what they built as 'theatres'. The stages were temporary, lath-and-plaster affairs, obviously regarded as belonging to the same genre as the sets made for carnivals and triumphal entries. In 1452, for instance, Alberti is mentioned as having built a '*theatrum*' for Pope Nicholas V. And there survives an interesting page of drawings by Leonardo da Vinci showing his set for a play called *Il Paradiso* by Bernardo Bellincioni, performed in a room in the Castello Sforzesco, Milan, in 1490. Leonardo invented a typically ingenious 'mountain' which moved on a revolving turntable and opened to reveal an interior.

In 1486 there are records of a performance of Plautus' *Meneachmi* at Ferrara on 'a stage of wood with five crenellated houses, each with a door and a window'. Later, in 1515, we hear of a stage erected on the Capitol at Rome, the back of which consisted of a 'wall divided by four columns into five compartments, each closed by a curtain'. It is exactly this arrangement which is illustrated in the well-known edition of Terence published at Lyons in 1493 [Pl. 37]. The sets vary to a certain extent, but all have four or five doors with curtains and written above them are the names of the characters who own the houses. The illustration of the whole theatre is less realistic [Pl. 38]. It has three tiers of seats, though it is hard to see how they are meant to be imagined in practice. But this theatre may not be as fictitious as is often assumed. A certain bourgeois of Lyons, named Neyron, is recorded as having built in 1540 a theatre which had three rows of galleries, or boxes, and a *parterre* furnished with benches. On the ceiling were paintings of Heaven and Hell.

Pls. 37, 38. Two illustrations to the Lyons Terence *of 1493. The theatre (right) is a strange case of classical data interpreted in medieval terms. It is a six- or eight-sided building, with the audience seated in a parterre and two galleries. The stage, on the right, has a kind of miniature* scaenae frons *with four doorways, which appear again in the smaller woodcuts illustrating particular plays. The one (left) shows a scene from* The Girl from Andros. *Above the doors are the names of the characters whose houses they represent. (The strange scene in the foreground of the large picture is explained by the fact that* fornix, *an arch or vault, also came to mean a brothel, and was evidently understood in this sense by the artist.)*

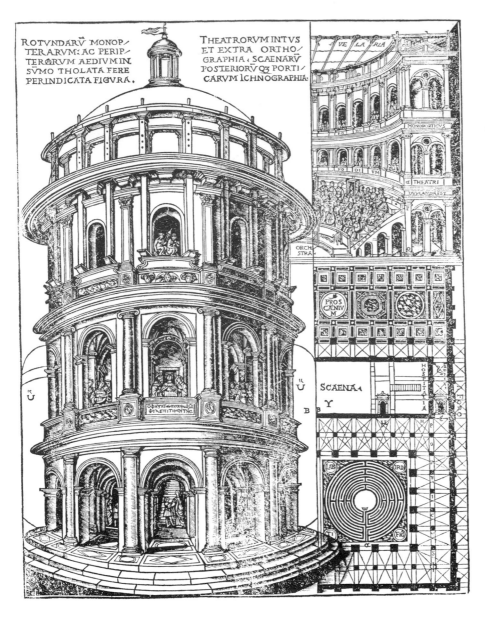

ROTVNDARV MONOP
TERARVM: AC PERIP
TERORVM AEDIVM IN
SVMO THOLATA FERE
PERINDICATA FIGVRA.

THEATRORVM INTVS
ET EXTRA ORTHO/
GRAPHIA. SCAENARV
POSTERIORV Q3 PORTI/
CARVM ICHNOGRAPHIA

Pl. 39. Cesariano's reconstruction (1521) of a Roman theatre based on the description by Vitruvius. The exterior is roughly correct: a semi-circle of three storeys with open arches. But Cesariano imagined the interior to be divided into parterre and galleries, as in the court-yards that he probably knew in Italy.

The publication and translation of Vitruvius gave rise to many attempts at reconstituting his description of a theatre—Fra Giocondo (1511), Cesariano (1521) [Pl. 39], Serlio (1551) and Barbaro (1556). The idea of actually building such a theatre was therefore very much in the air. Records are too scanty to enable us to decide who first carried it out. A sketch-plan by Antonio da Sangallo, dating from about 1515–30, may be connected with some such scheme. He shows a stage flanked by large *periaktoi* (captioned *machine*) and faced by a semi-circular *orchēstra* and *teatro*. In the accompanying elevation it is not clear how he intended the *periaktoi* to work. A theatre built for the Paduan humanist Alvise Cornaro in 1528 at Loreo may have been an attempt in the same direction. Constructed of stone to the design of a Veronese architect, Falconetto, it was apparently more substantial than Palladio's, but no trace of it survives today.

Architects trying to be faithful to Vitruvius found themselves faced in practice with two irreconcilable choices—either the *scaenae frons* or the perspective sets ('tragedy', 'comedy', 'satyr play'). The latter were obviously simpler and easier to erect in a hall or courtyard. It is known that Cardinal Bibiena's *Calandra*, performed in 1513, had a stucco set of this kind, and a revival the next year was in the hands of no less an artist than Peruzzi. Serlio was Peruzzi's pupil and no doubt inherited many of his drawings. When he came to build his own theatre in 1539 in the courtyard of the Palazzo Porto at Vicenza, it followed the earlier pattern [Pls. 40, 41]. 'For the city of Vicenza, rich and glorious among all the cities of Italy,' he writes, 'I built a theatre and a stage of wood, greater perhaps than any that had previously been built.' The plan, as he published it, shows an attempt to combine several Vitruvian features, such as the plan based on a circle, with a perspective set, though he must have known (since he published the plans of several) that no Roman theatre was like this.

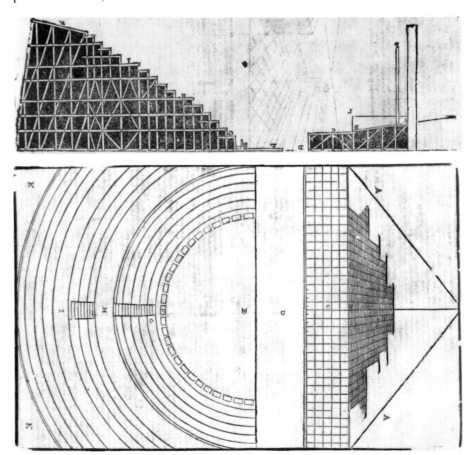

Pls. 40, 41. Plan and section of the theatre built by Serlio in a palace courtyard in 1539. The stage is divided into two areas, one flat, for the actors, the other sloping, upon which the perspective scenery was placed. In the auditorium Serlio retains the classical semi-circle and orchēstra, *though his drawing shows no way by which the actors could enter it.*

The most common form of theatre, however, continued to be the *teatro da sala*, the converted hall with seats round three sides and scenery at one end. The action would be projected forward into the middle of the room, using the 'stage' merely as a point of entry and as a backcloth for scenic effects. Buontalenti, for instance, built such a theatre in the Uffizi in 1585 which was noted for having a sloping floor, apparently an innovation. The theatres themselves, at this date, were decidedly less exciting than the sets. Buontalenti was among the most inventive of designers. The opening scene of one Florentine entertainment, for example, showed a vast city; the clouds over it descended, bearing a company of Virtues; these floated away to be replaced by Vices; the city of Dis appeared 'all in flames and smoke', etc., etc. The theatre of illusion is here well and truly launched, contrasting sharply with the contemporary 'academic' theatre, which was still wholly a theatre of convention. From the architectural point of view, one should note a theatre designed by Giorgio Vasari the Younger in 1598 as part of an ideal city [Pl. 42]. It is essentially still a *teatro da sala* with a shallow Serlian perspective at one end. What is remarkable is Vasari's conception of the theatre as a free-standing monument, articulated on the exterior by deep niches and entered by a staircase which, though small in scale, contains the seeds of future grandeur.

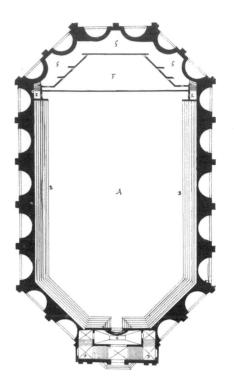

It is Daniele Barbaro who provides the link between Vitruvius and Palladio, through the Accademia Olimpico at Vicenza, a cultural society founded by the wealthy humanist and patron of the arts, Count Giangiorgio Trissino. The Academy invited lecturers, organized poetry readings and put on performances of classical plays. Palladio, the only non-aristocratic member, whose real name was Andrea di Pietro della Gondola, provided the illustrations for Barbaro's Vitruvius. One of his drawings showed the plan of a Roman theatre, based more on Palladio's own study of Roman ruins than on Vitruvius. It is interesting to see his treatment of the *periaktoi*, which he places unconvincingly inside each of the three doorways.

Next year the Academy began to sponsor actual stage performances and Palladio is recorded to have designed a *scena centrale* (i.e. presumably a Serlian perspective) in the courtyard of a palace where Terence's *Girl from Andros* was acted. In 1561, more ambitiously, he built a theatre inside the great hall of the Basilica at Vicenza. This was repeated the following year for Trissino's tragedy *Sofonisba*, which had a cast of eighty and two elaborate scenes, one in the town and one in the country. These temporary theatres are recorded in frescoes painted thirty years later in the Teatro Olimpico. In 1564, Palladio was called to Venice to build another in the cloister of a monastery, but it was not until 1579 that the Academy voted to build a permanent theatre in Vicenza, purchased the ground and commissioned Palladio to design it. He was now an elderly man—seventy-one. Work started in February 1580; in August he died. It was taken over by his pupil Vincenzo Scamozzi, who carried it to its conclusion in 1585, when it opened with a performance of Sophocles' *Oedipus*. 'There were more than 3,000 spectators', says our only account of the occasion. 'People came early . . . The performance began at 7.30 and was over by 11. Some, including I and my friends, stayed there perhaps eleven hours, not getting tired at all . . .'

Palladio cannot have supervised much of the actual building of the Teatro Olimpico, but his drawings survive and we know that the finished work is basically his [Pl. 45]. What he was trying to do was to create a Roman theatre—indoors, of wood, and on a small scale, but fundamentally faithful to classical models. It is ironic that this theatre, which is often cited as marking the beginning of a new age, in fact marks only a dead end. Already, in the court of Florence and elsewhere, the *teatro da sala* was experimenting with the use of the picture-frame stage and movable perspective scenery which would render the old pseudo-Roman *scaenae frons* a mere academic exercise. That this was in fact exactly what Palladio was aiming at was no doubt due to the nature of his commission. Nevertheless, late though it is, the Teatro Olimpico is almost our only vestige of that brief moment of true Renaissance drama, before opera, before Baroque, before the theatre of illusion.

The *scaenae frons* at Vicenza is therefore a conscious imitation of a Roman model [Pl. 44]. It has the conventional three doorways, the central one

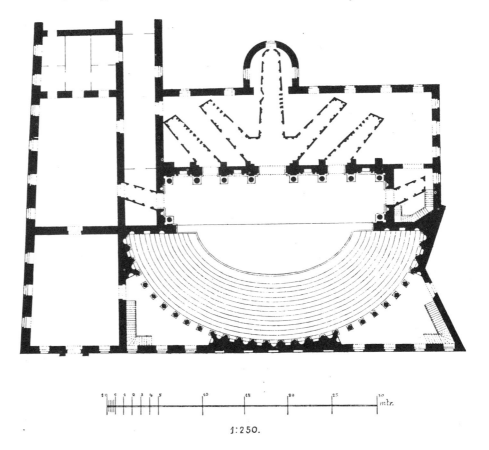

Pl. 43. The most famous Renaissance theatre is Palladio's Teatro Olimpico at Vicenza. The plan shows how the seven perspective sets are arranged inside the five doorways. The shallow curve of the auditorium, making it wider than it is deep, was forced upon Palladio by the restrictions of the site. The audience entered by the two doors at the back and climbed the corner staircases to reach their seats.

1:250.

much larger than classical prototypes warranted, free-standing columns, pilasters, pedimented niches and statues. The auditorium, slightly less than a semi-circle, abuts rather awkwardly on to the stage. There are twelve rows of seats. The back is formed by a colonnade which at the ends and at the centre is filled in and provided with niches and statues, but which is left open in the direction of the corners. The fact that the auditorium is semi-elliptical, not semi-circular, was probably due to the site. Palladio's solution to the problem which was to trouble nearly all subsequent theatre designers, of how to fit a curved hall into a square building, was to use the corners for staircases.

It is not clear how Palladio intended to treat the ceiling. As Scamozzi completed it, the whole of it may have been originally like the part over the stage, in a heavy, coffered, so-called 'Ducal Palace' style. In the nineteenth century it was covered by a pseudo-tent roof, imitating the *velarium* of the Romans (this can be seen in some of the old photographs). In 1914 the coffered roof was reinstated over the stage and the rest painted to represent the sky.

The present perspectives that fill the arches are also by Scamozzi. Did Palladio plan them from the beginning? The issue is complicated by the fact that when the Vicenza theatre was begun there was actually no room behind the *scaenae frons*; it was only after Palladio's death that the Academy acquired the ground on which they are built, and the fact that the masonry between the old and the new work shows a straight joint supports the theory that they were an afterthought. On the other hand, the Academy's very first proposal mentions perspectives, though Palladio's drawing now at the R.I.B.A. shows nothing in any of the arches [Pl. 45].

At any rate, Palladio can only have intended scenery in the central arch, the other two being too small. It was Scamozzi who enlarged them so that they were big enough for perspectives. The final set consists of five radiating streets, diminishing sharply as they recede [Pl. 43]; the effect from the auditorium is convincing but of course it is impossible for the actors to do anything with them. They represent a heroic attempt to combine practicality with Vitruvius.

The Accademia Olimpico, however, was satisfied. Around the central arch stand statues of Vicentine heroes, generals, scholars and the rich citizens who had contributed towards the building. Above them is a painting of the theatre, the words HOC OPUS and an inscription which means: 'Through their virtue and genius the Olympian Academy raised this theatre upon its foundation in 1584.' By a fantastic piece of luck the Academy still exists and so, therefore, does the theatre. The festivals of classical drama that are held in it become annually more popular, despite the crippling discomfort of its seats.

Scamozzi's later career was busy and successful. In May 1588 he was commissioned by Vespasiano Gonzaga, the ruler of Mantua, to build a

Pls. 44, 45. The Teatro Olimpico, Vicenza. Within a relatively small space Palladio creates an impression of grandeur. Through the central arch one of the perspective streets can be seen. Although actors entered through these doorways, the whole action had of course to take place in front of the scaenae frons. Right: one of Palladio's original designs. No provision is made for permanent perspectives, and Palladio probably envisaged painted screens or periaktoi in their place.

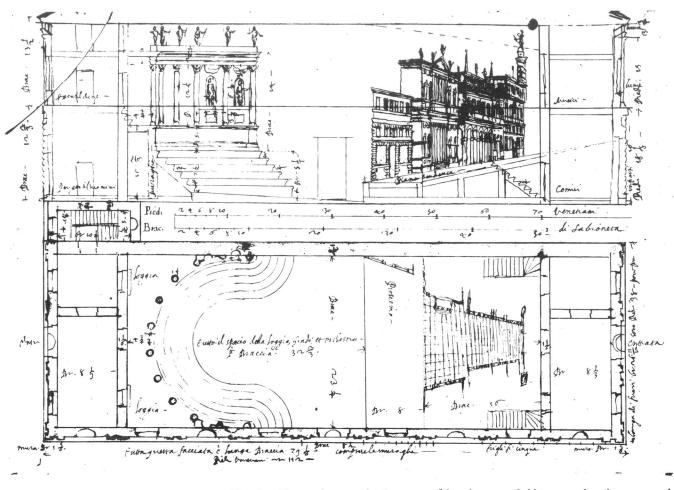

Pl. 46.   *Plan and section by Scamozzi of his theatre at Sabbioneta, where he gave up the* scaenae frons *and constructed a single perspective set filling the whole back of the stage.*

theatre at his new model town of Sabbioneta. Scamozzi's design relies heavily on that of his master but it had to be adapted to a completely different shape. The theatre at Vicenza is wide and shallow, at Sabbioneta narrow and deep. Consequently the semi-circle of seats has to be pinched in until it is almost a horseshoe. It is even smaller in scale, with only five rows of seats, but still manages to retain something of the dignity of its Palladian model. At the back of the seats is the same colonnade linked by a balustrade and surmounted by statues, and on the walls are excellent frescoes by the school of Veronese showing architectural motifs, Roman emperors and painted spectators leaning over an upper balustrade enjoying the play with the audience [Pl. 47].

Scamozzi's stage was later demolished but can be (and is being) reconstructed from drawings [Pl. 46]. It was a curious compromise. He gave up

Pl. 47. *The Sabbioneta theatre as it is today. Stepped seats originally occupied the space below the colonnade, and more spectators could sit behind the colonnade at the back.*

the *scaenae frons* and made one single arch (or rather a flat frame) embrace the whole stage. It was not yet a proscenium arch in the modern sense, however, since behind it he built a perspective even more elaborate than the one at Vicenza. It represented a piazza with a '*strada nobile*' leading off into the distance, lined by palaces and rich houses and again rising and diminishing in scale as it receded. It was larger than the Vicenza perspective, but was still so much wasted space as far as the actors were concerned, since they had to remain most of the time in front of it. Evidently it proved too hampering for later producers and an open space with movable flats was substituted.

Unlike the Vicenza theatre, which is hemmed in on all sides by other buildings, that of Sabbioneta is almost free-standing and Scamozzi could give it three imposing façades, severe enough in style to be called Palladian: a plain ground floor with rusticated quoins, doorways and windows, and a *piano nobile* with coupled pilasters and niches. There are three bays on the two short sides, nine on the long. It is at first rather misleading to find that the doorway in the centre of the long side leads straight into the space between the stage and the auditorium. The main entrance, through a vestibule, is by one of the narrow sides.

If one turns from Vicenza and Sabbioneta to the rest of Italy and of Europe, the picture is at first bewildering. There seems to be an unending variety of theatrical forms bearing little or no relation to each other. It may help to keep in mind four basic types: Firstly, the revived classical theatre, as exemplified at Vicenza; secondly, the medieval arrangement of scaffolds making up a multiple set; the third type was the temporary platform-stage with a simple backcloth, used for travelling shows and ceremonial occasions; and then there was the *teatro da sala*, or indoor auditorium, which developed from the converted nobleman's hall.

The last type I leave for the next chapter. It was here that the proscenium arch developed and here accordingly that we must seek the source for the standard European theatre of the next 300 years. Features from the other three occur in strange and often unexpected permutations. The three, or five, doors of a Roman theatre, for instance, which in classical drama stood for particular houses, had a function very similar to the *mansiones* of a medieval play. The remains of Roman theatres, therefore,

Pl. 48. A stage erected at Louvain in 1594 for a play on the Judgement of Solomon. The set, made of wood on canvas, is a poor man's scaenae frons, resembling the canvas triumphal arches and elaborate pageant architecture so popular in the Renaissance.

Pl. 49. A French seventeenth-century theatre, possibly the Hôtel de Bourgogne in Paris, until 1675 the only licensed French public theatre. Here, multiple sets of the medieval type continued to be used in what was essentially a modern theatre.

could readily be adapted to the performance of Miracle or Morality plays. Those at Orange and at Bourges (the latter no longer extant) are recorded as having been used in this way. Conversely, a medieval set using a Renaissance style of architecture can look like an anticipation of Palladio, for example the Valenciennes stage of 1547 [*see* p. 40 and Pl. 31], or even more strikingly, a stone theatre for a Passion play at Velletri dating from 1500.

A further complication is introduced by the combination of the revived classical stage and the platform on trestles. Examples are stages set up at Ghent, Antwerp and other towns in Flanders by the Rederyker Kamers, or Societies of Rhetoric, and particularly a stage for the *Judgement of Solomon*, performed at Louvain in 1594, a drawing of which has survived [Pl. 48].

Germany made few notable contributions to theatre architecture, though interest in classical drama was keen. Terence's plays were translated into German as early as 1486 with a frontispiece that envisages (if it does not commemorate) actual performance. One very forward-looking venture was the Ottoneum at Kassel, built by the Landgrave Maurice in 1610 in the shape of an Italian amphitheatre. But the Thirty Years' War (1618–48)

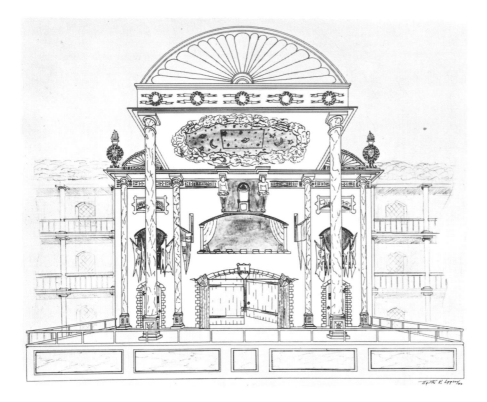

made sustained cultural activity impossible and it was not until the second half of the seventeenth century that German theatres began to claim the prominence that belongs to them in the eighteenth.

In Spain a vigorous native school of playwrights was growing up, but for some time there was no architectural form to match it. Plays were acted on temporary stages or in the courtyards of palaces, sometimes sheltered from the sun by sailcloth like a Roman theatre. These dignified *patios*, surrounded on four sides by loggias and windows, were to have some remote influence on Spanish theatre design of later centuries.

In France, characteristically, theory was a long way ahead of practice. Vitruvian studies were almost as advanced as in Italy. The engraving of a reconstruction of the Theatre of Marcellus by Béatrizet, made about the middle of the sixteenth century, is extremely creditable. Du Cerceau, a little later, includes five theatres in his *Livres des édifices antiques romains*, though they are less accurate than that of Béatrizet.

No French theatre in the least resembling that of Vicenza, however, was ever built. The reason was partly the monopoly still held by the old Confrérie de la Passion. At the beginning of the fifteenth century this semi-professional company moved into indoor quarters in the Hôpital de la Trinité. This meant squeezing their *mansiones* on to a narrow stage and

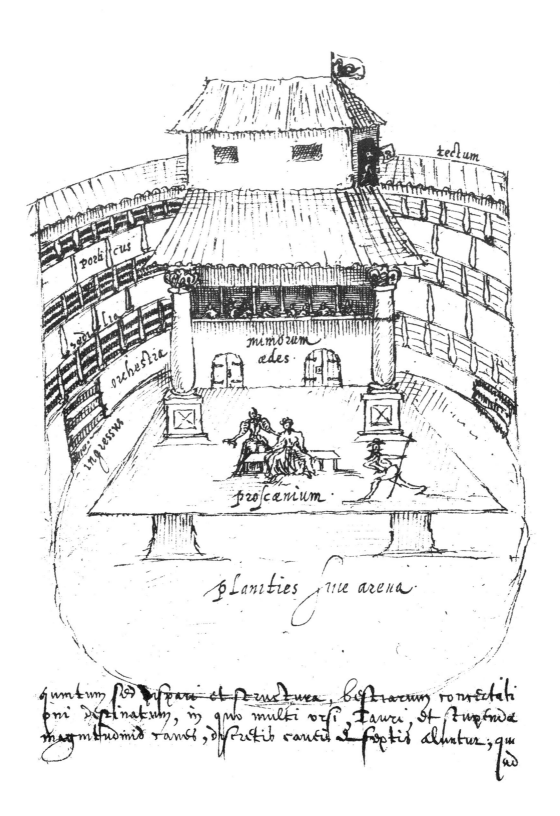

tectum

porticus

orchestra

mimorum
aedes

ingressus

proscænium

planities sive arena

quintum sed disparu et structura, bestiarum concertati
oni destinatum, in quo multi ursi, tauri, et stupenda
magnitudinis canes, diversis catenis & septis aluntur, qui
ad

possibly in two storeys. It must have looked rather like the Cologne *Laurentius*. In 1548, they moved again to a specially converted room in the ruins of the palace of the Dukes of Burgundy, and this hall, the so-called Hôtel de Bourgogne, saw the whole transition of French drama from medieval to modern. The confraternity was forbidden to act religious plays in that very year but they retained the theatre and licensed it to visiting companies. The monopoly lasted until 1675. Drawings of many seventeenth-century sets used in the Hôtel de Bourgogne have survived [Pl. 49]. They show the influence of Serlio, but also keep some of the conventions of the old multi-location sets. There was almost certainly no proscenium arch.

One national drama remains to be examined, that of England, where the years 1580 to 1620 saw an extraordinary flowering of literary talent and an almost equally unexpected development of theatrical form. The reason lies partly in social conditions. Companies of players, only nominally in the service (and therefore under the protection) of noblemen, found that the best place for acting a play was the yard of an inn, with its galleries running round three or four sides and its open space in the middle for the stage and standing spectators. A few such inn yards still exist and it is easy to visualize the arrangements. When players became prosperous enough to build theatres of their own, this was the model that they followed [Pl. 50]. (An alternative theory is that they copied bear-baiting arenas. Probably both came into it.)

There were never very many of these open theatres, and they were all in London. The first, called simply the Theatre, was built in 1576. The Curtain followed in 1577; the Rose in 1587; the Swan (of stone) in 1595; the Globe in 1599 (with timber from the Theatre, demolished at the same time); the Fortune in 1600; and the Hope in 1613. The Globe was burnt down in 1613 and rebuilt the next year. Our knowledge of what these theatres looked like is limited to one copy of a drawing of an interior [Pl. 51], and a few engravings of exteriors [Pl. 52], some descriptions by foreign visitors, one building contract, and what can be deduced from the plays performed in them. The pictures reproduced here are helpful but do not tell us as much as we should like. Of descriptions, one of the best is the earliest, that of Samuel Kiechel, a German, who went to the Theatre in 1585: 'Comedies are given every day; it is particularly amusing to go when the Queen's Men play, but for a foreigner who does not know the language, annoying not to understand. There are some odd houses with three galleries one on top of the other, so that a large crowd of people always comes to watch this kind of entertainment.'

Another visitor, a Swiss, had this to say about the Curtain in 1599: 'The theatres are so built that the players are on a raised platform and the whole audience can see everything quite well. There are separate galleries and places where you can sit in greater comfort, but you have to pay more for it.'

Pl. 52. *Part of Visscher's panorama of London, of 1616, with the Bear Garden and the Globe Theatre in the foreground. Their similarity lends some strength to the view that the Elizabethan theatre owed its peculiar shape as much to bear-baiting pits as to inn yards.*

The stage seems to have been raised about six feet from the ground, and the space beneath was boarded or curtained from view. Actors entered from doors at the back or at the sides. Some theatres had a space at the back that could be used as an inner room and closed off with a curtain. Above it, at first floor level behind the stage, was a gallery which could represent the upstairs of a house or a town gate. The stage itself projected forward into the audience and contained a trapdoor by which characters could also enter and exit. Around the central yard rose tiers of galleries, usually three; they and the back of the stage were roofed (although the Globe, we know, was thatched).

The most exact information on any of these theatres is provided by the contract for the Fortune Theatre, drawn up between Henslowe and Alleyn, theatre-managers, on the one hand, and Peter Streete, carpenter, on the other. (Streete's firm had also built the Globe, and the contract is tantalizingly full of specifications saying 'according to the manner and fashion of the said house called the Globe'.) The Fortune was to be square in plan, with sides eighty feet long. There were to be three galleries twenty-five feet in width and varying in height from nine to twelve feet. The stage was to reach to the middle of the central space and to be forty-three feet wide (in some theatres this had to be removable, so that they could be converted into bear-baiting pits).

The conditions that these theatres imposed upon dramatists are easy to recognize in the works of Shakespeare and his contemporaries. The projecting 'apron stage' meant that an actor could come forward into the centre of the audience, talk to them directly in a soliloquy or throw *sotto-voce* remarks to them which the other characters did not hear. The convention of the 'aside', now so awkward, must have seemed perfectly natural. Characters also appear 'above' (i.e. on the gallery over the stage); they are 'discovered' (i.e. the curtain at the back is drawn back revealing them); ghosts can 'ascend' (i.e. come up through the trapdoor) or 'descend', as the witches' cauldron does in *Macbeth*.

What relation, if any, was there between the Tudor playhouses and the Italianate fashions which were already strongly influential in Flanders? This is a question that has been much discussed, but the evidence provides no satisfactory answer. The form of the theatres themselves seems to owe nothing to foreign example. The stage is another matter. The records and descriptions make it clear that something more than plain oak-joinery was attempted, and there are frequent references to 'columns'. Whether they looked at all like the elaborate street theatres of Flanders we have no means of knowing.

In the histories of English drama much less attention is paid to the indoor 'private' theatres, although these had existed as long as the outdoor ones. The Blackfriars dates from the same year as the Theatre, 1576. It must have been a variant of the *teatro da sala* which was the normal setting for aristocratic entertainments both in England and on the Continent. They offered greater scope for scenery and illusionistic effects than the so-called 'public' theatres. An inventory of the public theatre manager Henslowe lists the props available at the Rose in 1598—a rock, three tombs, 'Hell's mouth', 'a tree of golden apples', an altar, a bedstead, two 'moss banks' and even 'a chain of dragons'. But these were humdrum affairs compared with the 'divers towns and houses', 'monsters', 'great hollow trees', 'battlements', 'prisons', 'clouds' and so on that appear in the accounts of the Office of Revels at the Court. This meant that a different kind of play tended to be written for the indoor theatres. The Blackfriars, for instance,

Pl. 53. Inigo Jones's masque designs show that he was already using the proscenium arch, and he was clearly aware of contemporary Italian practice. This drawing for 'The Queen's Masque of Indianos' (1634) represented only a temporary structure. Some other drawings by Jones seem to be sketches for a more permanent proscenium stage.

put on the plays of Lyly, whose delicacy and erudition would have been swamped in the robust surroundings of the Globe. A second Blackfriars Theatre (actually the converted refectory of a Dominican convent) was opened by Burbage in 1596. Shakespeare's later plays were written for this theatre, and it is no accident that they are more intimate in feeling than the early ones. A scene like the opening of the *Tempest*, which takes place on the deck of a ship, or a later one when a table of food appears and disappears, would also have more effect in such surroundings. One point of interest is the early use of the front curtain in English private theatres, at a time when it was not at all common even in Italy.

The key figure in the English court masques is Inigo Jones, who brings us back closer to the Palladian orbit than any artist outside Italy. Jones studied the Vicenza theatre carefully on his second visit to Italy, and undoubtedly nursed the hope of erecting its counterpart in England. His sketches survive. Like the Teatro Farnese (which he cannot have known), the design has one large arch instead of five smaller ones, with a permanent perspective set inside it. Other sketches show fully-developed proscenium arches, possibly temporary structures for masques [Pl. 53]. In the event, the only real offspring of the Teatro Olimpico seems to have been Jones's Cockpit-

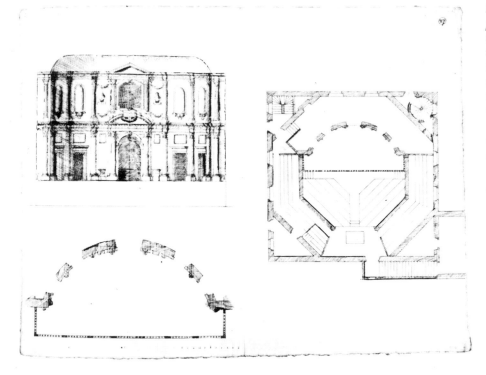

Pl. 54. The Cockpit-in-Court Theatre, probably by Inigo Jones. On the right is the plan of the whole theatre, on the left the plan and elevation of the scaenae *frons. The design, though miniature in scale (the width of the stage is only thirty-five feet) is a most interesting variation on Palladio's theatre at Vicenza, with the special subtlety of a concave back to the stage. The window over the central opening is no doubt the 'music room', still in its old Elizabethan position.*

in-Court Theatre at Whitehall. Much uncertainty still surrounds this building, but the following is a plausible interpretation. The Cockpit (i.e. a real pit for cock fighting) had been part of the rambling Whitehall Palace since Henry VII's time. Under James I it came to be used for private performances of plays and under Charles I (in 1630) it was remodelled by Jones as a permanent theatre. A plan and elevation at Worcester College, Oxford, is thought to represent this remodelling though the drawing is actually in John Webb's, not Jones's, hand [Pl. 54]. It is a small-scale variation on the plan of the Teatro Olimpico, with the seating arranged as a half-octagon and the *scaenae frons* curved. Five arches are framed in an elaborate classical façade. What was to happen behind them? There is hardly room for perspectives and the arrangement of five independent painted flats would have presented difficulties. The fact that Jones was never able to realize his more ambitious plans is much to be regretted. Those opportunities came only after the Restoration, when first Webb and then Sir Christopher Wren brought England into the mainstream of Continental theatre building. Neither, however, had the blend of fantasy and inventiveness that Jones possessed. The Baroque theatre never took root here. For that we must return to Italy.

V

THE PICTURE AND THE FRAME

The first half of the seventeenth century saw the formation of all the essential features of what one calls the modern theatre (though that term is now out of date)—the picture-frame stage and its horseshoe-shaped auditorium with tiers of galleries or boxes. The spread of Italian methods of staging meant that the theatre was increasingly seen as a place of illusion, of make-believe. The illusion depended on scenery; scenery made a picture; the picture required a frame. Hence the proscenium arch.

The crucial moment of transition can be excellently studied in the Teatro Farnese at Parma. It was commissioned in 1617 by Duke Ranuccio I, the great-great grandson of Paul III, the Farnese Pope who had established the family at Parma. The designated site was a hall on the first floor of Ranuccio's vast Palazzo Pilotta, a palace which, though unfinished and partly destroyed by bombing, is still large enough to house the archaeological museum, the city art gallery and half the municipal offices of Parma. The theatre plan, a long rectangle, was therefore not a free choice on the part of the architect, Gian-Battista Aleotti, and he was denied the possibility of the more manageable square.

Aleotti was an experienced and versatile engineer-architect (he was seventy-one years old in 1617), who had earlier served the Estes of Ferrara and had, among a multitude of other activities, already built a theatre there—the famous Teatro degli Intrepidi of 1606, altered in 1640 and burnt down in 1679. Although also constructed within an existing building (a granary), this embodied the most up-to-date features of Italian theatre design, in particular the proscenium arch, or 'picture frame', embracing the whole stage, which had probably developed first in Florence. At the same time Aleotti in this earlier design had followed Palladio in retaining the architectural elaboration of the *scaenae frons*, though placing the acting area behind it rather than in front; the set seems to have been a permanent 'tragic' street scene painted on a backcloth. The auditorium was semi-circular.

Ranuccio's theatre at Parma was to be on a larger scale and altogether richer in its decoration. Associated with Aleotti in its construction were a noble amateur, the Marchese Enzo Bentivoglio, the Lombard sculptor Marco Luca Reti and the Bolognese painter Lionello Spada. Aleotti himself was called away on legal business before it was completed, and there is reason to think that some of the planning should be credited to Bentivoglio.

Pl. 55. The Teatro Farnese, Parma, by Aleotti. Sadly damaged during the war, it is now being repaired to some of its old splendour. The arch on the right, surmounted by an equestrian statute, was originally one of the entrances.

The work suffered several setbacks. It was not finished until ten years later, after Ranuccio's death, and the first performance in fact celebrated the wedding of his son and successor Odoardo to Margherita de' Medici on 21 December 1628. (These spectacular celebrations, incidentally, also included the building of a temporary wooden theatre by the Baroque architect Rainaldi in the courtyard of the palace; all that history records about this is that the audience was so cold that the stamping of feet drowned the music.)

The basic shape of the Teatro Farnese has much more in common with Buontalenti's Uffizi theatre than with Palladio's at Vicenza. It is almost two and a half times longer than it is broad. Aleotti utilized this extra length by making the auditorium a deep U-shape. As at Sabbioneta, there is a space between the auditorium and the stage (where the orchestra pit of a modern theatre would be) into which two doors open, surmounted

Pl. 56. *The stage of the Teatro Farnese. In contrast to the Teatro Olimpico at Vicenza of some forty years earlier, there is now a single proscenium arch framing a deep space where flats could be manoeuvred.*

by equestrian statues of two earlier Farnese dukes, Ottavio and Alessandro. The stage itself is set back in a monumental composition of giant Corinthian columns on pedestals, with niches between them holding allegorical statues. On the cornice perch other allegorical figures and *putti*, two of whom hold the Farnese coat of arms over the centre of the stage [Pl. 56].

Movable scenery was intended from the beginning, a mark of modernity in 1617, and the stage is deep enough to accommodate nine or ten rows of sliding flats. The action, however, was not intended to be confined to this area; it could spill forward into the arena in front of the *scaenae frons* and even into the middle of the U-shaped ranks of seats.

The auditorium, which has fourteen rows of seats, could hold 3,000 spectators [Pl. 55]. The seats descend not to ground level but to a point six feet or so above the floor, where they are enclosed behind a balustrade.

This may be one of Bentivoglio's modifications to Aleotti's plan. A model now in the museum at Drottningholm shows the seats coming right down to floor level. Behind the seats rises a two-storey arcade, following the precedent of antique theatres and of the Teatro Olimpico, but based more specifically on Palladio's 'Basilica', a re-casing of the Town Hall, at Vicenza. At the back of the room it is a genuine arcade with space behind, but at the two sides it is merely applied to the wall, giving a strong sense of architectural unity to the whole design.

The opening performance was one that tested the theatre's resources to the full. It was an extravagant opera-ballet called *Mercury and Mars* by Achillini. Among the composers invited to Parma to provide music was Monteverdi, but his contribution is lost. It included a display of horsemanship and ended with a scene in which Neptune, enraged at the hero's escape, flooded the stage and central arena to a depth of two feet; storms, shipwrecks and fights between sea monsters ensued, to be pacified only by the descent of Jupiter from the sky with a hundred attendants.

The Teatro Farnese did not stand alone. By about 1640 every Italian court of any pretensions could boast a permanent theatre. Rome had many splendid ones. That of the Palazzo Barberini (1632) is said to have held 3,000 spectators and may have been designed by Bernini. It had a proscenium arch supported by two grand Corinthian columns, and (as at Parma) steps down to the *parterre*. Bernini's work for the theatre was far more prolific than his surviving drawings would suggest. John Evelyn, on a visit to Rome, attended an opera for which Bernini had written the words, composed the music, painted the scenery, invented the machines and built the theatre.

More significant for the future than these private court theatres were the public theatres which were coming into existence in Venice. (The earliest is in fact not in Venice but in Yugoslavian territory that was then Venetian—the plain little theatre on the island of Lesina, now Hvar, of 1612 [Pl. 58].) These theatres were financed either by noble families or by shareholders, but in either case the motive was profit. The owners rented out the boxes, leaving the income from the pit and galleries to pay the expenses of the actors. This system had an immediate effect on architecture. Instead of elegance and ostentation and the close association of stage and auditorium (since at masques the audience often joined in themselves), the overriding consideration was now the need to accommodate as many customers as possible. Instead of one, or at most two, tiers of galleries centred on the royal box, with the *parterre* often left empty, the new theatres crowded in three or four tiers, divided them up into boxes, filled the *parterre* with benches and put the orchestra (in the modern sense) in the space which at court often linked the stage and the auditorium. The Teatro San Cassiano (1639), by Benedetto Ferrari, was traditionally the first theatre designed in this way. Between then and 1699, at least sixteen

Venetian public theatres have been traced, known mostly by the names of the parishes where they were located. Only the Teatro San Moise partially survives as a cinema. Throughout this time the commercial theatre became more competitive and better organized. Prices of admission went steadily down, government regulations were issued to control safety and hours of performance. Evelyn attended one in 1645 and decided that 'taken together it is one of the most magnificent and expensive diversions the wit of man can invent'. Another observer, about 1672, found the theatres 'large and magnificent', the decorations 'superb and varied, but very badly lit'.

Pl. 57. This eighteenth-century plan of the Teatro Farnese, Parma, illustrates how not only the stage but the whole central arena was used for performances. On this occasion the attraction was a horse ballet, part of an elaborate pantomime called Neptune's Wedding.

Lighting of the auditorium, to judge from such scanty records as survive, was by a single large chandelier which was drawn up during the performance.

From Venice, the public theatres spread to the other Italian cities. In Rome the original Teatro Tor di Nona, of 1660, seems to have been the first. Like the Venetian theatres, those of Rome tended to have a bad reputation morally, and Pope Innocent XI ordered all the partitions between the boxes to be taken down.

At Bologna, in the Teatro Formagliari (1640), Andrea Sighizzi placed his boxes *en escalier*, rising behind each other to give a better view. He repeated the idea at the Teatro Malvezzi in the same city in 1653, and it was adopted at Genoa that year by G. A. Falcone in the Teatro Falcone (which survived until World War II), but it had fewer imitators than one would expect. Other celebrated theatres of around the middle of the century were the Teatro della Sala at Bologna, rebuilt after a fire in 1639; and the theatre at Piacenza, another Farnese city, designed in 1644 for a hall in the Palazzo Comunale by Cristoforo Rangani, with a proscenium arch and curtain, an auditorium lined with twenty-two Doric columns in imitation marble and two tiers of boxes between them.

In 1676 the first modern treatise on theatre architecture appeared, Fabrizio Carini Motta's *Trattato sopra la struttura de' teatri e scene*. The author deals with the differences between private and public theatres, with acoustics, problems of sight-lines and the need to provide the maximum number of seats, advising (as in fact seems to have been the practice, beginning with Lotti's Spanish theatre [Pl. 66]) that partitions between

Pl. 58. The small theatre at Hvar, Yugoslavia, (1612) is our best surviving example of the early seventeenth-century Venetian public theatre, a type which now took its place beside the much more lavishly decorated court theatres. It is on the first floor of the old Arsenal. Hvar (Lesina) was at the time Venetian territory.

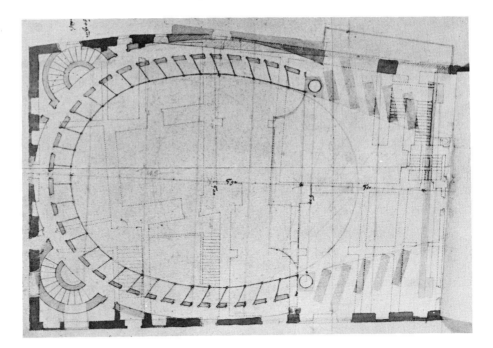

the boxes should be placed along the axes of the sight-lines instead of at right-angles to the balustrade. It is interesting to find Motta already giving attention to the segregation of social classes by providing separate entrances to the various parts of the house. This is a point which was increasingly to occupy architects during the next hundred years. A theatre is indeed an obvious symbol of the social hierarchy and was from the start recognised as such. Motta was also much enamoured of the 'acoustic curve', a shape which, when found, had to be reconciled with optical and structural requirements. Like later Italian theorists he was comparatively uninterested in decoration.

By 1700 nearly all possible shapes for the auditorium had been tried. One can get a good idea of their variety by comparing the plans (which have fortunately survived in Sir John Soane's Museum, London) of some of the most important—the Pergola, Florence, by Ferdinando Tacca, 1656, still basically intact, complete with its equipment for raising the floor to serve as a ballroom; the SS. Giovanni e Paolo, Venice; the Intronati, Siena; and above all the second Tor di Nona, Rome, of 1671 [Pl. 59]. For this a number of projects were prepared by Carlo Fontana, or possibly his pupil Alessandro Specchi, varying not only in the geometry of the auditorium but also in such things as the placing and form of staircases. The shape finally chosen was the horseshoe, a compromise between the favourite Baroque oval and the fan.

With the Tor di Nona the transition between the Renaissance and modern is complete. Almost all theatres, for the next two centuries, will conform to this pattern, and before going on to look at individual examples, it may be profitable to summarize what they have in common. Most important, since it determines much of the rest of the theatre, is the proscenium arch. The traditional account of the genesis of the proscenium makes it a development from the central arch of the Teatro Olimpico, which is bigger than the other two and contains most of the scenery. By the time of the Teatro Farnese, runs the story, this central arch has expanded to embrace the whole stage, and has moved forward, so that instead of forming a background for the actors it becomes a frame round them. Such an explanation no longer seems convincing. Picture-frame stages were being made for masques with movable scenery at the very beginning of the seventeenth century, if not earlier. The sequence from *scaenae frons* to picture frame no longer looks like an evolution, but a simple replacement of one by the other.

Once accepted, however, logic might seem to demand that the auditorium should adapt itself to the new requirements by making all the seats face directly forward. This did not happen. Long after the action had retreated behind the picture frame, the seats continued to be arranged as if it were still out in front of it. The reason is by no means simple. It was partly social pressure. A seventeenth- or eighteenth-century audience came as much to be seen as to see, and if all the seats faced in the same direction nobody could see anybody else. Not until Wagner's Bayreuth do we find side seats entirely abandoned. Beyond this, one perhaps enters the realm of group psychology. An audience in a typical old-fashioned theatre feels united, even if not all its members can see the stage properly. An audience in a more rationally planned house feels separately alone. One has only to attend a live performance on the stage of a cinema to know this to be true.

The proscenium arch was due primarily to the demands of the scene designer, and it was a long time before actors could be induced to keep within it. In England especially, what is now called the 'thrust' or 'apron' stage persisted until the nineteenth century, when theorists began to insist on a distinction between 'real' space and 'stage' space. Indeed, the arch itself was consciously treated as belonging to both spaces and uniting the two, being built in false perspective in order to lead the eye inwards and having side boxes incorporated in it. By the nineteenth century this fraternization was frowned upon and a rigid apartheid policy operated.

The curtain came naturally with the proscenium. It enabled set designers to reveal their pictures with dramatic suddenness, and to hide them when they had to be changed. Where it was first used in this way it is impossible to say. The English private theatres seem to have had curtains around 1600.

What is lacking in almost every theatre before the eighteenth century is any concern with circulation and refreshment and any ambition to give the theatres impressive exteriors. A few, however, had façades (e.g. the Dorset

Pl. 60. Opernhaus in Salvatorplatz, the private theatre of the Elector of Bavaria, in Munich. In 1685 it had been remodelled by the Italian architects Domenico and Gasparo Mauro. The Elector's box is its most conspicuous feature, the parterre still being left open so that the action could come forward 'in the round' if desired.

Garden Theatre in London) and there are projects by Fontana with monumental elevations all round.

The Baroque theatre spread to the rest of Europe from Italy, either through the visits of Italian designers to foreign courts, or, more rarely, the visits of northerners to Italy. One of the most interesting of the latter was Josef Furttenbach, who spent some time in Florence with Parigi (the designer of the Teatro Mediceo which succeeded Buontalenti's) before going back to his native Ulm and building a theatre there in 1641. This had a plain rectangular plan, was filled with raked seats facing the stage (i.e. it was unlike the standard court theatre) and used *periaktoi* in the scenery. Furttenbach had few opportunities for putting any more ambitious ideas into practice, but he was a prolific author. In one volume he puts forward a revolutionary design for an octagonal theatre with four stages facing each other on the alternate sides. The audience stood in the middle and turned from one stage to the other as the action required. This is a fascinating throwback to medieval practice, using Italianate motifs—just as contemporary northern architects were doing—purely as ornament. The stages were to be fully Baroque, with *periaktoi* scenery.

In the decade after the Thirty Years' War, German and Austrian princes began providing themselves with theatres and opera houses. That at Munich, the Opernhaus in Salvatorplatz (1654), built by a local baumeister in collaboration with the Venetian Francesco Saturini, was actually the first German theatre outside the walls of a palace. It was old-fashioned by Italian standards, but three galleries and a royal box were added in 1685 by Mauro [Pl. 60]. Dresden's first opera house, 1664, was by a German architect who had studied in Italy, Kaspar von Klengel; here the proscenium arch was combined with sweeping staircases to the gallery, an interesting attempt to bring the grand staircase inside the auditorium. That of Vienna (1652) was by Giovanni Burnacini. It had two arcaded levels of galleries and the acting area, as usual, spilt forward on to the floor of the house. As rebuilt thirty-five years later by Giovanni's son, Ludovico, it had three tiers of galleries on an awkward rectangular plan, but a splendid *trompe-l'œil* ceiling which made it seem larger than it really was. None of these exist today. The oldest surviving court theatre is the Schlosstheater at Celle, Hanover, of 1670. Germany, however, was laying the foundations of an art which, in the next century, was to make her the supreme exponent of Baroque theatre.

France was far less adventurous. The early theatres were all built in existing halls (tennis courts being particularly convenient) and embodied few architectural features: the Théâtre du Marais of 1629, the Petit Bourbon, 1635, and Richelieu's theatre in the Palais Cardinal of 1641. The last was by a famous Italian, Torelli, and had a large classical proscenium frame, the first in France. In 1661, Mazarin invited Torelli's rival, Gaspare Vigarani, to build a theatre in the Tuileries. This opened in January 1662 and lasted for many years in spite of serious deficiencies. The deep stage (132 feet) gave wonderful opportunities for scenic invention. Many architects, despairing of ever seeing their schemes actually built, had the consolation of building them in canvas on Vigarani's stage. The machinery was of such elaboration that it became known as the *Salle des Machines*, but the acoustics were so bad that few of the 5,000 spectators could ever hear what was going on. Vigarani's son returned to France later and collaborated with Le Vau in building theatres for *fêtes* at Versailles [Pl. 61].

Corneille, Racine and Molière were creating one of the great dramatic repertoires, but the conditions of performances remained primitive. A smaller theatre in the Palais Royal, designed in 1660 by Lemercier, had at least drawbacks different from the *Salle des Machines*, its stage being too shallow and hemmed in to accommodate elaborate scenery. Molière's troupe performed here until they moved to another mediocre theatre, the Théâtre de Guénégaud, but that was replaced in 1689 by the first French theatre to win any kind of international reputation, the Comédie Française by François d'Orbay. This was modest in scale, with a U-shaped auditorium, spreading slightly to the stage. There were benches at the back of the *parterre*, standing room in front, and more benches on the stage. To an Italian it would have seemed provincial, but it had a refreshment room and other amenities.

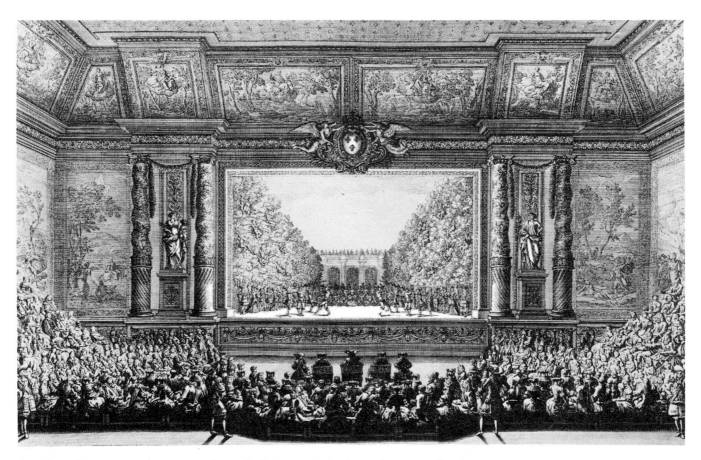

Pl. 61.   *A temporary theatre erected by Carlo Vigarani in the park at Versailles in 1672. The engraving probably exaggerates the scale, but clearly no expense was spared. Vigarani has modelled his side columns on Bernini's baldacchino at St. Peter's.*

In England the restoration of 1660 was the signal for a theatrical boom. Etheridge, Wycherley and Congreve gave the English stage a new comic style, and theatres on the French model sprang up in London and in a few provincial towns. Drama in England had fewer courtly connections than it had on the Continent. Theatres were plainer, smaller, noisier. Few of them had any architectural distinction. The Dorset Garden Theatre (1671) was supposed to have been designed by Wren; it had a proscenium arch of a sort, but the stage projected well in front of it, with stage doors at the sides and boxes over them. The first Theatre Royal, Drury Lane, was built as early as 1663, but only tantalizing descriptions (including some by Pepys) remain. It was replaced in 1674 by the second Drury Lane Theatre by Wren, about which controversy still rages. Wren certainly gave theatre design considerable thought (one of his earliest projects, after all, was the Sheldonian), and a collection of plans and elevations now at All Souls,

Oxford, show that he had many interesting ideas. One of them features an auditorium shaped like a scallop shell facing a conventional deep stage, into which only a third of the audience could possibly have seen [Pl. 63]. Another, which has been convincingly connected with Drury Lane, is far simpler—a rectangular hall with a stage facing curving rows of seats [Pl. 62]. At the back was to be a row of boxes, the royal box being isolated, and galleries above. Again, nothing much was made of the proscenium arch; the stage projected in front like an Elizabethan apron stage (a fashion which the actors were probably reluctant to give up) and receded behind to create a space which has been christened the 'vista area'. The side walls contained a double range of boxes between giant pilasters. Later alterations to Wren's theatre are known to have had the effect of pushing the stage back inside the proscenium arch, a tendency common to the whole of Europe. Another London theatre about which one would like to know more is that built in the Haymarket by Vanbrugh as part of his career as an impresario. It had tiers of boxes on a horseshoe plan, and the auditorium was covered by a dome. The immense segmental proscenium arch was much admired by the public, but was considered too grandiose by the actors. Colley Cibber says that 'this extraordinary and superfluous space occasioned such an undulation from the voice of every actor that generally what they said sounded like the gabbling of so many people in the lofty aisles of a cathedral.' A monumental exterior was designed by Vanbrugh but never materialized; he did, however, provide a foyer for patrons of the boxes, and a large salon with a fireplace.

Finally two examples from opposite ends of the theatrical spectrum. At Amsterdam, Jacob van Campen's Schouwburg of 1637 was an extraordinary combination of old and new [Pls. 64, 65]. The auditorium had rows of boxes between pilasters (which Wren may possibly have known), but the stage was a sort of multi-locational *scaenae frons*, with several vestigial *mansiones* grouped together on an open platform without a proscenium arch, but providing space for painted flats. Near Madrid, five years earlier, Philip IV's theatre at his palace of El Buen Retiro was built by an Italian architect, Cosimo Lotti [Pl. 66]. This was as amazingly advanced as the Schouwburg was backward. While not competing in scale with theatres in Italy, it embodied all the latest devices, including sliding flats and box partitions on the axes of the sight-lines.

I have so far avoided anything but the barest mention of stage spectacle, since this is a history of the theatre as architecture. But at this point the two subjects are so closely interconnected that it would be pedantic to keep them apart, not only because nearly all the architects of theatres were also outstanding scene designers (usually, indeed, more famous for this than for their architecture), but also because Baroque art itself was indivisible to an extent that has rarely been true of any art before or since. Architecture, painting, sculpture, music, poetry, drama—all merged with each other and

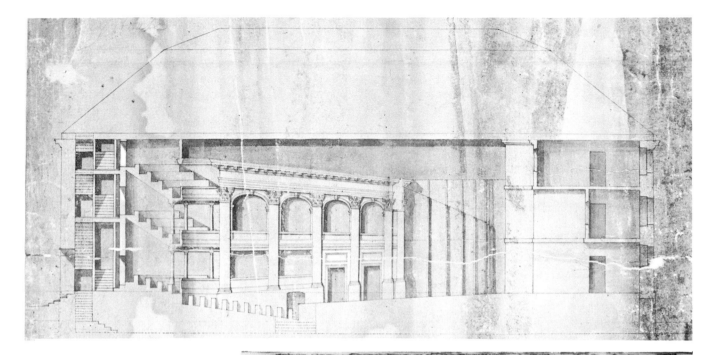

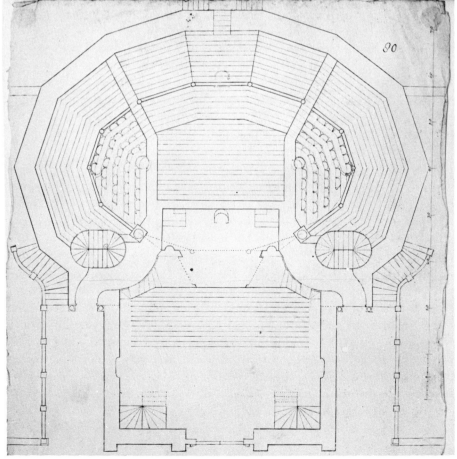

Pls. 62, 63. Two theatre designs by Sir Christopher Wren. Above: section believed to be of the old Drury Lane Theatre. The straight sides of the auditorium are lined with boxes and articulated by pilasters. There was a proscenium arch (sketched in another drawing) but the stage projected more than two bays in front of it, and was provided with two doors on each side. Right: projected plan, comparable in some ways with the Cockpit-in-Court (Pl. 54). An eleven-sided auditorium is focused on an apparently tripartite stage, but it is not clear how the space behind this was meant to be used. Obviously only those sitting in the centre section of seats would be able to see into it.

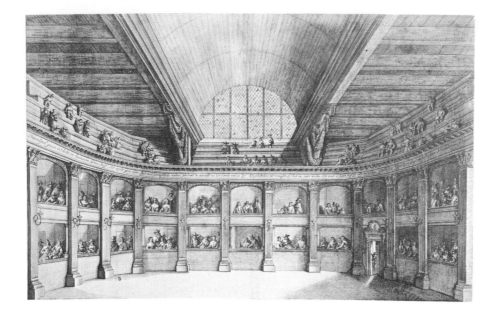

Pls. 64, 65. The Old Schouwburg at Amsterdam, of 1637, marks an interesting moment of transition. The auditorium (left) has classical pilasters, two tiers of boxes and (most advanced of all) a spacious raked gallery at the top. In the parterre, there is standing room only. The stage (right) consists of a permanent multiple set based on the Rederyker 'frontispiece' stages that were set up in the street or in courtyards. (The Rederykers were oratorical societies who held competitions in plays and recitations.) But painted flats in the modern Italian style could be fitted between the columns.

served a single purpose. This makes it difficult to judge. Baroque plays and operas taken on their own seem flimsy and artificial; what is missing is the magic which came from the union of all the arts. In fact all Baroque art, it used disparagingly to be said, was 'theatrical'. Bernini, like Verdi, saw no reason to change his style when he turned from the stage to the church. The Cornaro Chapel is even overtly suggestive of a theatre. Pozzo saw the ceiling of S. Ignazio very much in terms of a theatrical problem. The Asam brothers, whose altarpieces at Rohr and Weltenburg can only be described in theatrical terms, whether to praise or to blame, specifically called one vital element in their art *scenographia*.

There was little room for magic on the Vitruvian stage. As Inigo Jones observed of the Teatro Olimpico: 'In this scene there are no apparitions of *nugole* (clouds) and suchlike, but only the artifice of the scene in perspective carrieth it.' We have seen how the open, Serlian stage gave more opportunity for scenic invention, but it was still on the whole static. Scene designers, prodded by erudite patrons, went on trying to make sense of the *periaktoi*, though they receded further and further from any classical precedent. Sometimes there were as many as six of these 'revolving prisms' on either side of the set, each painted with a small section of scene, which fitted together like three-dimensional jigsaw puzzles. But their limitations were insurmountable. They were cumbersome to construct and install, they could make only three changes of scene, and they were unconvincing from most parts of a large theatre. The superiority of sliding scenery—flats standing one behind the other—was so obvious that it soon won the day. The idea goes back well into the sixteenth century. As early as 1544,

Pl. 66. In Spain, Philip IV's theatre in his palace of El Buen Retiro is completely in what was to become the later seventeenth-century style. It was built in 1632 by Cosimo Lotti, a Florentine and an associate of Parigi. One advanced feature for that date is the arrangement of box partitions along the sight-lines.

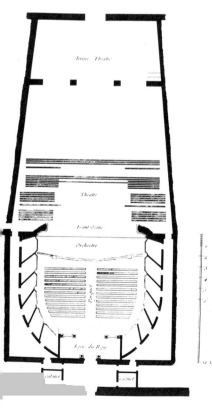

Philander was suggesting the transformation of the stage 'through panels drawn to the sides, so that this or that scene is revealed within'. By 1645, when Evelyn was in Venice, the theatre of magic was in full swing—'the history was Hercules in Lydia, the scenes changed thirteen times.'

There are several seventeenth-century accounts of stage illusionism. Andrea Pozzo, already mentioned, wrote a treatise on perspective scenery in 1693. Furttenbach's books were published between 1626 and 1663. Most illuminating of all was Nicola Sabbatini's *Prattica di fabricar scene e machine ne' teatri* (1638), which gives a full exposition of how to create a whole range of marvellous effects—how to make a sky, how to light the scene with colour, how to make houses, doors, windows, arches, etc., as if receding, 'how to arrange that the scene is suddenly darkened' (you lowered shades mechanically over all the candles at once), '*come si posse fare un Inferno*', how to get people quickly on and off the stage, how to make mountains, seas (his machine for producing waves is particularly ingenious [Pl. 67]), storms, rivers, fires, and so on. Most or all of this must have been common practice in Italy, and one can see Inigo Jones imitating it as well as he could in his masques. How far it succeeded is hard to say; the drawings always make it seem perfect, but in fact the elaborate perspective sets could only have looked convincing to a small section of the audience. Sabbatini in fact advises that, when a particularly tricky transformation scene is taking place, a man should be stationed in the back of the theatre to make a disturbance and distract people's attention.

Lighting also grew more and more complex, though of course it was still limited to candles and oil lamps. They were placed above or beside the scenery and reflected in various ways for special effects. Sabbatini also describes footlights—a short parapet in front of the stage with lights hidden behind it. These did not come into common use for over a century. As time went on, more and more lamps and candles were used, built up in great banks against huge reflectors. The heat was overpowering and, for both actors and playgoers all through the eighteenth and early nineteenth centuries, the risks of being burnt to death were by no means negligible.

Sabbatini could also, of course, turn his hand to architecture, and built at least one theatre, the Teatro del Sol at Pesaro. The history of Baroque theatre is full of such versatile geniuses, often moving from city to city and country to country, who regarded architecture only as an extension of their work as scene designers. Aleotti, who built the Teatro Farnese, was one of the reputed inventors of flats, or 'wings'. Gaspare Vigarani and Giacomo Torelli, who introduced Baroque scenic effects into France, both also designed theatres in Italy—Vigarani the court theatre at Modena in 1654, Torelli the Teatro della Fortuna at Fano in 1661. We have seen how Vigarani founded a theatrical dynasty in Paris. The Burnacinis achieved the same sort of position in Vienna. Greatest of all, in talent as well as in numbers, were the Bibienas, whose story includes the whole development of Baroque theatre from its origins in seventeenth-century Italy to its consummation a century later in Germany. They may fittingly lead us forward to that period by beginning a new chapter.

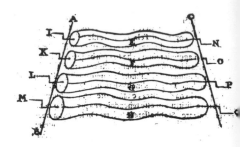

Pl. 67.   Nicola Sabbatini's wave machine. Four cylinders, bent in the way shown, have iron handles (I, K, etc.) fixed to their ends which rest on two wooden beams, The cylinders are covered with cloth painted blue and black, with a touch of silver. Each is turned by one man (if the stage is very large it will take a man at each end), standing of course out of sight. The cylinders should be placed about a foot apart, except when an actor has to stand between them in order to appear swimming or rising from the water. (See also Pl. 79.)

VI

COURT THEATRES
OF THE BAROQUE

The grandfather of the Bibienas was Giovanni Maria Galli-Bibiena, born in 1619. His famous sons (born in the late 1650s) were Ferdinando and Francesco. The third generation—omitting those of less note—consisted of Ferdinando's three children, Alessandro, Giuseppe and Antonio, and Francesco's one, Giovanni Carlo (all born between 1687 and 1700). The fourth had only one outstanding member, Giuseppe's son Carlo (1725–87). Throughout practically the whole of the eighteenth century they were in constant demand, as scene designers and arrangers of lavish shows much more than as architects. One comes across them in nearly all the leading towns of Italy and Germany, as well as in Prague, Buda, Belgrade, Lisbon, and Barcelona. Large numbers of their superb stage designs have survived, but few of their theatres. They represent the last great flowering of architects who were also men of the theatre. After the mid-eighteenth century the two professions diverged, and no one has been able to bring them together again.

The most widely admired Bibiena theatre was probably the Teatro Filarmonico at Verona, built by Francesco Bibiena between 1715 and 1729, and famous for its projecting boxes [Pl. 68]. The Filarmonico became something of a model to the Neoclassical generation. Francesco Milizia, who we shall meet in the next chapter, praised it in 1771 as being 'one of the best conceived theatres in Italy'. It had a fine staircase with four landings, and Milizia especially approved of the stalls entrance being placed next to the orchestra, 'as in the ancient Greek and Roman theatres, not exactly opposite the stage, since this point is the best for seeing and ought never to have been wasted on a doorway.'

Antonio's masterpiece, visually at least, was the Teatro Comunale at Bologna of 1756, built by a group of Bolognese noblemen after Sighizzi's Teatro Malvezzi had been destroyed by fire. Most of the planned amenities, such as a concert hall and gaming rooms, had to be sacrificed to economy, but the auditorium had a sort of Piranesian grandeur, with the lowest terrace of boxes resting on rusticated arches, grouped in pairs by means of rusticated pilasters; in the upper levels the pilasters were replaced by coupled columns. A splendid model of Antonio's interior remains [Pl. 69], but the actual building was altered in 1818–20 to the relatively unexciting form that it has today. Only his oval ceiling, pierced by twenty-two lunettes (forming gallery boxes) remains more or less intact. Pierre Patte, another critic of the late eighteenth century, found it '*mesquine et peu agréable*'. In spite of, or more probably because of, its architectural distinction, the Teatro Comunale was a conspicuous failure acoustically. This did not prevent Antonio from repeating it on a slightly smaller scale in the Teatro de' Quattro Cavalieri at Pavia in 1773 (now the Teatro Fraschini), where the gay mixture of classical motifs and excessive rustication can hardly have pleased the more purist critics of that date [Pl. 70]. Another work of Antonio's to survive is his relatively small-scale Teatro Scientifico at Mantua [Pl. 71]. Opened in 1769, it is now being restored. Leopold Mozart wrote to his wife that he had 'never seen a more elegant little theatre'.

Antonio's brother Alessandro built the court theatre at Mannheim in 1742. This had a graceful bell-shaped plan, the second section of seats being set back behind the first, so that the space receded in steps. The boxes

Pl. 68. Interior elevation of the Teatro Filarmonico, Verona, by Francesco Bibiena. The auditorium consisted of five tiers of boxes, each box slightly raised above the one in front— a scheme devised in the seventeenth century by Andrea Sighizzi. The boxes do not abut directly on to the proscenium columns but are divided by a space containing the entrance doors.

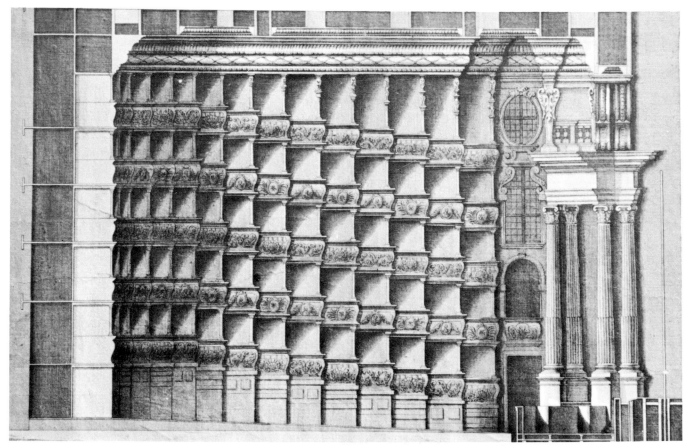

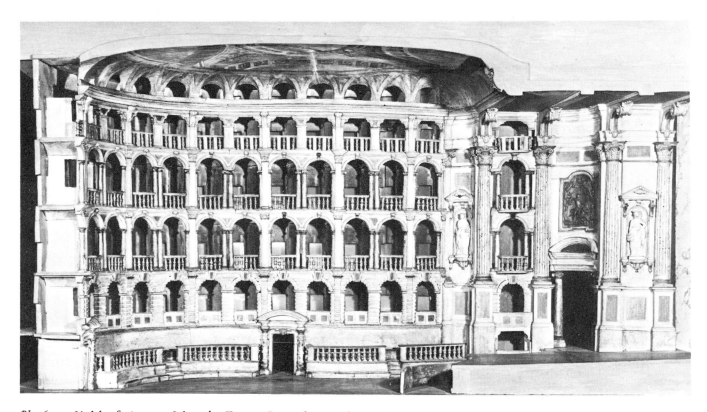

Pl. 69. *Model of Antonio Bibiena's Teatro Comunale at Bologna. The architectural elaboration of both proscenium and auditorium is not too far removed from the sets that the Bibienas designed in two dimensions for the stage. In many eighteenth-century pictures one is struck by the aesthetic continuity of audience-space and drama-space (see, for example, Pl. 75).*

themselves were separated in the northern fashion, by low partitions only, and were arranged on the Sighizzi method '*en escalier*'. Altogether it was one of the most originally conceived of all the Bibiena theatres. The stage was set well back inside the proscenium arch and had no fore-stage—signs of the Neoclassical taste that was to come.

By a stroke of extreme good fortune, one of the Bibienas' most perfect works survives absolutely intact, the Margrave's Opera House at Bayreuth [Pl. 72]. This was a family affair, begun by Giuseppe, probably working from a design by his uncle Francesco, and completed by his son Carlo. The stage is in fact very large—until the nineteenth century the largest in Germany—but the auditorium, which had to cater only for the court, is small in scale, constructed almost entirely of wood and relying as much on painted as on sculptural decoration. It is a work of irresistible charm. The showpiece of the whole theatre is the Margrave's box, which is covered by a canopy held by flying angels, its columns wreathed with gilded vines. Four tiers of galleries manage to squeeze themselves between floor and ceiling, the top one running right over the Margrave's box, and the bottom one, only slightly raised above floor level, connected with the *parterre* by a double flight of steps. More steps lead down from the stage, so that again the whole space could become a festive ballroom lit by rows of candles. Next to the stage are the so-called 'trumpeters' boxes', from which fanfares announced the arrival of the Margrave and the beginning of the play. (The contemporary façade of the theatre, incidentally, a dignified Neoclassical work by a French architect, provides an object–lesson in stylistic contrast.)

In 1740 Giuseppe Bibiena was called upon to design sets for Metastasio's *Arsace*, set to music by Francesco Feo. The occasion was the opening of the King of Piedmont's new court theatre, attached to his palace at Turin, the Teatro Regio [Pls. 73–5]. King Carlo Emmanuele III's original project had been for a theatre by Juvarra. But the latter departed for Spain in 1733, leaving his plans unfinished, and it was eventually built by someone who was by early training neither a man of the theatre nor an architect— Benedetto Alfieri, a lawyer. Like all great amateurs, Alfieri managed to keep up with the professionals by a combination of enthusiasm and diligence, and in fact was later appointed First Architect to the King in succession to Juvarra. Before embarking on the Teatro Regio he went on a tour of other Italian theatres, gathering ideas and learning from failures. Very little that he did is entirely original, but he united all that was best in contemporary theatre design. He increased the size of Juvarra's plan,

Pls. 70, 71. Two surviving theatres by Antonio Bibiena. Left: the Teatro Fraschini, Pavia, designed in 1773 (originally the Teatro Quattro Cavalieri). Right: the Teatro Scientifico, Mantua, of 1769. Both use a rusticated ground storey to support rows of superimposed columns (in correct classical sequence), with balconies on consoles between them. Note, in the Fraschini, the two statues high on the sides of the proscenium representing Music and Poetry.

turning it from a horseshoe into a more pronounced ellipse. There were 152 boxes, their different levels distinguished by contrasting styles of décor. In the centre stood the *corona*, the royal box, but except on special occasions the court occupied the proscenium boxes. (The *corona* had doors lined with mirrors so that the King could watch the stage even when his back was turned.) Heating was by hot air conveyed in pipes under the first level of boxes and then discharged into the stalls through two outlets fitted with regulators by which the temperature could be controlled. The main lighting consisted of a huge chandelier which could be raised and hidden behind painted panels during the performance. Alfieri adapted this device because 'those in the boxes were dazzled by the light shining in their faces and those in the stalls covered with falling dirt'. He thought also that a hole left open in the ceiling would interfere with the acoustics. Underneath the orchestra pit was a semi-cylindrical basement used as an acoustic reflector, with the bottom of the stage as the sounding board. A project for a façade was vetoed by the king, who wanted to keep the symmetry of the arcaded square.

From the very beginning the Teatro Regio set a standard, and it is interesting to note that although it was a court theatre the initiative was not entirely royal. It was begun in April 1738 by the forty-strong Società dei Signori Cavalieri of Turin, who wanted a new theatre for plays, operas and ballets and who paid an advance to the king of 100,000 lire. In return they received a seven-year financial interest in the sale of tickets, refreshments, libretti, etc. It served, in fact, as a sort of aristocratic civic centre. A platoon of soldiers was permanently on duty in the auditorium and adjoining gaming rooms to prevent disorder and to supervise the conduct of the public.

Galeotti of Florence and Milocco of Piedmont painted the ceiling with scenes showing the triumph of the gods. The stuccoist Domenico Ferretti was responsible for the royal box. The top of the proscenium was modelled in *scagliola*. Scenery was in the hands first of Giuseppe Bibiena and then of Fabrizio and Bernardino Galliari; Bernardino designed the drop-curtain with scenes of Bacchus and Ariadne.

Small wonder that the Teatro Regio became the admiration of Europe. It was probably studied more closely than any other theatre and, as the years went by, its restraint and the relative austerity of its decoration only recommended it the more to visitors nourished on the doctrines of Neoclassicism. Patte came here in 1750 and was to base his *Essai* very largely upon what he learned. Dumont in 1763 and later Diderot (in the article 'Théâtre' in the *Encyclopédie*) devoted many whole-page diagrams to it [Pls. 73, 74]. Another writer, J. J. Lalande, in 1765, found the theatre 'the most scholarly, the best laid out, and the most complete of any to be seen in Italy, and the most richly and nobly decorated of any in the modern style'. The innovation that most struck him was the concavity of the

Pl. 72. *The best preserved of all the Bibiena theatres is that at Bayreuth (1745–48), by Giuseppe and Carlo. Its finely calculated plan, brilliant colouring and profusion of rich Baroque decoration make it a uniquely enjoyable interior.*

ceiling, 'contrary to the custom of most theatres, which always have flat ceilings'. This noble theatre was destroyed by fire in 1937. (Alfieri, it may be of interest to record, went on to make architectural history by applying the horseshoe plan to a church, S. Giovanni Battista at Carignano. Why not?)

Italy and Italians were still clearly in the theatrical lead, though they were not long to retain it. In Germany, the Baroque tradition took firm root, blossoming into its own Rococo, and its jealous courts were ideal providers of patronage. But in the early years of the century, German theatres still seemed provincial. Mauro's opera house at Dresden of 1719 had a cramped auditorium with galleries, not boxes, the benches arranged in such

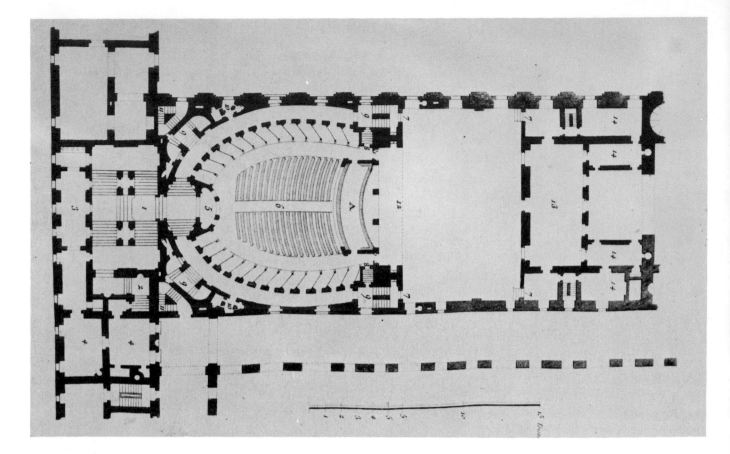

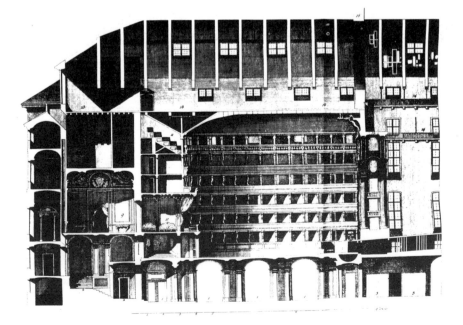

Pls. 73-75. The Teatro Regio, Turin, one of the most admired of European eighteenth-century theatres. The plan and section (above and left) come from Diderot's Encyclopédie. Right: a painting by P. D. Olivier of the opening night, December 26, 1740, when Metastasio's Arsace was performed with sets by Giuseppe Bibiena. Five tiers of boxes are fitted into the sides of the proscenium, one even perched over the semi-circular pediment. The painting is full of interesting details—the orchestra (without a conductor), the girls distributing refreshments, the armed guard keeping a watchful eye against disorder.

a way that only those in the centre faced the stage. When the theatre was rebuilt by Zucchi in 1738, he replaced the galleries by boxes, but transferred the same seating arrangements to the floor of the house—an indication that the court still looked for a hall theatre, with the performing area (potentially at least) in the middle.

For the true flower of German Rococo we must go to Munich. Here in 1750 François de Cuvilliés, Court Architect to the Elector Maximilian III Joseph, was commissioned to add a theatre to his master's palace, the Residenz [Pls. 76–8]. Few architectural careers can have followed a stranger course than that of Cuvilliés. Born in Flanders in 1695, he had come to Bavaria as a professional dwarf, then trained as an engineer, and had then been sent to Paris to study architecture under Jean François Blondel. He returned to Munich as the ambassador of a new style, uniting in a seemingly effortless way the energy and richness of the Germans with French daintiness and discipline. He remained essentially a decorator, unable to challenge his German contemporaries (Neumann, Fischer, Zimmermann) in pure architectural virtuosity, the moulding and manipulation of space.

To create the Residenztheater some of the best craftsmen in Germany were appointed to assist him—the court joiner, Adam Pichler, to do the woodwork, the sculptors Joachim Dietrich and Johann Baptist Straub, the painter Johann Baptist Zimmermann. Stage machinery was in the hands of an Italian, Paolo Gasparo. The new theatre opened three years later, on 12 October 1753, with Ferrandini's *Il Catone in Utica*.

Cuvilliés' ground-plan is not of any special interest. His auditorium was the conventional U-shape, with four levels of galleries. His proscenium arch rested on pairs of red imitation marble columns, with the stage itself projecting as far as the outer pair, and the ceiling above them diminishing in perspective (the inner pair were therefore slightly shorter than the outer). The space between each pair held two boxes, so that it belonged equally to the actors and the audience. In the modern, rebuilt, theatre, this space has been given to the orchestra, which originally sat further forward. Staircases were functional rather than ostentatious and, apart from the auditorium, only the apartment behind the Elector's box received any elaborate decoration. As there was no space behind the stage for the actors, their rooms and those of the property men and scene painters lay along the sides of the theatre behind the boxes. All these arrangements were swept away when the theatre was rebuilt on a different site (though still within the Residenz) in the 1950s.

The distinctive glory of the Residenztheater is its decoration, conceived by Cuvilliés and executed by artists of superlative talent. Its leitmotiv is the arabesque curve, which everywhere accompanies and softens, though it never conceals, the main architectural lines of the building. The second tier is the most lavishly treated. Swags of gilded fruit and foliage hang above the

Pls. 76, 77. Cuvilliés' Residenztheater, Munich: the restored auditorium.
Completed only a few years after Bayreuth, this is as purely Rococo as the other
is Baroque. Colour is limited to red, gold
and white, and the frothy arabesque
lines are thinner and more delicate. An
engraving published in 1771 (right)
shows the perspective effect aimed at in
the double proscenium columns, and at
the bottom the machinery for raising the
auditorium floor to the level of the stage.

boxes, which are separated from one another by caryatid figures ending in candelabra. Over the balustrades crimson velvet drapery, edged with gold, has apparently been carelessly thrown. The climax of the whole scheme is the Elector's own box [Pl. 78]. Supported on two over life-size caryatids and framed by fantastic golden palms, it is surmounted by a blazon of heraldic motifs, cupids and crowns, while an angel leans out into space and blows a long golden trumpet. The theatre is lit by candelabra projecting from the galleries at each level and by chandeliers hanging from the ceiling. The stalls were slightly raked but for special occasions it could still be turned into a ballroom by raising the floor of the auditorium to the level of the stage.

The details of this whole rich ensemble are a constant delight, overflowing with wit and unexpected invention. Here a Turk's head, with flowing moustache and golden turban, peeps out from a cartouche; there a spray of wheat or oak leaves climbs unnoticed over a moulding, or a group of perfectly carved pipes, drums and violins hangs waiting for some exuberant musical *putti* to snatch them up. Not all of it is original. The theatre was gutted in 1944, but enough of its decoration was saved to make possible what has been probably the most loving and successful of all postwar restorations. Only the ceiling, by Johann Baptist Zimmermann, has been lost for ever.

Two other court theatres, as far apart as Sweden and Bohemia but completed in the same year, 1766, share the distinction of still possessing their original stage machinery and painted sets. The first is part of the Summer Palace of Drottningholm, five miles outside Stockholm, and was built on the initiative of Queen Lovisa Ulrika, the wife of King Adolf Fredrik and the sister of Frederick the Great [Pl. 79]. Her architect was a Swede, Carl Fredrik Adelcrantz, but she drew upon French talent (Adrien Masreliez) for the painted decoration and Italian (Donato Stopani) for the machinery. The auditorium, while far simpler than the other examples described in this chapter, is more ingeniously planned for the convenience of the monarch. The whole front half of the room, which swells laterally in plan to form a curved space wider than the stage, becomes in effect the royal box. Here the royal family had an intimate view of the stage, but were separated from the rest of the audience, who occupied a single ramp of seats at the back. There are no galleries, but if complete privacy was required the king could retreat into one of two corner boxes which were completely screened by lattice grilles.

Drottningholm remains miraculously untouched, the only major alteration being a new foyer added in 1791 by the French architect Louis Jean Desprez. After neglect in the nineteenth century, it was re-opened in 1922, using the original furniture, the original movable stage (worked by a giant windlass), the original hoists and pulleys above the wings, and the original scenery, of which over thirty complete sets survive, by such artists as Carlo

Pl. 78. Right: the Elector's box in the ▶
Residenztheater, Munich. Much of the sculpture (in wood) was saved when the theatre was destroyed in 1944 and a thorough restoration has been possible. The putti holding up the crown, the angel trumpeters, the caryatid figures and the decoration of the canopy are the work of Johann Baptist Straub. The capitals, imitation drapery and architectural features are by Joachim Dietrich.

Pl. 80. Contemporary with Drottningholm is the small theatre in the palace of
Český Krumlov, near Prague: a single
box, a narrow balcony and flat parterre.
The decoration is all painted.

◀ Pl. 79. Left: the royal theatre at
Drottningholm, near Stockholm, (completed 1766) viewed from the back of the
stage into the auditorium. Drottningholm preserves its original eighteenth-
century scenery, and one backcloth is
seen upside down at the top of the photograph, ready to drop into place. In the
foreground are waves exactly like those
illustrated by Sabbatini [Pl. 67]. In the
auditorium the front section was reserved for the royal family, the narrower
part at the back for the courtiers and
servants. Where the room narrows can be
seen the small screened boxes into which
the king could retire.

Bibiena, Johann Pasch and L. J. Desprez. Zeal for authenticity now goes to such lengths that the members of the orchestra, usherettes, and programme-sellers wear eighteenth-century costume and powdered wigs. The former dressing-rooms house a notable museum of theatrical history.

The Bohemian example, at Ceský Krumlov, near Prague, is inside the Schwarzenberg Palace and was reputedly designed by the son of one of the princes, Johannes Schwarzenberg [Pl. 80]. It boasts a single gallery with a central box, but most of its decoration, apart from the shallow pilaster strips, is painted in trompe-l'œil. The surviving sets are fewer than at Drottningholm, mostly rather uninspired work by Johan Wetschel and Leo Merkel.

The emphasis in this chapter has inevitably been on the decorative qualities of the Baroque theatre, but it was also a period of continuous experiment in planning and organization. In Italy, the boxes now commonly projected to give a better view, and the Sighizzi system of 'stepping' them came into wide, though never universal, use. We have noted Alessandro Bibiena's theatre at Mannheim in this connection; the same was true of Francesco Bibiena's Teatro d'Aliberti in Rome, of the theatre of Reggio, 1736, and of Pozzo's new Filarmonica in Verona when the original theatre burnt down in 1749. Of Roman theatres, Juvarra's auditorium for Cardinal Ottoboni in the Cancelleria (1712) and Teodali's Teatro Argentina (1732) were the most influential. The old San Carlo at Naples (1737, by G. A. Medrano), though on the grand scale, retained the gracefully curving staircases connecting the royal box with the body of the house which we have seen, for instance, at Bayreuth. Pöppelmann's Neues Opernhaus at Dresden, built in 1719 as part of the Zwinger, moulded the stalls into a

Pl. 81. The Manoel Theatre, Valletta, Malta, of 1731. Theatres like this, with no great architectural pretensions but much charm, were typical of most European cities. The top floor originally consisted of five boxes in the middle and galleries at the sides.

bowl, the banks of seats rising towards the back to meet the lowest range of boxes, a charming and practical idea rarely imitated. The Manoel Theatre at Valletta, Malta, of 1731, must also be mentioned here simply because it survives unscathed [Pl. 81]. Baroque was indeed the most fitting and fertile of all styles for the theatre of magic. Even its revival in the nineteenth century, though inevitably debased and often sadly lacking in subtlety, still has a kind of persuasive glamour to which only the most austere playgoer can be entirely immune.

VII

THE NEOCLASSICAL IDEAL

The change from Baroque to Neoclassicism is easier to recognize in architecture than in the other arts, but this does not mean that it was primarily an architectural movement. If it had any specific origin, it was literary. Writers like Shaftesbury in England, Diderot in France, Lessing in Germany, argued for a more serious, moral approach on the part of the poets, painters and architects, and pointed once again to the ancient world as the model to be imitated. The invocation of classical authorities, the formulation of rules, became favourite occupations. In the theatre a precise distinction is harder to draw (though not impossible—are not Handel's operas, for instance, Baroque, Gluck's Neoclassical?), and one can hardly claim that the Neoclassical stage took shape in response to the demands of a new drama. Both, however, reflected the same principles.

An age of principles is an age of books. In the history of the theatre, the second half of the eighteenth century parallels the Renaissance in the fertility of its ideas and the way in which these ideas were expressed as criticisms or as 'ideal' projects. I begin this chapter, therefore, with a brief survey of critical writings between 1755 and the French Revolution, since this gives the background of comment and controversy against which the buildings themselves were judged.

Count Francesco Algarotti, the Italian scientist, author of *Neutonianismo per le Dame*, published his *Saggio sopra l'Opera* in 1755. The fabric of theatres, he advises, should be of brick or stone as a safeguard against fire, but the auditorium should be of wood, 'the material from which we make musical instruments', for reasons of acoustics. His preferred plan is the semi-circle, since this was the shape favoured by the ancients, but he realizes that with modern scenery this would make the proscenium inconveniently wide, and so compromises on the ellipse. He advocates the Sighizzi method of stepping, and urges moderation in the ornament, even to the extent of not using the orders, on the grounds that these could not be given their proper dignity.

Algarotti's views were typical of the cultivated public of his time, and are echoed, with varying emphases, by other writers. Jean-Georges Noverre, in his *Observations sur la Construction d'une Nouvelle Salle de l'Opéra* of the early 1760s, argues for a theatre which would take its place as a civic monument, if possible free-standing on all sides, both for ease of access and to reduce the dangers of fire. He condemns the boxes inside the proscenium arch because 'the front of the stage should be regarded as a huge frame, ready to receive the varied pictures which the arts have to offer'. Decoration should not be obtrusive, or the actors and scenery will be 'crushed by the ornament and richness'.

Count Enea Arnaldi, a gentleman of Vicenza, entered the controversy in 1762 with his *Idea di un Teatro*. Arnaldi represents the old-school humanist. For him Palladio has said the last word, but his book in fact demonstrates all too clearly the need for a new solution. Retaining as much as possible of Palladio's *scaenae frons* and classic semi-circle as he can, he is obliged to extend his auditorium upwards into four tiers of balustraded galleries, with boxes grouped awkwardly by means of pilasters supporting statuary.

Charles-Nicholas Cochin (*Projet d'une Salle de Spectacles pour le nouveau Théâtre de Comédie*, 1765) also looked back to Palladio, but his revisions were far more radical [Pl. 82]. In the conventional horseshoe theatre, he notes, those seats from which one sees best are furthest from the stage, while the nearer ones give a bad view. His solution is to retain the oval, but to place the stage on one of the long sides, not at the end. His auditorium thus becomes wide and shallow, and he is faced by the same problem recognized by Algarotti—how could people at the sides see the stage? By bringing the stage forward, says Cochin, and making the back of it concave. He proposed a fixed *scaenae frons* of three wide arches, with perspective scenery inside them. Thus every member of the audience would be looking directly into *one* arch, and as long as the actors remained in front of the concave *frons* they were easily visible to everyone. The three arches could, in fact, represent different places—e.g. a temple, a palace and a tomb—and characters could, with verisimilitude, seem to be unaware of each other's presence. Cochin's ideas were widely known and aroused interest though, as we shall see, only one architect made a serious attempt to put them into practice (Cosimo Morelli at Imola [Pl. 98]). They seem to have been partly anticipated by Inigo Jones' Cockpit-in-Court [Pl. 54], though we know too little of this to be quite sure.

By the 1770s many French cities were erecting public theatres on a large scale, and the theorists' terms of reference become correspondingly more grandiose. The *Description des Arts et Métiers*, the rival in many respects of the *Encyclopédie*, gives a careful review of theatre architecture from ancient Greece onwards and concludes with a project for an ideal theatre drawn up by A. J. Roubo the Younger. The sources of Roubo's design are easy enough to find (mostly at Versailles, Bordeaux and Lyons) and he adds little in the way of original thought. Circulation is badly worked out, two triangular staircases being squeezed into the spaces left in the corners. By choosing a semi-circular auditorium he is faced with the familiar problem of the width of the proscenium, and only partially solves it by stipulating a fore-stage in the English style. The *parterre*, however, is steeply raked—something often advocated but hardly ever carried out. Roubo's intention

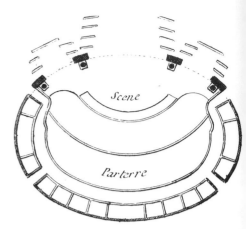

Pl. 82. *A revolutionary theatre design proposed by Charles-Nicolas Cochin in 1765. The back of the stage is concave and divided into three arches by pillars. Every spectator has a good view of the fore-stage and can see into at least one of the arches.*

was to produce a theatre adaptable to 'many kinds of spectacle, such as tragedies, comedies, operas, concerts, balls and public festivals', which has a familiar sound today.

One of the most ambitious of such ideal schemes was that proposed by Francesco Milizia in his *Trattato completo, formale e materiale del Teatro*, of 1794 [Pl. 83]. Here the theatre forms the climax of a huge cultural complex containing academies of painting, sculpture, architecture and literature, halls for music, dancing, gymnastics and tennis, and even an arena for ballooning. The theatre itself was largely conceived by his colleague Vincenzo Ferrarese. It is contained in a monumental colonnaded building covered with a dome. Circulation is well managed—a *porte cochère*, two large staircases, two entrances to the stalls (each with a ticket office) and extra exits for emergencies—and there was to be a ballroom over the entrance court and two cafés. Utilizing Cochin's idea of the concave *scaenae frons*, Milizia proposes a single circle divided almost equally into stage and auditorium, and united by the use of a giant order in both. In the auditorium the columns would hold boxes; on the stage they would form three openings 'according to the ancients and according to the best taste which deserves to be revived'. Behind the central arch Milizia's plan shows perspective scenery, but the whole concept is so beautifully geometrical

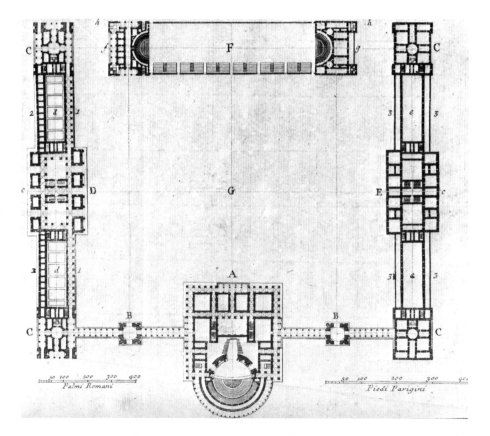

Pl. 83. The ideal 'Teatro Nuovo' of Milizia and Ferrarese, first published in 1771. The key is as follows: A, the theatre; B, lateral entrances; C, academies of painting, sculpture, architecture and music; D, shops on the ground floor, public rooms above; E, academy of music; F, balloon court; G, piazza for riding displays and public shows. The design of the theatre itself, with its semi-circular façade and entrances at the sides, looks both back to Roman models and forward to Semper.

that one feels he did not really want to spoil it with real actors and sets. The same might be said of G. P. M. Dumont and J. N. L. Durand, both of whom included theatres in their schemes for ideal cities, but who approached the matter entirely from the point of view of public effect. Soufflot's project for a circular Comédie Française surrounded by colonnades belongs to the same family.

Another French architect, however, named Damun, makes a commendable attempt to return to the dramatic roots of the theatre. In his *Prospectus pour un nouveau Théâtre tracé sur les Principes des Grecs et des Romains* (1776) he tries to reconstruct the beginnings of theatres, rather as Laugier was doing in a wider context with his 'primitive hut'. Look, he says, at travelling performers doing a play in the street. 'These actors deliberately stand with their backs to a wall, and the people naturally form a semi-circle round them. Those at the back stand on tiptoe so as to see as well as those in front. This was how the ancients arrived at the plans of their theatres, and this is how modern architects ought to begin. What he proposes is a simple raked semi-circle ending in a colonnade. No place here for elaborate perspective scenery, which, in any case, only gets in the actors' way. Why ask for more than the Greek *periaktoi*?

Most fantastic of all such ideal schemes was E-L. Boullée's plan for an opera house, put forward (though never published) after the Opéra fire of 1781 [Pl. 84]. Boullée saw the theatre as '*un monument consacré au plaisir*'. From outside, his building was a huge domed peristyle of Corinthian columns on a stepped base with four square plinths for statues. It was to stand in the midst of a garden. The public should converge from all directions, attracted by the prospect of a play. The interior was to be divided into stage and auditorium by a single complete semi-circular arch (the auditorium could thus receive a semi-dome contained within the

Pl. 84. The utopian theatre proposed by Etienne-Louis Boullée. The exterior was to be a perfect circle surrounded by a giant Corinthian colonnade. This section is cut to show the foyer and auditorium graphically but the stage (on the right) only as a diagram. The auditorium would have been a sort of demi-Pantheon, with three tiers of spectators looking awkwardly through the coffering of the dome.

Pl. 85. Until the eighteenth century, theatres were hidden away reticently behind un-assuming façades or in the recesses of palaces. Frederick the Great's opera house at Berlin (1741) seems to have been the first theatre to be given prominence as a public building in its own right.

exterior hemispherical vault rather like the double dome of St. Paul's). The *parterre* rose in a gentle slope and behind it was the inevitable semi-circle of giant columns. In spite of the grandeur of his conception, Boullée was a severely practical man. He had interesting ideas on scenery and stage lighting, and was particularly concerned with fire precautions. 'Most of our theatres', he wrote, 'are frightful funeral pyres.' His opera house staircases led by self-contained circulation systems (to prevent panic) to four main vestibules. Everything except the stage and its furniture was to be made of stone or brick. Finally, he proposed a huge basin of water underneath the whole theatre, into which any burning substance could be made to drop.

In 1782 a book appeared which surveyed the whole scene of theatre architecture, actual and ideal, summing up the issues involved with a clarity which remained relevant at least until 1900 and is in some ways still relevant today: Pierre Patte's *Essai sur l'Architecture Théâtrale*. Patte's criteria are scientific—his sub-title is : *De l'ordonnance la plus avantageuse à une salle de spectacles, relativement aux principes de l'optique et de l'acoustique.* He considers all the proposed plan types—circular, semi-circular, oval, semi-oval, bell-shaped, racket-shaped, horseshoe-shaped, octagonal and rectangular—before deciding finally on the ellipse. Decoration, in particular the orders, is to be avoided. 'A theatre, in order to fulfil its function, must be made up of purely *optical and acoustic forms*.' Of all existing theatres, the Teatro Regio at Turin comes nearest to his ideal. Patte, with his acoustic diagrams, sight-lines, angles of reflection and so on, seems at first rather remote from the realities of drama, but he was sensitive enough not to be a slave to theory. He dislikes Sighizzi's 'steps', for instance, though he admits they 'do indeed aid the view of the spectator', because they 'break up the surface so that the sound is dispersed' and also because they 'present a very disagreeable appearance'. He insists that rows of boxes should be visually tied together, not left as 'a multitude of little holes'. Even more remarkable is his insight into theatre psychology. English theatres, he notes, tend to have deep galleries all facing forward, rather than circles of boxes. 'Most of the audience, it is true, find themselves placed in a position facing the stage, but nothing is less agreeable or less in conformity with good taste than this arrangement. It divides the house into separate parts and does

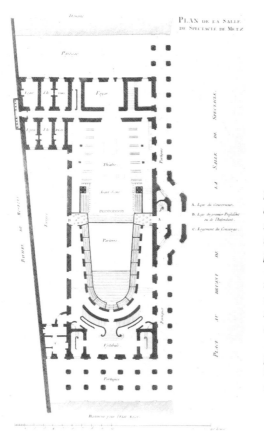

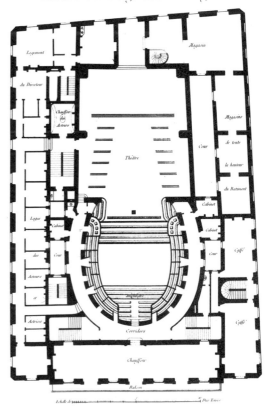

Pls. 86, 87. Two French examples that mark the rapid acceptance of the theatre as a focus of city planning. Metz (left), of 1751, had colonnades on two sides and a vestibule which was treated as a setting for a grand staircase. Lyons (right), of 1754, occupied an important island site and included numerous public rooms.

away with contact between members of the audience. Each one sees only those at his own level.' (As we shall see later, this actually seems not to have been true.) His purpose, however, is not closer contact between actors and audience. He criticizes schemes like those of Cochin and Roubo with pronounced fore-stages: 'The actors would find themselves isolated in the middle of the audience and too far away from the scenery. There would no longer be any illusion, and the dramatic action would seem reduced and ineffective.'

Patte's book was not the end of controversy on these matters (one of his opponents, an architect named Poyet, was inspired to suggest a trapezoidal auditorium which surprisingly prefigures Wagner's Bayreuth), but it is time now to study the theatres that were actually going up during this period.

The Berlin Opera House, of 1741, by Knobelsdorf seems to have been the earliest free-standing theatre building in Europe [Pl. 85]. It had a portico at one end and two other state entrances at the sides. Over the main entrance was the 'Apollo Hall', a large saloon whose windows formed part of the façade. All these features were to become standard in the great opera houses of a hundred years later.

The influence of Berlin can be traced in eastern France during the following decade, when many of the larger towns erected public theatres as part of a general movement towards prestige civic architecture. That of Metz (1751) adjoined the river Moselle on one side and the customs house at the back, but its other two sides were given monumental façades of porticos and columns [Pl. 86]. Here, too, a grand staircase occupied most

103

Coupe du nouvel Opéra de Stuttgardt esquissé pour en voir l'effet sans aucunes regles de Perspective.

Plan où Projet de la restauration de l'Opéra de Stuttgardt.

Pl. 89. *Philippe de la Guépière's remodelling of the court opera house of Stuttgart in 1758-59 increased the seating capacity of the auditorium (though not its overall size) and the depth of the stage to meet the demands of the new style ballet. A new foyer and staircases were added (left, on the plan) and to balance them a whole wing was projected on the other side.*

of the vestibule, beginning as a single flight and dividing at right angles half-way up, the prototype of Bordeaux. Montpellier followed, adding a concert hall over the vestibule. Front-of-the-house services often functioned independently of the theatre, and one bought one's ticket as one actually entered the auditorium. Nancy and Brest are other good examples. Grandest of all was Lyons (1754), designed by Soufflot, the architect of the Panthéon [Pl. 87]. Soufflot was a friend of Cochin and had travelled with him in Italy. His theatre stood on an isolated site, part of an ambitious piece of town planning, facing the Hôtel de Ville. Its huge stage was surrounded by rooms for the actors and theatre staff, while the audience were provided with a long gallery for promenading, three staircases to the different gallery levels and two cafés. It must have been a sober building, for Soufflot denied himself the use of the classical orders, both within or without. The auditorium, which was an almost complete oval, had three tiers of galleries and a panelled ceiling.

The authority of Soufflot and the theorists might have discouraged the use of classical orders in theatre interiors had it not been for a formula invented by Luigi Vanvitelli for the court theatre at Caserta, near Naples, of 1752–9 [Pl. 88]. Here, on a relatively small scale, Vanvitelli showed how they could be used with a new grandeur. The lowest level of boxes is treated as a series of pedestals, on which stand giant Corinthian columns embracing three more rows of boxes. The theatre has that odd feeling of frigidity which often affects Italian Neoclassicism, but it was a brilliant idea handled with undeniable confidence. Its influence in Italy can be seen in the Teatro Comunale (1788) at Faenza by Pistocchi, and continued as late as 1863 in the rebuilt Teatro della Fortuna at Fano by Poletti.

Germany could never free itself entirely from the charms of Baroque. At Stuttgart the court architect to the Duke of Wurttemberg, Philippe de la Guépière, produced in 1759 plans for an opera house as monumental as any project by Durand [Pl. 89]. In front and behind the central block, which contained stage and auditorium, were vast halls serving as foyers, cafés and reception rooms, including one octagonal room behind the stage almost as big as the auditorium. The interior elevation, however, was almost frivolously Rococo, with boxes held up on thin spindly supports and a top gallery supported on caryatids. Yet De la Guépière evidently knew the literature; another design of his, made probably between 1765 and 1768 for the same patron, is a serious attempt to adapt Cochin's theatre to court use. The three wide concave arches face a shallow auditorium rising in stages through the 'amphithéâtre des princes' and the 'amphithéâtre des seigneurs' to the 'loge du prince'. There was to be a row of boxes level with the prince's and above that a gallery also supported on caryatids. It would have been an odd mixture of the sublime and (one suspects) the ridiculous.

The Baroque spirit, though not necessarily Baroque forms, lingered on in Germany after it had been superseded in France by a purer Neoclassicism.

Pls. 90, 91. The royal opera house at Versailles, by Jacques-Ange Gabriel: the stage (left) and part of the auditorium (right). The decoration of the theatre is everywhere of the highest quality— Neoclassical, in contrast to the Rococo of the Residenztheater—but what makes Gabriel's theatre especially interesting is the stepping back of levels. Instead of boxes rising vertically one above the other, he places an amphithéâtre *behind the stalls, a row of boxes behind that, another row on corbels behind and above that (including the three royal boxes with grilles), and finally a promenade encircling the auditorium behind the colonnade. Within a decade these ideas were to be developed on a far larger scale by Ledoux.*

A Frenchman, for instance, could hardly have taken completely seriously the theatre built in the Neue Palast at Potsdam (1763–9), with its extraordinary palms and lattice patterns (one of the architects, J. G. Büring, had built Frederick II's Chinese Pavilion). The one added in 1766 to the palace of Schönbrunn by Nikolaus Pacazzi has more dignity and its classicism is in detail perfectly correct. Yet even here the numerous projecting balconies give it a rhythm which a Frenchman would have found too nervous.

By 1770 we have reached the beginning of one of the most important decades in the history of theatre architecture. Interest moves emphatically to France and in particular to three men, who between them almost sum up the achievements of Neoclassicism: Jacques-Ange Gabriel, Claude-Nicolas Ledoux and Victor Louis. Appropriately, we begin at the centre of European culture, Versailles.

Until 1770 Versailles had no theatre. The king, it is true, had long been pondering the matter. His architect, Gabriel, prepared schemes and listened to learned advice from travellers who had seen Vicenza, Parma and Turin. He was by now an old man, with a highly successful career behind

him. His taste was for Neoclassicism tempered by a certain softness and ease of proportion that recalls the English Palladians. What finally made up Louis' mind was the forthcoming marriage of his grandson, the future Louis XVI, to Marie Antoinette. A new theatre that could also serve as a banqueting hall must be prepared. Gabriel, after twenty years of royal indecision, was told to have it ready in twenty months.

The contrast between Gabriel's Opéra and Cuvilliés' Residenztheater is highly instructive. At Munich the eye goes at once to the decoration and the details, at Versailles to the noble symmetry of the whole. At Munich, it is the swirling arabesque line, the unending play of surface that first claim the attention; at Versailles simplicity, restraint and immediate grandeur. The last is deceptive. Gabriel would doubtless have liked to build the whole theatre in marble. Shortage of time and money prohibited that, so he used painted wood disguised as marble—a loss, perhaps, in authenticity, but a gain in comfort and acoustics.

Gabriel's design is a good deal more sophisticated than that of Cuvilliés [Pls. 90, 91]. For the auditorium he chose the oval dying into straight lines where it joins the stage. Whereas Cuvilliés' galleries simply rise one above the other, differing only in their decoration, Gabriel creates a real architectural sequence, spreading back in widening circles, as well as rising vertically. Behind the seats of the *parterre* runs a continuous balustraded section (the *amphithéâtre*). Behind and above that is a row of boxes; above that (on corbels) another row, including the king's own box. This row is slightly narrower than the row below, since it does not completely overhang it, so to give it the necessary depth the wall behind it is set back in a series of square niches. At the uppermost level, dominating the whole room, is a semi-circle of Ionic columns forming, behind it, a gallery backed by mirrors. The cornice which these columns support, and which is interrupted in the centre, over the king's box, by a coffered niche, is surmounted by a coved ceiling with oval windows and finally by the flat ceiling containing a huge oval painting. The effect is extremely subtle, combining a sense of enclosure with one of spaciousness. The stage is emphasized by giant Corinthian columns rising the whole height of the room, while above the flat proscenium arch two flying angels hold the royal *fleur-de-lys*.

The decorative details are full of interest, providing a sort of cross-section of current styles. The ceiling, painted by Durameau, is still entirely Rococo. The panels in the royal box, on the other hand, while still light-hearted in mood, show a definite awareness of Pompeii, plus an element of *chinoiserie*; while Pajou's carving, with its chaste medallion profiles, its eagles with outstretched wings and its sphinxes beside the round windows in the coving, looks forward to the Empire style.

The theatre was officially opened on 16 May 1770 with a banquet to celebrate the wedding. The next day its theatrical inauguration took place with a performance of *Persée*, an opera by Quainault and Lully, described in

Pl. 92. Right: the monumental entrance ▶ *to Ledoux's theatre at Besançon (1778), all that now remains of one of the most influential theatres of the eighteenth century.*

a contemporary source as '*le triomphe du machiniste*'. The feasting lasted a week, with further operas and plays. For twenty years it was the scene of brilliant events, musical, dramatic and social. In 1775, Horace Walpole, attending a wedding there, called it 'the bravest in the universe, and yet taste predominates over expense'. Then came the Revolution. Napoleon ignored it. Under Louis Philippe it was altered for the worse (the enclosed royal box was taken out and an open balcony substituted), though under Napoleon III it enjoyed some revival of its early splendour. It was he who built new rooms for the royal family and enlarged the circulation space. Queen Victoria and Prince Albert were entertained there in 1855. In 1871, Paris being in the hands of the Commune, the National Assembly met here. Durameau's ceiling-painting was taken down, unceremoniously rolled up at the back of the stage, and replaced by a skylight. The floor was raised to the level of the *amphithéâtre*. In the early part of this century the theatre presented a depressing sight. Paul Valéry wrote a moving plea for its restoration: '*Une nation possède le plus beau théâtre du monde . . . La France le conserve, le balaye, et l'ignore . . . Il n'est point un théâtre mort, il n'est qu'un théâtre enchanté. Je rêve qu'on l'éveille.*' In the 1950s it was, slowly and with great care, 'awoken', and now takes its rightful place among the most endearing theatres of Europe.

Less charming, but ultimately more intriguing, was the theatre at Besançon, conceived by Claude-Nicolas Ledoux in 1775 and built between 1778 and 1784 [Pls. 92–4]. Ledoux was a planner of ideal cities, like others mentioned in this chapter, but at the same time a man who went back to first principles and based his theories firmly on the ground. He was the only such planner actually to begin his ideal city (at Chaux). For current theatre design he had little admiration: the planning made it impossible to see or hear, the decoration was vulgar and distracting, the orchestra was placed in the middle of the audience—'*quelle incohérence de conceptions!*' Like Damun, Ledoux goes back to the crowd of peasants in the street: 'They form a circle, the strongest get to the front, the weak remain further away—each takes a place where he can see best, unimpeded by the people around him.'

Ledoux's solution is not dissimilar to Gabriel's, though his auditorium is larger and is planned with a more conscious functionalism. The three semi-circular tiers of seats (Ledoux abolished boxes) recede as they rise until they reach the theatre's most monumental feature, the curving colonnade (Doric, without bases) supporting a frieze [Pl. 94]. Never before had classical architecture been adapted so inventively and logically to the requirements of a large modern theatre. Ledoux published a haunting representation of this auditorium reflected in the pupil of a huge eye [Pl. 93].

The semi-circle was in fact narrower than the stage. Where the first tier met the proscenium it opened out, making a bell-shaped plan. Behind this tier ran a sculptured frieze with subjects connected with tragedy, comedy

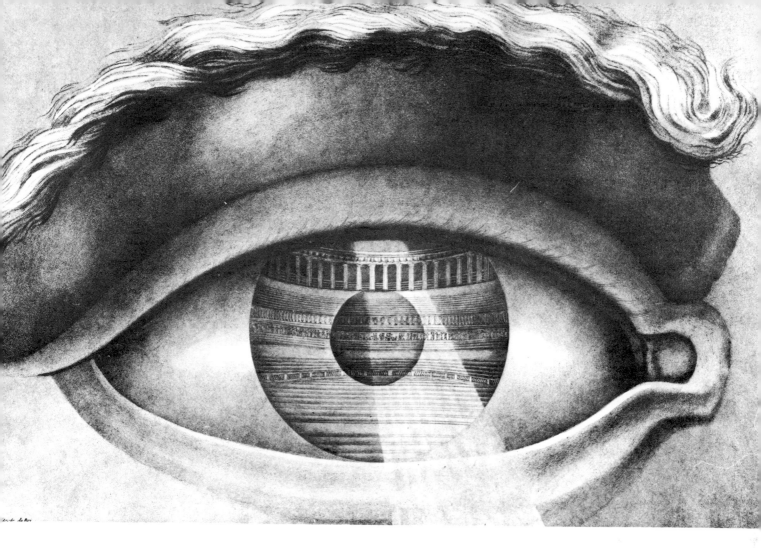

Pls. 93, 94. Two plates from Ledoux's own edition of his works, showing the Besançon theatre. Above: a typical Ledoux conceit—the auditorium reflected in the pupil of an enormous eye. Gazing into it, we see that seats fall into two main divisions which are behind, not simply above, each other: first the parterre, divided by a balustrade; then (behind a sculptured frieze) the amphithéâtre, ending in a Doric colonnade with more seats behind that. Right: section showing the orchestra pit hidden from the audience and half under the stage.

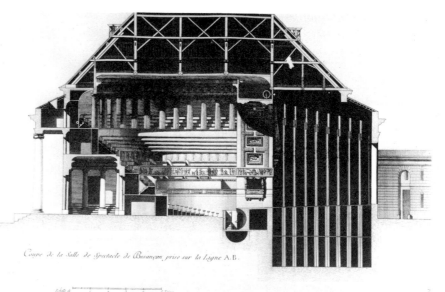

Coupe de la Salle de Spectacle de Besançon, prise sur la Ligne A.B.

and the dance. The tier behind it was more than a gallery: it was an *amphithéâtre* steeply raked and receding far back, holding more people than the *parterre*.

The proscenium arch was a wide, nearly semi-circular, coffered barrel vault, supported not on columns but on giant rusticated walls, and it held boxes at the sides. This was the *avant-scène*, a space which Ledoux believed to be vitally important—it should 'link actor and audience, not stand between them'. There were bas-reliefs of chariots in the spandrels.

Nothing proves Ledoux's boldness more than his placing of the orchestra. 'The orchestra, considered as an instrument like the voice, should not be displayed.' Perhaps some of his ideas on this subject derived from his master Blondel, who had proposed bringing the audience close to the stage by dividing the orchestra into two and placing them at the sides ('rather difficult to conduct', comments Patte). An obscure writer called De Marette, whose *Mémoire sur un nouvel orchestre de salle de spectacles* was written, but apparently not published, in 1775, advocated a position underneath the stage. Ledoux hid the orchestra in a pit which went partly under the stage and was screened from the audience by a hood—an exact prefiguration of what Wagner was to do at Bayreuth. A vaulted space underneath added resonance.

The hot air heating system was even more elaborate than that at Turin. It had six stoves, two of brick on either side of the orchestra pit, and two, covered with tiles, to warm the vestibule and passages.

After surviving with relatively minor alterations, this noble theatre was burnt down in April 1958, only the great Doric portico remaining [Pl. 92].

Ledoux designed two other theatres, neither of which was built. That for La Guimard (1772) was small in scale, a rising amphitheatre plan ending in a semi-circle of columns. That for Marseilles (1785) was extremely ambitious, and was conceived as part of a major town-planning operation. It was to be free-standing on all sides, with shops on the ground floor behind colonnades. In front, a portico without pediment supported a quadriga. This led into a columned vestibule, from which one either descended to the café or ascended to the level of the *salle*. The auditorium embodied the same principles as those at Besançon.

The third of our key architects is Victor Louis of Bordeaux. Louis was a brilliant and interesting man, a friend of Beaumarchais and Mme Geoffrin, who had studied at Rome, built a palace in Warsaw and made additions (now regretted) to Chartres Cathedral, before returning to Bordeaux in 1772. The story of his long and acrimonious dealings with the city council during the next eight years reminds one strongly of the building of Blenheim. Like Vanbrugh, he was forced to relinquish control before the building was finished and departed to Paris embittered and angry. A request for a pension was turned down with the excuse that he had already involved the city in unnecessary expense with his 'peristyles and painted ceilings'.

Pl. 95.   Façade of the Grand Théâtre at Bordeaux (1773–80)—a watercolour drawing by the architect, Victor Louis. Although it is not immediately clear from this drawing, the columns form an open portico, with space for carriages to drive in behind them.

For the façade, in fact, Louis had adopted the simplest and grandest of all motifs, a long colonnade of twelve tall Corinthian columns supporting a flat entablature [Pl. 95]. Originally the ground sloped up so that carriages could drive inside this colonnade. It is continued round the side elevations as a pilaster order. Upon entering, one finds oneself in a low vestibule supported on Doric columns, which leads to the grand staircase hall—one of Louis' boldest ideas, the importation into a theatre of a feature hitherto mainly characteristic of palaces. The hall itself rises to the whole height of the building and is covered by an oblong domical vault ending in a skylight. To left and right the elevation consists of an arched, rusticated ground storey and a gallery of Ionic columns. In the centre the staircase ascends until it meets the far wall where a door flanked by caryatids leads into the *Grande Salle*, the auditorium; then it divides left and right and goes up to the gallery [Pl. 97]. Above the cornice, lunettes cut into the panels of the vault reveal a view of small domes over the galleries. Over the low vestibule, just as at Soufflot's Lyons theatre, is an oval concert hall.

The *Grande Salle* itself looks to Italy rather than to Versailles or Besançon, but its originality is immediately apparent [Pl. 96]. Louis rests his domed ceiling on four main supports forming a square. Two of them coincide with the sides of the proscenium arch; the other two are giant Ionic columns which divide the auditorium into three segments. These segments are articulated by further Ionic columns, holding three rows of

Pl. 96. *The auditorium of Louis'*
Bordeaux theatre. Besides achieving an
interior of unparalleled dignity and
grandeur, Louis foreshadowed future
developments by his handling of the
ceiling and the upper level of seats. The
shallow dome rests on four very wide
arches, leaving space underneath them for
an extension comparable to Ledoux's
amphithéâtre.

boxes, so that at first sight they form a continuous colonnade, i.e. the motif of Caserta. But above the cornice the three segments become galleries under wide segmental arches. The plinth of the whole colonnade is a solid rusticated wall. The stage is framed by the usual paired columns holding boxes. Patte called this 'the most magnificent of our modern theatres'.

In Paris, Louis built two more theatres—the Théâtre Français (it went by many names before settling down to the one it is now known by, the Comédie Française), and the Théâtre National (or Théâtre des Arts). In the first he made theatrical history by using cast-iron for most of the structural members—vaults, supports of galleries, etc.—and hollow-tile construction for the floors. The site was too restricted for another grand staircase, but in the auditorium he used a variant of the Bordeaux system, with a giant Ionic order uniting two (not three) tiers of boxes. Between boxes and *parterre* was a gallery, perhaps a small version of Ledoux's *amphithéâtre*, and spacious seating at the top level was another glance in the direction of Besançon. This interior was remodelled in 1822, when the columns were replaced by posts to improve the view, and destroyed by fire in 1900. Louis' second Paris theatre opened at an inauspicious moment (August 1793, the height of the Terror) and was demolished in 1820. Here Louis went back to the idea of supporting the ceiling on four large arches resting on four main columns, this time coupled. A contemporary description tells us

Pl. 97. *Right: the grand staircase at* ▶
Bordeaux, ancestor of a host of other grand
staircases that were to follow in the nine-
teenth century. Louis' overall design is one
of restraint and simplicity but he adds
richness by a careful use of sculpture and
architectural subtlety by the views he
allows through the lunettes at the top
into domed spaces beyond.

Pls. 98, 99. Left: Cosimo Morelli's theatre at Imola, 1779. The stage is concave and divided into three by the two large columns carrying caryatid figures. Each division could have a different set, thus putting into practice the ideas proposed by Cochin fourteen years earlier (see Pl. 82).
Below: auditorium of the theatre built in the Hermitage, Leningrad, by Quarenghi. In spite of its small scale it has all the leitmotives of Neoclassicism—marble columns, heads in medallions, statues in niches.

that the proscenium columns, instead of holding boxes, were 'entirely architectural, adorned with statues and bas reliefs, forming a very pronounced line of demarcation between the stage and the audience. This is a sacrifice made by the management in the interests of art. The illusion is preserved, since one does not see the people in the boxes confused with those on the stage.'

By the 1780s the key ideas had been formulated and the key innovations made. Theatres built in the following years can be grouped fairly easily according to the precedents they chose to follow. Largely for structural reasons, the most common type continued to be the horseshoe of boxes or galleries vertically one above the other, the ceiling resting on posts or columns supported by the top level of the horseshoe itself. Most of the Italian opera houses to be described in Chapter XI will be of this type. The elevation can (as at Caserta) be articulated by a giant order without affecting the structural scheme. A variant, however, (e.g. Bordeaux) was to rest the ceiling on four main piers, leaving the intervening spaces unencumbered by supports. The alternative (represented by Versailles and Besançon) was to make the auditorium go back in a series of steps, virtually without overhangs. Such a design demands greater floor area and presents correspondingly greater difficulties in roofing, since the roof has to rest on the outer walls.

Pl. 100. Smaller still but even grander than the theatre in the Hermitage is the court theatre of Gripsholm, Sweden, of 1781. From its interior one would hardly suspect that it occupies one round tower of a medieval castle. Mirrors between the columns at the sides make it seem larger.

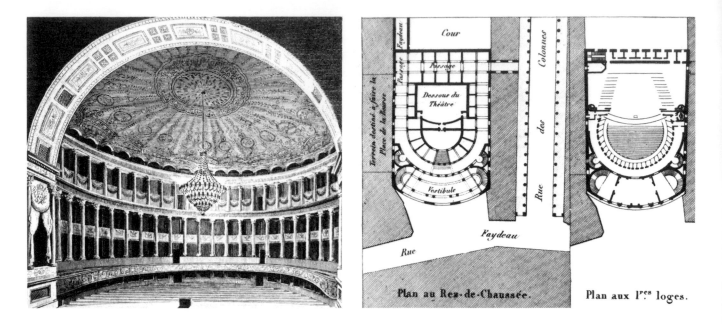

Pl. 101. *Faced with a narrow site, the architects of the Théâtre Faydeau, Paris, adopted a curved façade and vestibule, following the line of the back of the auditorium. The latter was Italianate in its verticality and almost obsessively classical in its array of giant columns.*

The fluctuations of fashion and influence are not easy to summarize briefly, though they give the period a special variety of interest. When Peyre and de Wailly, for instance, put forward a design for a circular Odéon in 1778, they were thinking in terms of Durand or Soufflot at his most ambitious. The theatre as built (1779–82) shows the influence of Louis and the dominating giant order. And when that theatre, having been burnt down in 1799, was rebuilt by Chalgrin, admiration had shifted to the school of Ledoux, especially obvious in the exterior.

Cosimo Morelli's theatre at Imola (1779) has already been mentioned as an attempt to put Cochin's ideas into practice. The frame of the stage consisted of three arches on a concave plan [Pl. 98]. As Cochin proposed, these were used to represent three different locations. Actors entered from one or other scene, thus indicating where they were supposed to be, but the acting area was the fore-stage enclosed by three arches. This was a radical innovation in the days of deep stages and elaborate, frequently changed, perspective sets.

Ledoux's design for the theatre at La Guimard prefigured or (just possibly) provided the model for two attractive court theatres in northern Europe, both still extant. One is Quarenghi's theatre in the Hermitage, St. Petersburg [Pl. 99]. The motif of the semi-circle of columns became widely popular: it is seen again in the little private theatre at Ostankino, outside Moscow. The other example is the tiny theatre built into a round tower of the Swedish castle of Gripsholm [Pl. 100]. It was commissioned by Queen Lovisa Ulricka's son Gustavus III and is as well preserved as that at Drottningholm. The architect was Erik Palmsted. The semi-circle of columns, following the shape of the tower, gives it a dignity out of proportion to its size. In the centre the intervals between the columns hold boxes but those at the sides are panelled with mirrors, creating a most unclassical effect of shimmering space. Gustavus III enters theatrical history in another way: his murder in the royal box of the Stockholm Opera House (by Adelcrantz) forms the subject of Verdi's *Ballo in Maschera*.

France continued to produce bold and interesting designs—Heurtier's Théâtre Italien of 1784 (later the Opéra Comique, but not the one we know); Legrand and Molinos' Théâtre Faydeau of 1788–91, with its grand quadrant-shaped vestibule ending in two flights of stairs in apses [Pl. 101]; as well as a number in the provinces—Amiens (1780), Rheims (1785) and Nantes (1788). This classical French tradition in the theatre lies behind the next important development which took place in Germany under Schinkel and Semper. But as a postscript to the 'Neoclassical ideal', let us briefly return to the realm of the unrealized and perhaps the unrealizable.

In France under Napoleon a more archaeological classicism asserted itself, combined with an almost megalomaniac grandeur. Brongniart's project for a Théâtre Napoléon had an exterior that was a replica of a Roman temple. Percier and Fontaine's Salle des Spectacles in the Tuileries was something quite without precedent—a sort of classical cathedral with the emperor's box in the centre of a huge apse. Germany produced one architect who was potentially the equal of Boullée or Ledoux—the *enfant*

Pl. 102. Gilly's project for a National Theatre in Berlin, 1798. The stage building is a cube, the auditorium a half-cylinder about three-quarters the size of the cube. At the back is a matching half-cylinder, probably intended for rehearsal rooms and administration.

Pl. 103.   Between 1789 and 1791 a developer named O'Reilly tried to organize a scheme for a new opera house on the north side of Leicester Square in London. His efforts came to nothing, but the designs of his chosen architect, Sir John Soane, survive. They show exteriors strongly influenced by Victor Louis but with the addition of domed corner pavilions. The entrance portico led into a spacious vestibule with staircases on each side reached through colonnades.

prodige Friedrich Gilly, who died in 1800 at the age of 29, leaving a series of astonishing designs, none of which was ever built. His sketch for a National Theatre at Berlin (1798) is composed with meticulous clarity from a cube, half-cylinders, hemispheres and quadrants [Pl. 102]. The interior would have been scarcely less austere, though the coffered decoration and the unifying effect of its clear geometrical lines give it a pure Greek kind of humanism.

In England the only man capable of understanding such ideas fully was Sir John Soane. His projects for an opera house to be built in Leicester Square in 1789 [Pl. 103] show considerable study of French models, particularly Bordeaux. In one scheme, it was to have an entrance colonnade of twelve giant columns, two grand staircases dividing and doubling back, and an oval auditorium.

Mention of Soane may remind us that England has been neglected in the last few chapters. We must retrace our steps by a decade or so to repair the omission.

VIII

GEORGIANS AT PLAY

In the eighteenth century Englishmen went to the Continent to look at theatres; foreigners came to England to look at acting.

England had nothing to compare with the court theatres that we have been examining in the last two chapters. When a Hanoverian king wanted to see a play, he went to a public theatre. True, he had a private royal box with its own entrance and could 'command' a particular play if it happened to be in the repertory, but what he saw was the standard theatrical fare of the day, not a court entertainment. Some of the nobility had cultural ambitions, but their achievements were meagre—the little theatre added by Wyatville to the Duke of Devonshire's Chatsworth in the early nineteenth century is practically all that patriotism can point to.

On the other hand, public theatres thrived as nowhere else in Europe, producing a *rapport* between playwrights, actors and audience which was broad-based, genuine and fertile. The buildings themselves are not impressive, precisely because, to their credit, they did not need to be. George Saunders, one of the few English architectural theorists of the theatre to meet the French and Italians on their own ground, wrote in 1790: 'By attentive observation we shall find that the massive columns and pilasters, together with the many ornaments accompanying them, engage the eye from the scenery and occasion it to have a comparative littleness.' Theatre designing in France by the end of the century was perilously close to an abstract exercise. The circumstances of the building of a typical English playhouse which happens to have survived will immediately make clear the difference between such an architecture imposed from above by architects and patrons, and one springing from the simple requirements of actors and spectators.

The Theatre Royal, Bristol (which gained its title by royal licence some twelve years after it opened on 30 May 1766), owes its existence to the initiative of a group of playgoing businessmen. Fifty shareholders paid £50 each, another forty-seven subscribed £30, and a further £1,046 was raised by other means. This meant a capital of nearly £5,000. Shareholders had the right of free attendance (though not necessarily a seat) at any performance. The theatre was to be leased to the actors at a rent of £300 per annum. Since the season at first only lasted from June to September, it was evidently expected to make a handsome profit.

The architect was James Paty, who was said to have taken as his model Wren's Drury Lane Theatre [Pl. 62]. The two theatres do indeed resemble each other not only in the general plan but in the use of tall pilasters linking both tiers of boxes. At Drury Lane these went right round the theatre, at Bristol they are confined to the boxes flanking the stage. We know the names of all the craftsmen who worked on it—carpenter, mason, smith, tiler, painter and upholsterer. The scenery was the work of John French, formerly of Covent Garden, and a pupil of Philip de Loutherberg.

The floor of the auditorium, known in France as the *parterre* and in England, and hereafter in this chapter, as the pit, was provided with benches and surrounded by two tiers of boxes. The nine lower, or dress, boxes, were each named after an English dramatist (Shakespeare in the middle) and held 267 people. The upper boxes were confined to the sides of the theatre, three on each side, holding 104 people, the space in the centre being left as an open gallery.

The flat proscenium arch was supported on paired columns framing the doors by which the actors entered and above those were additional boxes, holding eleven people each. The stage itself formerly projected one bay further than it does now, and the fact that it has been set back has meant that one pair of pilasters lack the bottom of their pedestals. Both these features—proscenium doors and projecting stage—were typical of English theatre design. At the back of the stage is a large arched recess in the wall, probably to accommodate the extremity of very ambitious perspective sets.

The painted scenery flats, of which part of one set survives, ran back and forth on grooves. Other relics of this early period still in existence include the elaborate system of winches and trapdoors which used to be under the stage and the 'thunder run', a wooden trough above the auditorium down which iron balls were rolled to imitate thunder.

In 1800 the roof was raised and a new tier of seats, the present gallery, built above the upper boxes [Pl. 105]. The pretty plaster ceiling dates from this time and some of the original benches of the gallery are still *in situ*. The colour scheme then was stone-colour for the walls, with panels in pale green, and cornices and capitals picked out in gold. Most of what we see now is Victorian, but the earlier 1800 décor seems to be largely intact underneath. The stage and staircases have been rebuilt and most of the box divisions removed. Originally without a façade at all, it was given one in 1903, but this has recently been demolished [Pl. 104].

In London, the only two licensed theatres during the early eighteenth century were those of Drury Lane and Covent Garden, later joined by the smaller Haymarket theatre managed by the comedian Samuel Foote. Vanbrugh's Opera House was used exclusively for opera and ballet. None of these, except the last, made any pretensions to great architectural merit, and indeed in England generally a visit to the theatre had few pleasures to offer outside those of drama proper. Most had several entrances, leading to different parts of the house, each with its own 'paying place'. Drury Lane had five, in three different streets. Contemporary records are full of

Pls. 104, 105. The Theatre Royal, Bristol. The auditorium closely resembles Wren's Drury Lane (Pl. 62) except that small columns here replace giant pilasters everywhere but at the sides. The stage would originally have projected as far as the second pilaster, with proscenium doors on each side. The two lower galleries were divided into boxes. Right: the newly built façade, replacing that built in 1903, with next to it the eighteenth-century Coopers' Hall, now used as a vestibule to the theatre.

accounts of the disagreeable pushing and shoving that had to be endured before one found oneself satisfactorily inside. The lobbies where the playgoer waited for the doors to open were normally far too small. Before 1775 London had nothing resembling the elegant public rooms of French or Italian theatres, but some had cloakrooms, and all had lavatories of some sort. There was normally also a room where gentlemen could wait for their carriages—one of the few parts of a theatre to be heated, though a fireplace was installed in the royal box at Covent Garden in 1796, 'to the great surprise and no less satisfaction of their Majesties'.

Narrow passages and staircases led to the actual auditorium which was opened about an hour before the performance began. Here the dangers of being crushed were very real. In 1794, before a command performance at the Haymarket Theatre, fifteen people were trampled to death. Seats were not numbered, so there was another scramble to find a good place. When all the seats were taken, more people stood round the sides of the pit. Sometimes the doors would be closed and *locked* to prevent more people from coming in (an experience known as being 'screwed in'), with of course catastrophic results in the event of fire. The seats in the pit and galleries were simply benches without backs, about one foot nine inches apart. Boxes were more comfortable but still contained three or four rows of seats.

Chandeliers and candles made the auditorium almost as bright as the stage, which was lit by candles behind the wings with reflectors behind them, and a row of footlights along the front which could be lowered and raised. Scene designers like De Loutherberg also experimented with coloured and transparent gauzes. Stage machinery in general was probably equal to anything to be seen abroad. In the words of Dr. G. W. Stone: 'There were pulleys in abundance with ropes manipulated by the strength of the sceneman's arm over a windlass. There were springs to catapult objects aloft, or from one side of the stage to another. There were trapdoors for disappearances. There were platforms of different elevation for mounting different groups, as well as swinging platforms properly counterbalanced. There were cloud effects concealing baskets capable of holding actors. There were smoke effects, used sparingly. There were transparencies and an abundance of coloured lighting.' Many English theatres had, at each end of the footlights, an iron grille called 'the spikes' to prevent members of the audience from climbing on to the stage.

Wren's Drury Lane remained substantially intact until 1775, when major alterations were made by Robert Adam [Pl. 106]. How far this affected the building structurally is hard to say; he certainly enlarged the auditorium by extending the gallery backwards, but it was the decoration which aroused most comment—the dainty panels in front of the boxes and the *trompe-l'œil* ceiling suggesting a shallow dome. 'The pillars which support the upper boxes and gallery', wrote a contemporary, 'are inlaid with plate glass on a crimson and green ground . . . The ceiling is heightened by twelve feet whereby the voice of the performers is greatly improved.' Adam enlarged the proscenium a little by removing 'the old heavy square pillars on each side of the stage', but this was still fairly small by foreign standards—thirty feet wide and 130 feet deep. A fine new Neoclassical façade was also built.

Saunders' *Treatise on Theatres* of 1790, already briefly quoted, shows that Englishmen were aware of theatrical developments on the Continent. He discusses the merits of the circle, the oval and the horseshoe as forms for the auditorium, judging them for acoustics as well as for vision. He observes, sensibly enough, that the horseshoe has a pleasing appearance, but for those sitting at the side 'occasions a very painful position of the head'. He also disapproves of excessive height—an angle of forty-five degrees is the most that anyone should be expected to look down. It is interesting to find Saunders arguing against the English projecting apron stage and advancing the French theory that 'a division is necessary between the theatre and the stage, and should be so characterized as to assist the idea of their being two separate and distinct places.' We learn, incidentally, that in 1790 'the saloon, or what we generally term coffee-room, is so necessary that the managers of the present theatres find their account in adding one.'

Such thought and study were to bear fruit in the first English theatre to be seriously comparable with the great theatres abroad—Henry Holland's rebuilding of Drury Lane between 1791 and 1794 [Pl. 107]. While it lasted, this was among the largest and most splendid theatres in the world, with a reported capacity of 3,611 (the present Drury Lane theatre holds 2,226). The auditorium must have been very impressive, with its four tiers of boxes arranged in a semi-circle, converging by straight lines towards the stage. Here Holland preserved a modified apron, with proscenium boxes but no doors. The proscenium itself was supported not on pillars but on tiers of ornamental pilasters set with oval mirrors, reflecting the audience back at itself, and ending in huge acanthus consoles. Boxes and galleries were supported on cast-iron columns.

Holland gave much thought to the comfort and convenience of his audience. Circulation was admirably managed, with wide corridors and ingeniously placed staircases avoiding monotony. The main front formed the pit entrance which led through a semi-circular vestibule to a grand 'Egyptian hall', segmental in plan (probably suggested by Molinos' Théâtre Faydeau of a few years earlier [Pl. 101]), with nine bays of Doric columns, lined with arcades housing shops. Stairs at each end led upwards to the upper tiers, and in the middle downwards to the pit. It must have been a composition comparable in every way to Louis' foyer at Bordeaux. The boxes had their own entrances on the north and south (traditionally the King's side and the Prince of Wales' side), each with its vestibule and a saloon above. On the exterior, Holland planned an Ionic colonnade 'affording shelter and convenience below and forming a terrace before the theatre above', but this was

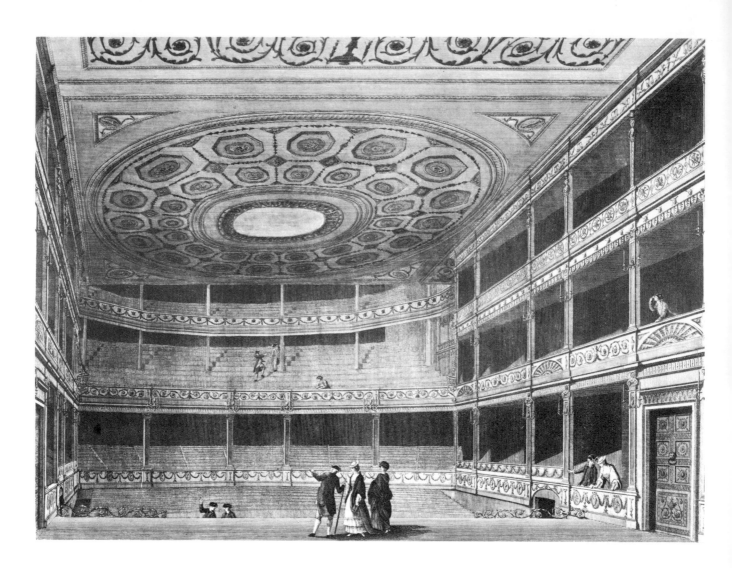

never completed; there was also to be a ventilation tower modelled on the Tower of the Winds, crowned by a ten-foot high statue of Apollo. The theatre, however, was not to be an isolated public monument. Its frontages were integral parts of their streets, with shops, coffee-houses, etc., on the ground floor.

Holland incorporated the latest safety devices from France—an iron curtain and four huge tanks of water in the roof. To no avail. Less than twenty years later it was burnt to the ground, to be replaced by the theatre which still partially survives, by Benjamin Wyatt.

Wyatt's theatre, built partly on Holland's foundations, was begun in 1811 and opened the following year [Pl. 108]. The shape of the auditorium, almost a three-quarter circle, was influenced by Saunders' theories of

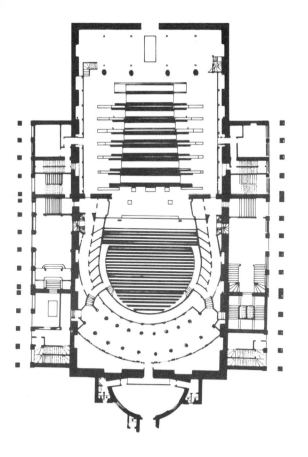

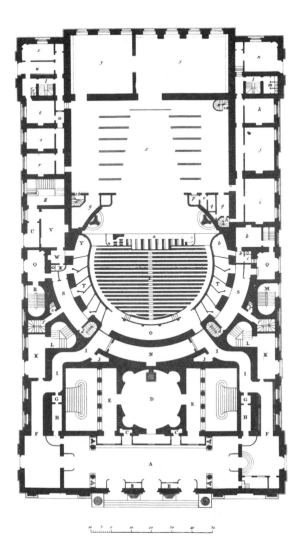

Pls. 106-109. Opposite: Drury Lane Theatre in 1775, after Robert Adam's alterations. Above left: plan of Henry Holland's rebuilt Drury Lane, 1794. This ambitious theatre was full of interesting and original features, both in the accommodation of stage machinery and in the provision of circulation space for the audience. Benjamin Wyatt's Drury Lane succeeded Holland's in 1812 (above right), and the foyers and staircases of this still survive. Right: section through the domed rotunda of Wyatt's theatre (D on the plan), from which, through colonnaded screens, stairs lead to the upper floors.

acoustics and by the example, according to Wyatt, of the Grand Théâtre at Bordeaux (though in fact this is quite different—three segmental curves separated by columns which, as we have seen, form the corners of a square). It had a flat ceiling, which disappointed those who had hoped for a dome. Wyatt retained the boxes beside the stage but beneath them, instead of the traditional English doors, he placed classical tripod altar lamps, similar to those still to be seen outside the main entrance. During the first season they were kept alight but were then removed because they were disturbed too much by the rising and falling curtain. In spite of Wyatt's attention to theory, the acoustics and sight-lines were not good and the auditorium was substantially rebuilt in 1822. (The present interior dates from exactly a hundred years later.) However, his entrance and public rooms remain intact. Three doors open into a vestibule, which in turn leads into a domed rotunda with niches for statues. To left and right rise two grand staircases (King's and Prince's). The rotunda is open through two storeys, with a gallery at first-floor level, and the stair arrangements are repeated at both levels, producing spatial effects smaller but no less subtle than at Bordeaux [Pl. 109]. Over the central vestibule is a saloon, as was standard in France, with column-screens and statues. Wyatt took pains to segregate the various parts of the audience. Respectable patrons were spared 'being obliged to press through lobbies, rooms and avenues, crowded with the most disreputable members of the community, and subject to scenes of the most disgusting indecency.'

The exterior was soberly Neoclassical. Set back above the façade one saw the semi-circular line of the auditorium rising like a clerestory (only without windows). Wyatt's planned portico remained unexecuted. The present rather squat porch was built in 1822 to the design of Sir John Soane, and the colonnade along the north side somewhat later.

The first Covent Garden Theatre, begun in 1731, was based partly on Vanbrugh's Haymarket Opera House, but with a more pronounced fan-shaped auditorium. 'All the spectators in the side boxes', complained a contemporary newspaper, 'were turned away from the stage.' In 1782, it was remodelled by making the sides parallel at right angles to the stage. Surviving plans show how this was surrounded by dressing-rooms (many with stoves), rehearsal rooms and rooms for the storage of scenery. But typically for England at this time, no attempt was made to provide an impressive exterior or comfortable circulation inside. It was entirely hemmed in by houses and shops, and access to its various parts was by dingy and depressing alleys.

This theatre was replaced by one designed by Holland in 1792. Although more ambitious than its predecessor, it did not rival the same architect's Drury Lane, a few hundred yards away. The main entrance was still by an inconspicuous door in Covent Garden Piazza. Holland was an unlucky man. Both his London theatres burnt down within six months of each other

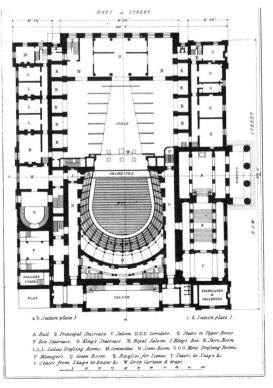

Pls. 110, 111. Robert Smirke's Covent Garden Opera House, completed in 1809. The main front (above) was in fact the flank of the building. Entering the portico (on the right-hand side of the plan), one ascended a long staircase to reach the back of the auditorium. Above the windows of the façade are Flaxman's reliefs representing ancient and modern drama, later re-used on the present theatre. The strange features of the upper storey are merely the eaves of the roof projecting through openings in a screen wall.

(September 1808, February 1809). The task of rebuilding Covent Garden was entrusted to the young Robert Smirke, future architect of the British Museum, then in the first flush of neo-Greek enthusiasm.

His design gave London its first monumental public theatre, exposed on all four sides and with a dominating façade in Bow Street [Pls. 110, 111]. The auditorium, for which Greek models provided no recipe, was conventional. Smirke introduced the Continental type of boxes, completely enclosed on all sides instead of being merely divided by low partitions, but these were not popular. Three tiers of boxes were surmounted by two galleries, the upper one being squeezed into the lunettes of the ceiling ('ranges of dens', says one contemporary account, 'sometimes tenanted by no unfit inhabitants'). In spite of, or perhaps because of, his ingenuity in finding room for 2,800 spectators, Smirke's auditorium was not a success. Various alterations had to be made, including raising the proscenium arch from segmental to semi-circular in order to give patrons at the back of the gallery a view of the stage, and it was almost totally rebuilt in 1847.

Smirke's best ideas undoubtedly went into the public rooms and the exterior. The site was still constricted, so that he was obliged to place his principal entrance at one side of, instead of directly behind, the auditorium. From the vestibule one turned left, ascended a long staircase that rose with no change of direction under a Greek tunnel vault lined with Doric columns, and at the top turned right into the saloon. From here one reached the back of the auditorium in the usual way. The exterior was perhaps the most impressive of any in English theatrical history. The central accent was a tetrastyle Doric portico uniting two storeys; this was flanked on each side by rusticated walls with three bays of windows (a sculptured frieze by Flaxman running above them), ending in slightly projecting corner bays with niches for statues by Rossi. The classical symmetry was completely artificial, since the theatre lay at right angles to it. Above the cornice was a high wall concealing windows, rather like Wren's screen-wall at St. Paul's. Behind that, and set back by the depth of the vestibule and staircase, rose the bulk of the auditorium roof, crowned by another wall which was pierced by six segmental arches, through which portions of the eaves of the roof projected, to be held on corbels—a strange, Ledoux-like, even Piranesian, effect.

Vanbrugh's Opera House on the west side of the Haymarket (see p. 76) perished by fire in 1789. Schemes for the rebuilding of it included one by Robert Adam which, had it been executed, would have put London in the architectural forefront of theatre building [Pls. 112, 113]. It was to lie, like its predecessor, lengthwise along the Haymarket, with the stage end facing Pall Mall, where Adam envisaged a curved façade. The long Haymarket front was to be an assemblage of all his favourite motifs—a rusticated ground storey, numerous projections and recesses, columned screens under arches and a central dome. All this would have disguised rather than

Pls. 112, 113. Right: plan and elevation of Robert Adam's projected Haymarket Opera House, never built. Adam had no innovating ideas concerning stage and auditorium, but his reception rooms would have been of unparalleled elegance. The oval saloon behind the auditorium, opening in four directions into rooms with equally subtle shapes, would have been particularly intriguing. Even the sides of the stage, normally invisible to the audience, were to have a giant order of columns.

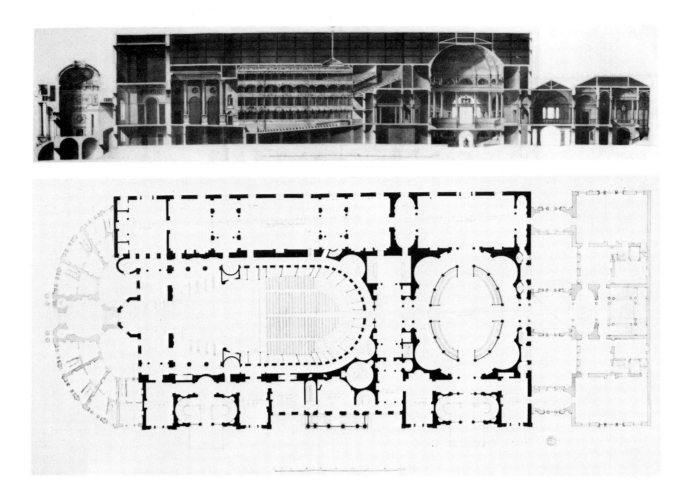

expressed the interior, which was to have had an oval vestibule and a horseshoe auditorium.

The building actually erected was by a Polish scene painter called Novosielski. His theatre, which incorporated several ideas apparently plagiarized from Adam, opened in 1793. When John Nash laid out the surrounding streets as part of his new townscape between Regents Park and the Mall, he and Repton redesigned the street frontages and added a colonnaded pavement similar to those of old Regent Street. It is to this 'face-lift' that we owe the Royal Opera Arcade behind the theatre. Novosielski's building burnt down in 1867, and its successor was demolished in 1896, when the present theatre, rechristened Her Majesty's, was built.

One other London theatre which perhaps deserves a mention is the Pantheon, Oxford Street. It had been built by James Wyatt in 1772 as a place for masquerades and concerts, and was based with surprising fidelity on Hagia Sophia, Constantinople. In 1790, Wyatt converted it into an opera house by building a proscenium arch and giving half the total space to the stage and half to the auditorium, which contained five tiers of boxes. It was widely admired as a piece of architecture, though admitted to be cramped and inconvenient. It lasted only one season before being destroyed by fire. The ruins were incorporated into another theatre by the amateur engineer and architect N. W. Cundy, who modelled his interior on that of La Scala, Milan. It was later described as 'too large for any rational purpose'. In 1834 it was replaced by Smirke's 'Pantheon Bazaar', but Wyatt's façade in Oxford Street remained until 1937.

Outside London, theatres in the late eighteenth century were numerous but remained small and intimate in character. Many are known from engravings, but only a handful still stand and most of those have been converted to other uses. In recent years, attempts have been made to rescue some of them from their degradation as store-rooms or warehouses and to reconstruct them as they were. Their smallness, incidentally, may not have been simply the result of limited means. English audiences, according to Benjamin Wyatt, liked their theatres to be small and there were certainly loud complaints when Drury Lane and Covent Garden were enlarged. Dr. Richard Southern, speaking of the theatre at Richmond, Yorkshire, notes how in these subdued, almost domestic surroundings, the actors could 'reach out and hold, without the slightest effort, the attention of the audience in every corner. The sense of communication here is notable and delicate. One may well understand that the intimacy represented in contemporary caricatures is not exaggerated.'

The Richmond theatre was built in 1788, twelve years after Bristol [Pl. 114]. It is a tiny building with the plainest of exteriors, a simple stone rectangle with a gable roof, like a barn. There is no foyer. One goes straight in, past the paybox, up a short flight of stairs to the passage behind the lower tier of boxes. More steps lead to the gallery. To reach the pit, one goes down a narrow passage and emerges at the front, next to the stage. The theatre could be converted into a dance-hall by covering the pit with boards. The first tier of boxes was on the level of the substitute floor, but could easily overlook the occupants of the pit. Traces of the proscenium doors and boxes have been preserved, but not the proscenium arch, if there was one.

At Bath, the Theatre Royal rivalled that of Bristol. Built to a design of George Dance the Younger, its elegant façade still survives, but the rest was totally rebuilt after a fire in 1862. An ambitious theatre was built at Limerick, Ireland, by an architect called James Lewis. This had the usual three tiers of boxes but, if one can trust Lewis's drawings, they were cantilevered out from the wall rather than supported on columns—an astonishing advance for so provincial a place.

Across the Atlantic, American theatres were serving the same dramatic traditions and embodying all the familiar features of theatres in England. The first theatre in America seems to have been that at Williamsburg,

opened in 1716. Another at Charleston, the Dock Street Theater, is known from 1736. The first of which any detailed record survives was the Chapel Street Theater, New York, opened in 1761 and destroyed six years later. This held 116 people in the pit, 146 in its two tiers of boxes and 90 more in the gallery. Circulation was as inconvenient as in any English theatre. The upper boxes seem to have been accessible only from backstage, so that patrons used the stage door. The John Street Theater, New York, of 1767 again had two tiers of boxes and held a total of 1,000 people. It was described as 'an unsightly object, painted red'. No theatres were built during the War of Independence or for some time afterwards, but in 1786 Harmony Hall, Charleston, was greeted with delight and enthusiasm. It had the luxury of a complete semi-circle of boxes each with its own lock and key. Another Charleston theatre, built in 1793 by James Hoban, the architect of the White House, was the most lavish up to that date. It had three levels of boxes 'decorated with thirty-two columns, with a glass chandelier to each column', and was ventilated by an air-pump invented by a Mr. Edgar, the husband of a leading actress, which rendered the theatre 'pleasant and comfortable, even in cases of crowded audiences'. Its disadvantage was that 'it indeed takes up a little room in the gallery, which cannot hold as many as before'.

The next year, 1794, saw the opening of two large theatres which were to prove influential in the future. One was the Federal Street Theater, Boston, by Charles Bulfinch, one of the architects of the Capitol in Washington. It had a monumental façade, with a portico, three Venetian windows and three separate entrances. The auditorium was conventional, but the building included 'an elegant drawing room, richly ornamented with Corinthian columns and pilasters. There were also spacious card and tea rooms, and kitchens with proper conveniences.' In 1798 it was

Pls. 115, 116. *Philadelphia, the Chest-nut Street Theater. Its fine façade (above) was added in 1804 by Benjamin Latrobe, a pupil of Sir John Soane. The auditorium, built some ten years earlier, was based largely on the Old Theatre Royal, Bath, (not Dance's theatre) and had forty-five boxes in three tiers. It claimed to be the first in America to install gas lighting, in 1816.*

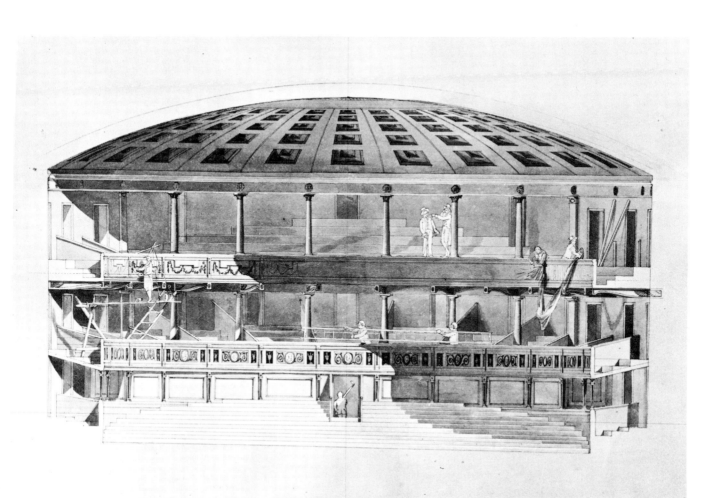

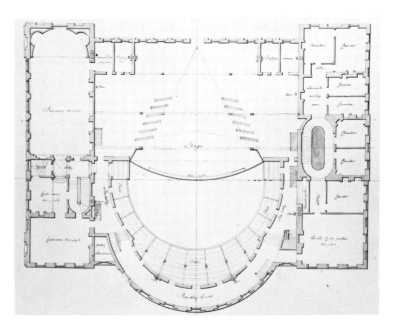

Pls. 117, 118. Latrobe's design for a theatre at Richmond, Virginia, (1798) was never realized but contained some amazingly progressive thinking. Like Foulston's theatre at Plymouth (Pls. 121, 122) of a decade later, it was envisaged as part of a whole community centre. The interior (above) would have been fairly modest, with one tier of boxes and a gallery, but the exterior, which echoes the curve of the auditorium and is flanked by straight wings, prefigures a popular type of theatre front in the nineteenth century.

remodelled by Bulfinch, who cantilevered the lower range of boxes, perhaps on the model of Lewis's Limerick Theatre, engravings of which had been published in 1788. The other theatre which opened in 1794 was the Chestnut Street Theater, Philadelphia, which had forty-five boxes in three tiers, some holding as many as thirty-five people [Pl. 116]. It had a lobby where in winter two fires were kept burning, a large three-tier auditorium, the usual apron stage and proscenium doors, and footlights that could be lowered and raised. The normal English arrangement was followed by which the boxes, pit and gallery each had their own entrances. This aroused the egalitarian anger of the new democracy: 'Shall the national spirit of America slumber under the degradation of European distinctions?' The management was forced to make alterations and provide a single entrance for everybody. The façade of the Chestnut Street Theater was not completed until 1804 when Benjamin Latrobe gave it a big pediment, a Venetian window and a colonnade [Pl. 115].

Latrobe himself, the most interesting American architect of the late eighteenth to early nineteenth centuries, built no theatres, but in 1798 he did produce designs for one at Richmond, Virginia, which contained some of the most original thinking so far to be seen on the subject in America [Pls. 117, 118]. It was to be entered by a quadrant vestibule, as in Holland's Drury Lane, but instead of being hidden behind a false front, this was expressed on the exterior by a segmental curve. Flanked by straight wings containing a hotel and public rooms, this produced a façade which was destined to become extremely familiar in Europe after Semper, but which

had no precedent in the eighteenth century. The auditorium was semi-circular, with two tiers of seating and a wide stage. The proscenium arch was hardly articulated at all, the interior walls leading straight into the stage. A coffered semi-dome, rather like Latrobe's House of Representatives, formed the ceiling. It is heartening to learn that, after 170 years, it is possible that Latrobe's theatre may now be built at Richmond.

In 1798 the Park Theater, New York (once attributed to Mark Isambard Brunel, but now thought to be by Joseph Mangin, in whose office Brunel was then working), took its place as the largest theatre in America [Pl. 119]. It held 2,000 people and boasted a fine classical façade. Seven years

Pl. 121. *John Foulston's Theatre Royal, Plymouth, of 1811, reconstructed from his own designs. Foulston used cast-iron for the balcony supports and had an iron safety-curtain. The stage still extends in front of the proscenium arch, but there are no boxes over the proscenium doors. Above the stage, the numerous hoists for 'flying' scenery foreshadow the later tall fly-towers.*

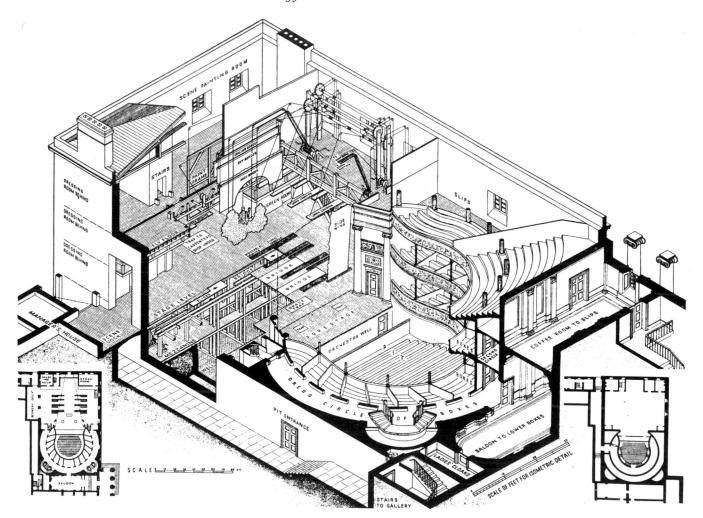

Pl. 122. The façade of Foulston's civic complex at Plymouth, of which the theatre occupied the right-hand wing, beyond the portico (two columns of this can be seen on the right of the diagram opposite). The whole building formed a large square with a courtyard in the middle. On the extreme right is the front of Foulston's Athenaeum, now also demolished.

later it was enlarged by 'a handsome colonnade with mirrors and fireplaces at each end . . . There are several coffee-rooms.' This building was destroyed by fire in 1820 and rebuilt by William Strickland on a large scale, with a stage forty-five feet across and a much reduced apron [Pl. 120]. An English actor, however, said that 'the exterior is the most prison-like looking place I have ever seen appropriated to such a purpose'.

By this time there were probably as many theatres in the United States as there were in Britain, and it was becoming normal for British companies to include America in their tours. Audiences seem to have been, if anything, rougher than at home. Frances Trollope has this description of an evening at Washington: 'One man in the pit was seized with a violent fit of vomiting, which appeared not in the least to annoy or surprise his neighbours; and the happy coincidence of a physician being at that moment personated on the stage was hailed by many of the audience as an excellent joke, of which the actor took full advantage, and elicited shouts of applause by saying "I expect my services are wanted elsewhere".'

Back in England, the first decades of the nineteenth century saw the plainness of the Georgian provincial playhouse developing into Victorian opulence. A specially interesting example of the period of transition was the Theatre Royal at Plymouth [Pls. 121, 122]. Designed by John Foulston, it was opened in 1811 and embodied several improvements stemming from France. Each part of the house, for instance, had its own coffee-room. Foulston's theatre was part of a large civic centre comprising a club, dining-room, assembly hall, hotel and stables, all built around a square courtyard and entered through a portico.

Pl. 123. The Theatre Royal, Bury St. Edmunds: a theatre that has recently been restored after serving as a warehouse. Designed by William Wilkins in 1819, it is a typical Regency theatre in a provincial town; its Empire-style decoration is quite ambitiously cosmopolitan.

The whole ensemble has succumbed to progress and greed, and now the only surviving theatre from the Regency period is the Theatre Royal, Bury St. Edmunds, built in 1819 to the design of William Wilkins, the architect of the National Gallery, whose father was the lessee [Pl. 123]. The façade has a heavy Tuscan porch with a frieze, but the interior (now restored) is delightfully relaxed—two rows of boxes (which held 360 people) and a gallery (120) round a semi-circular pit (holding 300).

Nash's replanning of the Haymarket area in London also included a new theatre of his own on the other side of the road, the present Haymarket Theatre (1821). Its interior was like a Neoclassical mansion crossed with Brighton Pavilion [Pl. 124]. It had an old-fashioned plan with straight sides, but the proscenium had columns ending in palm fronds, with the arch between them imitating the canopy of a tent. This was all remodelled in 1843 and again rebuilt in 1880, but the noble portico remains, its six Corinthian columns facing down the long street to St. James's Square—the only theatre setting in London worthy of its architecture.

Pl. 124. Right: Nash's Haymarket Theatre, as it looked on the opening night, July 4, 1821. The two proscenium doors with boxes above them can here be seen very clearly. At the back of the auditorium were two tiers of galleries. Nash, unlike Foulston, seems quite unaware of developments in theatre design during the previous forty years, but this interior obviously has a great deal of charm.

INTERIOR OF THE ROYAL as it appeared on the Night

NEW THEATRE HAY MARKET, of its opening 4th July 1821

IX

OPERA GOES GRAND

The opera house became recognizable as a distinct architectural type in Italy during the eighteenth century and spread all over the world in the nineteenth, reaching its climax with the Paris Opéra in the 1870s. During the period 1780 to 1870 it outshone every other kind of theatre building and may even have played its part in arresting the development of other forms of drama. By the early twentieth century its days were numbered. The great opera houses are maintained to serve the repertory for which they were built (from, say, Gluck to Puccini, but for special reasons excluding Wagner) and for little else.

Opera is an extraordinary phenomenon, still not given its due in histories of the drama. In our present context, we must face the fact that it makes nonsense of many cherished theories. In no other form of drama is the separation of actors and audience more complete, yet in few others does an audience feel so warmly drawn together in a shared emotional experience. And the physical setting must be relevant to this effect. The much prized 'atmosphere' of an opera house is essential to the experience of opera, which has never lost its connection with Baroque court entertainment. Examined by the cold light of day, these vast buildings—La Scala, the Fenice, San Carlo, and so on up to the Teatro Massimo of Palermo—are architectural monsters, lacking in spatial originality and, for the most part, devoid of real genius. But they work. They have a hold on our affections. We cannot properly have opera without them.

The basic structure remained that of the traditional Italian theatre, hardly influenced at all by Gabriel, Ledoux or Louis. The most favoured plan was the horseshoe, with tiers of boxes rising vertically one above the other, until they reached the ceiling where a gallery would be squeezed in. As opera lost its intimate qualities, and as the Romantic orchestra increased in volume, so the opera house increased in size and grandeur, its décor grew richer, its lobbies and staircases more luxurious, its amenities more ambitious. It was as if the opera house, beginning as one room in a nobleman's palace, had ended by eating up the entire palace.

The decade of the 1770s had been crucial in France. What was happening in Italy? On 26 February 1776 the old Teatro di Corte in Milan was burnt down. By 9 March a group of ninety box-holders met to plan a new one. Archduke Ferdinand, the Austrian ruler, favoured the enterprise, even urged the Milanese to build two theatres instead of one and suggested Giuseppe Piermarini as the architect. The result was the Teatro Cannobiana

Pl. 125. Left: La Scala, Milan, which opened in 1778, has been redecorated and restored many times, particularly after severe bombing in 1943. The royal box occupies its standard Continental position in the centre. This view makes very clear the limited seating capacity of the traditional opera house, a limitation that could only be overcome by making the theatre enormously big. Six tiers of boxes have been successfully integrated, but each is only two or three rows deep. Nothing more could be done until Ledoux's experiments with the amphitheatre (Pls. 93, 94) bore fruit, or (a century later) cantilevering made possible deep projecting galleries.

(demolished in 1894) and the Teatro alla Scala, so called because it was built on the site of the church of S. Maria alla Scala. On 22 August 1776, exactly six months after the destruction of the old theatre, the contract was signed. In May 1778 it was finished.

Architecturally La Scala had nothing particularly new to offer. The façade was, and still is, judged to be too unemphatic, but one must remember that it was originally part of a street, not the focal point of a large public square. The charm of the interior, upon which generations of opera-goers are unanimous, owes as much to the carefully supervised details as to the general planning, though the sight-lines are well managed and the acoustics excellent [Pl. 125].

There are six tiers of boxes. The parapet of each box was decorated according to an overall scheme worked out by Levati and Reina, who also painted the ceiling. But inside, the boxes were luxurious little private apartments, which could be cut off completely from the outside world by curtains, and which each box-holder could embellish according to his own taste. Some were fitted up in the frilliest Rococo, others in the severest classicism. That of the Meroni family, for instance, was painted by a pupil of Galliari with rural pictures recalling scenes from Cimarosa's operas. Others had gilded wood carving. On gala evenings, when everyone came to outshine their neighbours, the effect must have been dazzling. A few of these boxes remain intact, but many were ruined as early as 1796, when the short-lived Cisalpine Republic ordered the destruction of all heraldic insignia. Others perished in redecorations of 1807, 1830 and 1879. Finally in 1921 a rather drab uniformity was imposed, on the grounds that 'La Scala no longer has an aristocratic public, for whom the boxes were appendages to their mansions.' In fact, however, the records of box-holders show that even by 1840 nearly all of them were bourgeois. In the postwar reconstruction an attempt has been made to reinstate some of these boxes in their former glory.

The royal box occupies the most prominent place in the centre, with the main entry into the *parterre* (*platea* in Italian) beneath it. The stage is, as usual, flanked by pairs of giant columns holding tiers of 'proscenium boxes', topped by a section of classical entablature. This does not itself support the arch, however; that rests on pairs of enormous consoles springing from giant satyr heads.

Piermarini's stage, already large, was extended in 1814 by Canonica and Giusti, who took in some ground at the back belonging to a demolished monastery. In 1907 the orchestra pit was lowered, and throughout the years there has been a steady attrition of boxes and their replacement by rows of seats. Lighting was at first by candles on the parapets of the boxes, later improved by oil lamps with reflectors. In 1821 a large chandelier was installed with eighty-four oil lamps; in 1860 this was replaced by another using gas, which in 1884 was converted to electricity.

Pl.126. The Fenice Theatre, Venice. The interior was badly damaged by fire in 1836 and some twenty years later was again drastically remodelled. But the lively Rococo decoration applied to what is still basically an eighteenth-century structure vividly evokes the original theatre.

La Scala has always enjoyed a pre-eminence as the queen of opera houses. The others that might lay claim to the honour will have to be described more briefly. The opera house of Venice, the Fenice, was one of the last buildings to be erected by the old republic before it lost its independence for ever [Pl. 126]. Commissioned in 1788, it was completed by 1792. Its architect, Antonio Selva, was faced with a cramped, irregular site which precluded monumental planning. His solution was to separate the stage-auditorium section almost entirely from the ceremonial rooms, and to scale down the façade until it seems to promise little more than a rather lavish private house (there is also a canal entrance for those arriving by gondola). Within these limitations he was strikingly successful, and in fact they proved a blessing in 1836 when the fire which destroyed the main building was effectively prevented from spreading to the vestibules. Selva's auditorium had been soberly Neoclassical. The reconstruction by the Meduna brothers retained its basic form but substituted an exuberant neo-Baroque style of decoration.

At Naples, the old San Carlo opera house of 1737 was one of the largest and most splendid in Italy. It was praised by Patte in particular for its circulation. Three staircases led to a vestibule which ran along the whole front of the house. The horseshoe-shaped auditorium had six tiers of boxes, making up 184 altogether, of which seventy belonged to noble Neapolitan families who were forbidden to give them up without royal permission. Acoustically, however, it was open to criticism, and until 1810 it lacked an impressive façade. In that year King Joachim (Napoleon's general, Joachim Murat), as part of his efforts to gain popularity among his reluctant subjects, held a competition for its completion, which was won by Antonio Niccolini. Niccolini's design was perfectly calculated to appeal to the king—Italian display expressed in French revolutionary terms [Pl. 127]. It is divided horizontally by an emphatic projecting balcony. The lower zone consists of five giant rusticated arches, with panels of relief sculpture running above them; the upper of a long colonnade of fourteen Ionic

Pl. 127. The San Carlo Opera House in Naples, by Antonio Niccolini (1810) —one of the most original, logical and powerful of all theatre fronts, and a monument of Neoclassicism. Its massive rustication is relieved on the lower level by garlands and heads, on the upper by a series of reliefs alluding to music and poetry. Above the balcony, in complete contrast, a graceful Ionic colonnade shields the large windows of the salon. Largeness of scale is emphasized by such details as the six-foot-high bollards.

Pl. 128. The Teatro Regio, Parma. Already in 1828, Neoclassical severity has become out-dated and gold leaf, festoons, cherubs, etc., are returning. The royal box is surmounted by a crown. There are 112 other boxes, many still privately owned, and each with its original ante-room.

columns. The influence of French architects is unmistakable (Ledoux and Chalgrin have been suggested) but it is no mere imitation. Six years later a fire destroyed the old theatre. Niccolini (working now for the restored Bourbons) rebuilt it on conservative lines, so that the auditorium still conveys something of its eighteenth-century dignity.

During the middle and later years of the nineteenth century almost every large Italian city treated itself to a new opera house. (Those after 1870 will be considered in the next chapter). The Carlo Felice, commemorating the king of that name, in Genoa, was opened in 1828. Its most noteworthy feature, from the architectural point of view, was the huge Doric portico which its designer Carlo Barabino placed not on the façade but on the flank, facing the main square of Genoa, purely for visual effect. Parma acquired its Teatro Ducale, by Nicola Battoli, in the same year (called Teatro Regio since 1849). This is far less grand than the examples cited so far, but has the decided merit of having survived practically intact [Pl. 128].

Outside Italy, one finds opera houses on the grand scale confined to the capitals. France, well provided with theatres in the mid-eighteenth century, attempted nothing of the first rank until Garnier's Opéra. Before this, Paris had the Théâtre Impérial de l'Opéra in the rue St. Honoré, built in 1770 by Moreau, in a style (as Patte observed) definitely reminiscent of Italian examples. Its form was that of a horseshoe, but the floor was raked steeply so that it in fact overlapped the vestibule behind it. One entered, not at the back of the stalls, but near the middle. When this theatre was burnt down after only eleven years, opera was performed at the Académie de Musique, by Debret, in the rue le Peletier, which followed the model of Louis' Théâtre National.

The situation in England has been partly anticipated in the last chapter, but neither Wyatt's Drury Lane nor Smirke's Covent Garden came very close to the Italian prototypes. In 1846, however, the latter was transformed by an Italian engineer and ex-Carbonaro, Benedetto Albano, who entirely reconstructed the auditorium, inserting new lyre-shaped tiers of boxes and increasing the seating capacity to 2,243 [Pl. 129]. This theatre was greatly admired, as much for its acoustics as for its rich decoration and efficient planning. But it was fated to last only ten years before being destroyed by the inevitable fire.

Its successor is the present opera house by E. M. Barry, opened in 1858 [Pl. 130]. Barry enlarged the auditorium but economized in circulation

148

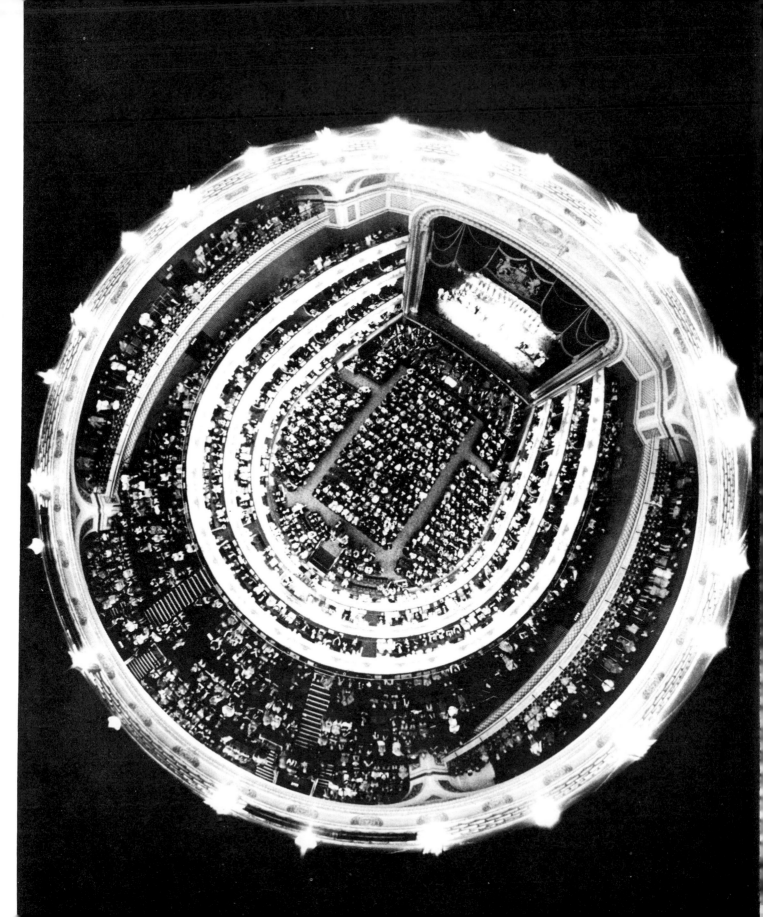

space. His interior owes more to Albano than to Smirke, though he was no doubt also acquainted with the best in French and Italian design. Structurally, this interior seems to utilize the system of Louis' Théâtre National, with a shallow dome resting on four segmental arches, one of which is the proscenium. Only seems, however. In reality, the dome, the arches and everything else are suspended from eight wrought-iron trellis girders nine feet high and ninety feet long resting on the inner shell. In spite of minor alterations (the substitution of continuous galleries for boxes, except at the sides, and the setting back of the formerly projecting stage), Covent Garden today is more or less as Barry left it. It is only a pity that the great gas chandelier ('gasolier'), with its three tiers of lustres, disappeared when electricity was introduced in 1892. For the façade, Barry seems to have gone to La Scala, uniting a grand portico with a basement serving as a *porte cochère*. The effect is now spoilt by the infilling of the ground storey and the erection of a conservatory behind the columns. But above this, on the upper part of the wall, are Flaxman's bas reliefs from the old theatre, and Rossi's statues, also salvaged, occupy niches to the right and left.

Pl. 131. Interior of the Chatham Garden Theater, New York, in 1825. The pit here recedes under the lowest gallery instead of using that space for a row of boxes.

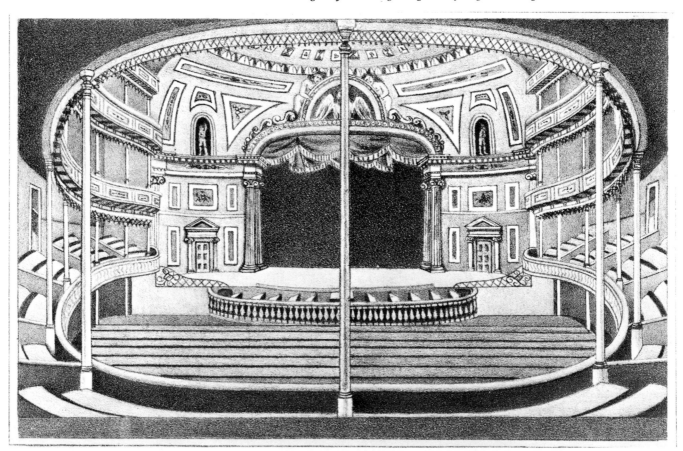

Pls. 132, 133. Fashions in façades: the Bowery Theater, New York, had a sombre Greek temple front (right) when it was built in 1826. After a fire in 1828 it was rebuilt in a semi-Egyptian style (below). The Bowery, with a capacity of 3,000, was for a time the largest theatre in America.

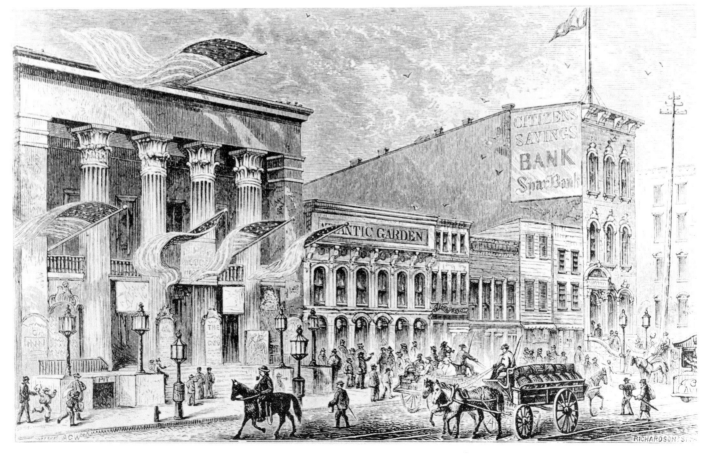

The United States, up to about 1880, could still be regarded as theatrically part of England, though an increasingly independent part. There were no opera companies and no civic theatres in the European sense, hence no opera houses. The Italian Opera House, New York, of 1833, came closest to its Old World models, with a second tier composed entirely of boxes, but it could not subsist on opera for more than two seasons. New York theatres such as Palmo's Opera House (1844), the Astor Opera House (1847), and Pike's Opera House (1869) served opera only in name.

New York seized the theatrical leadership early. In the 1820s, three very large theatres were built (not counting the rebuilt Park Theater): the Chatham Garden Theater (1824) [Pl. 131]; the Bowery (1826), then the largest in the country, lit by gas and with a capacity of 3,000; and the Lafayette of 1827, which had the most elaborate scenic machinery ever seen in the States. Frances Trollope noted: 'The Park Theater is the only one licensed by fashion, but the Bowery is infinitely superior in beauty; it is indeed as pretty a theatre as I ever entered, perfect as to size and proportion, elegantly decorated, and the scenery and machinery equal to any in London.' The façade was that of a Doric hexastyle temple, lacking, one would have thought, in gaiety, but it was

Pl. 134. The second St. Charles Theater, New Orleans, 1843. Theatres in America were more democratic than in Europe, and the St. Charles had no boxes. As a result, spectators had to sit behind the pillars, in positions occupied in European theatres by the partitions between boxes.

Pl. 135. *Moscow's Bolshoi Theatre was rebuilt after a fire in 1856 by Albert Cavos, but the portico and some of the outside walls were retained from the earlier building: this dated from the 1820s and was by two Russian architects, Bove and Mikhailov.*

widely imitated [Pl. 132]. The first Bowery lasted only two years. When it was rebuilt in 1828, an Egyptian style replaced Greek [Pl. 133]. The Lafayette followed it to ashes in 1829. In 1861 Wallach's Theater became the best equipped in New York, to be overtaken in 1869 by Booth's, which had a hydraulic lift for scenery, and in 1880 by the Madison Square Theater, whose whole stage was one huge lift [Pl. 156].

Outside New York, the most ambitious theatre was that of Boston, built in 1854 and seating an audience of 3,000. It was, by American standards, unusually well-provided with vestibules, smoking rooms and passages. Further west, drama came comparatively late. New Orleans acquired its St. Charles Theater in 1835, lit by a huge chandelier thirty-six feet in diameter. This was burnt down in 1842, but its successor was equally grand [Pl. 134]. The first permanent theatre in Chicago was not built until 1847. Perhaps the most intriguing of these 'pioneer' theatres was that of the Mormon Salt Lake City, erected under the auspices of Brigham Young in 1862. Inside it was 'light and airy, having no curtains and no boxes, save two in the proscenium . . . Peace and order reign in the midst of fun and frolic.'

Outside, it was 'a rough Doric edifice'—two Doric columns *in antis* between solid bays with pilasters.

Classicism, in fact, was *the* style for theatre façades all over the world. One might have expected some relaxation, some concession to frivolity, some flirtation at least—in this age of 'the battle of the styles'—with the exotic and the exciting (the history of cinemas is an object lesson in what might have happened). But the grip of classicism was too strong. It was not until the end of the century that theatre designers felt free to look elsewhere for their models.

Some of the noblest of these later Neoclassical theatres are in Russia. The Alexandrinsky, St. Petersburg, (now the Pushkin Academic Drama Theatre) was the work of an Italian, Rossi, in 1832; the Bolshoi, in Moscow, was by the son of an Italian, Cavos, in 1856 [Pl. 135]. The Mariinsky Theatre (now the Kirov) in St. Petersburg, also by Cavos, was built in 1860 and bears evidence that its designer had studied Wyatt's Drury Lane; the vestibule is in the form of a rotunda rising the full height of the building and flanked by oval staircases.

But it was in Germany that classicism achieved its real fruition. Already fully mature in theatres such as the Prussian National Theatre of Berlin by Langhans (1800) and the Munich Opera House of 1811–18 by Karl von Fischer (rebuilt after 1823 by Klenze but on the same lines), classicism reaches its climax in the work of Karl Friedrich Schinkel, friend and associate of Friedrich Gilly. Schinkel came to architecture from the theatre, having begun his career as a scene designer and romantic painter. In 1818 he was commissioned to build the new Schauspielhaus in Berlin as the centre of a grandiose new scheme of town planning. The façade is self-consciously monumental—an Ionic portico standing at the top of a steep flight of steps, flanked by wings on a rusticated basement with, rising behind it, another higher portico supporting a bronze quadriga [Pl. 136]. But the interior is more restrained; in the semi-circular auditorium the orders are conspicuously absent, decoration being pared down to flat panels, medallion heads and similar motifs. The left-hand wing of the building formed a smaller concert-room so cool and chaste that it could easily be a sculpture hall in his own nearby museum. Schinkel built no more theatres, but his thoughts on the subject continued to develop and to influence later architects. He came to believe in a much plainer setting, with the stage projecting into the auditorium.

His most notable follower, and the inheritor of his ideas, was Gottfried Semper, one of the most creative talents of nineteenth-century theatre design. Like Schinkel, he combined mastery of architectural theory and practice with a concern for drama and an informed interest in the ancient world. In 1836, he collaborated with the great Shakespearian scholar Ludwig Tieck in reconstructing the Fortune Theatre according to the original contract. The result looks hopelessly unconvincing to modern eyes, but represents more than an academic exercise. Later in his career (1856), he did a design for a Greek amphitheatre to be erected inside the Crystal Palace (after its removal to Sydenham). Since the space available was small, Semper had to slice off the sides of the semi-circle to fit into a square. Abortive as both these projects were, they are signs that men of the theatre were beginning to rethink the whole relationship of architecture and drama. One could also quote such enterprises as the wide stage with multiple set (medieval *mansiones* revived) built by Karl Immermann at Düsseldorf in 1852 for performances of *Twelfth Night*, the renewed interest taken in the Oberammergau play around this time, and various other experiments with projecting stages.

Semper's first major work, the Dresden Opera House of 1838–41, at once launched a new theatrical type [Pl. 137]. The façade consisted of a two-storeyed semi-circular loggia (Doric and Ionic), with the higher auditorium, also semi-circular, set back behind it and articulated with Corinthian pilasters. The plan clearly leaned heavily upon the French theorists of the eighteenth century—Durand and his school—and in particular upon a late Italian member of it, Pietro Sangiorgio, whose *Idea di un teatro* of 1821 works out the implications of the semi-circular front and side

Pl. 136. Façade of Schinkel's Neues Schauspielhaus, Berlin. The wing to the left of the portico houses the concert hall, that to the right a rehearsal room and offices.

Pl. 137. *Gottfried Semper's façade of the Dresden Opera House of 1838-41 revealed the semi-cylinder of the auditorium for the first time since antiquity, though it had been advocated in several eighteenth-century ideal projects. With its semi-circular foyers on two levels and staircases in 'transept' positions at the sides, this design was to prove influential for the next hundred years.*

entrances in some detail. Semper's own philosophy is best expressed in a description he wrote of a later project, the Rio de Janeiro opera house of 1858: 'Above all I have wished not to conceal the semi-cylindrical form of the auditorium, a form beautiful and varied in itself, and sanctioned moreover by theatrical tradition. I have not imprisoned it in a square cage, as most modern auditoria are.' At Dresden one could enter through the centre of the façade into the semi-circular vestibule, but the main staircases were at the sides, entered by way of separate lateral porches. The high roof of the auditorium was extended sideways over these porches, like the transepts of a cathedral. The auditorium, in deference to contemporary usage, was in fact not semi-circular but horseshoe-shaped.

In 1842, a young conductor of unorthodox views and dynamic personality was appointed to the new opera house—Richard Wagner. Between then and 1849, when both had to flee the city in the wake of revolution, Wagner and Semper were colleagues at Dresden, and the subject of the perfect opera house was discussed frequently and earnestly. Both were dissatisfied with the grandiose Italian plan then in vogue, and already Wagner was formulating his ideal requirements—a fan-shaped auditorium without galleries or boxes, a remote but clearly visible stage, and a hidden orchestra. Their association was continued at Zürich later in the 1850s, and finally at Munich under the patronage of Ludwig II of Bavaria, with results that were to be crucial to the history of our subject.

Before pursuing this theme, however, we must pause to look at the mightiest monster of them all.

X

THE AGE OF MAGNIFICENCE

The decision that Paris should have a new opera house worthy of the capital of France—one that would be the consummation of all that had gone before, a monument of architecture, a focus of city planning, a splendid setting for sculpture and painting, a shrine of opera and ballet—had been taken as early as 1840, but it was not until Napoleon III and Baron Haussman had begun their wholesale building programme in the 1850s that any practical move was made. Although a design by the resident Opéra architect already existed, it was announced at the end of 1860 that the project would be thrown open to a public competition. The idea is thought to have been the Empress Eugénie's, who expected her favourite, Viollet-le-Duc, to win. The time allowed was a single month, yet by 31 January 1861, 171 entries had been received. From the most promising a short list of five names was made, and to the Empress's annoyance Viollet-le-Duc's was not among them. His design, indeed, was a banal work, partly no doubt because the style had to be classical instead of his preferred neo-Gothic. The five successful competitors were asked to submit more detailed plans by the end of another two months. Two of them declined to go on. At the end of May, the name of the winner was announced—Charles Garnier, a promising but almost unknown young man of thirty-one.

Garnier came from a poor family, and as a student had actually helped to support himself by working in Viollet-le-Duc's office for seventy-five centimes an hour. In 1848 he won the much coveted Grand Prix de Rome, and spent four years in Italy, visiting also Sicily, Greece and Constantinople. But in the eight years that had elapsed since his return he had failed to make his mark, and was finding it hard even to support himself.

Victory in the competition elevated him to a height to which he was not accustomed. The story of his first visit to the Tuileries to show his plans to the royal couple is thus told by a friend: 'The Empress had a dry, dissstisfied manner, and a brusque tone, and as the Emperor was saying politely, "Very good, very good . . . beautiful", she broke in bitterly: "What style is it in? It's not in any style at all! It's not Greek, not Louis XIV, not even Louis XV!" "No", said Charles, "those are styles of the past. This is the Napoleon III style. Are you complaining about that?"—"The stage is too big, the auditorium is too small"—"But one has to leave space for the decoration and the sets . . . And the human voice has its limits", said Charles; "if the auditorium were bigger, who could make himself heard in it, and where would you find the crowds to fill it?" Charles' tone was becoming rather sharp, that of the Empress had been so from the beginning. The Comte de Cardaillac took Charles by the sleeve and said *sotto voce*, "Keep calm." The Emperor was smiling quietly behind his moustache . . . Approaching Charles he said very softly, "Pray don't get upset, she understands nothing".'

Work began on the building almost at once but progressed slowly. A year was spent draining a pond that was found to be under the foundations. It was not until 1867 that the south front was unveiled. The whole exterior was complete by 1869, but the interior was still unfinished when war broke out in 1870. During the war it was used as a warehouse. The two sieges of Paris and the terrible destruction that took place during the Commune made it out of the question to continue with it straight away. The fact that work was resumed and brought to a triumphant conclusion in January 1875 owes much to Garnier's own energy and administrative ability. The opening night was a psychological boost to the whole of Paris, a sign that the dark days were over. A varied collection of European notables was assembled for the occasion, including, besides the president of the new republic, the Lord Mayor of London, the King of Spain and his mother, the King of Hanover, and the Burgomaster of Amsterdam. Garnier's masterpiece, indeed, was built as a symbol of national glory, and has always functioned as such. Its record as an opera house is depressing, but as a flamboyant gesture, as an expression of its age, as an unquenchable assertion of gaiety, optimism and eternal youth, it has a place in the affections of the world. When Garnier said '*C'est du Napoléon III*' he was doing himself no more than justice.

In terms of its professed purpose, the Opéra is an extremely competent building [Pls. 138–42]. Standing free on all sides, its exterior form clearly expresses the divisions of the interior. The rectangular block in the front is the foyer and grand staircase; the central dome is the auditorium; the two flanking domes are the library and the entrance of the head of state; the large cubic mass behind that is the stage; and the block at the back is the artists' and administrative quarters.

The spectator's progress from the pavement of the Place de l'Opéra to his seat in the auditorium is an exhilarating experience—destined, possibly, to be his most exhilarating experience of the evening. He passes first through one of the arches of the façade, a vast polychrome composition which bears witness to Garnier's studies in Baroque Rome as well as to his talent for invention [Pl. 140]. Rich it undoubtedly is, but its richness does not get out of control. The carved decoration, contributed by a host of sculptors, was carefully worked out in advance by Garnier, who gave each the dimensions required and a rough silhouette of what he had in mind. The ornamental details both of this façade and of the rest of the exterior can be

Pl. 138.   Right: the Grand Staircase of ▶ the Paris Opéra. 'Unhappy is he', wrote Garnier, 'who becomes so wise that no grain of folly or fantasy can grow in his brain.' The staircase was at once recognized as a masterpiece—so much so that he grew almost tired of hearing it praised. 'People talk', he grumbled, 'as if the Opéra was nothing but the staircase, just as they see the Invalides as nothing but the dome.'

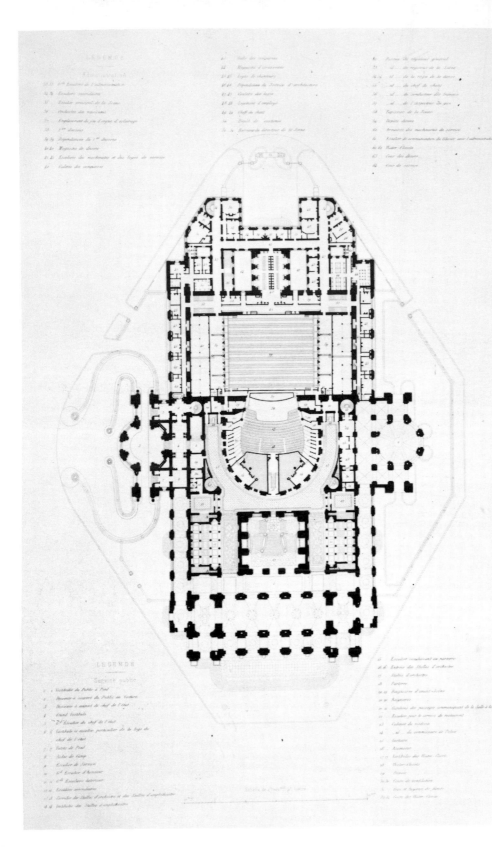

Pl. 139. Plan of the ground floor of the Paris Opéra. The entrance front is at the bottom. The Grand Foyer runs across the building above the lobby, then comes the staircase taking up the whole height of the building. It is interesting to see how relatively little of the total area is occupied by the auditorium. The rotundas to left and right contain on their upper floors the rooms of the head of state, and the library. Garnier prepared his plans with the utmost care, and beneath all the ostentation lies an extremely functional building, every requirement of the client (the Emperor) being taken into account and satisfied.

Pls. 140, 141. *Above: the façade of the Opéra. Garnier's critics, of whom there were many, complained that the base was too squat and the rest too rich, too highly coloured, and looked like a sideboard loaded with knick-knacks. 'The base is the same height as that of the Louvre's east front,' said Garnier; 'who complains about that?' As for colour, 'living every day and every hour in a world full of colour, why should we deny it to architecture?' Right: the auditorium, its form based closely on Louis' Théâtre National. 'The eyes begin to be gently charmed, then the imagination follows them into a sort of dream; one drifts off into a feeling of well-being.'—Garnier.*

a constant source of surprise, if not always of pleasure—the 'rostral' columns, for instance, bearing gas lamps and placards announcing the performances, which are ringed by the spiked prows of antique boats; or the lateral entrances which have giant caryatid figures holding laurel branches over the doors, topped by the imperial eagle.

Inside, the whole length of the façade is occupied by the Grand Vestibule, the central three bays of which lead into the Grand Staircase, the Escalier d'Honneur [Pl. 138]. On either side are subsidiary staircases, while if one goes down instead of up, one reaches a large circular waiting room directly underneath the auditorium. Both the Grand Staircase and the circular waiting room are derived from Victor Louis, the first from Bordeaux, the second from his Parisian Théâtre National—debts which Garnier cheerfully acknowledged. Circulation, supply of tickets and what the French call contrôles (barriers to check the tickets) are extremely well managed and there is never a feeling of congestion. The tiers of the auditorium, almost all divided into boxes, are reached from wide corridors running behind them. Services included cloakrooms, washrooms and lavatories in greater abundance than was usual in the 1870s, a reasonable ventilation system, a doctor's surgery, a bookshop, library, flower shop, even—most modern of innovations—an electric lift. Electricity was also used for the lighting (i.e. arc-lights, not incandescent bulbs, which were not used in the theatre until the 1880s) and Garnier installed a small generating plant beneath the Grand Staircase. When mains electricity became available he thankfully gave this up: not only were the vibrations endangering the marble columns but the water being pumped up from the wells underneath was slowly sucking up the subsoil with it.

The Grand Staircase, which is the showpiece of the whole design, is closely based on the Bordeaux staircase, but to compare the two is to become painfully aware of the change in taste between 1770 and 1870. Everything has grown bigger, tougher, more bulbous. The stairs themselves, and their treads, and the balconies between the columns, curve voluptuously; spaces are deepened and enriched by mouldings and colours; on either side of the main flight, punctuated at its beginning by groups of agitated statuary, stairs leading downwards create a new dimension.

The Grand Foyer, which occupies the *piano nobile* of the south front (the position taken by small concert rooms in some earlier French theatres), is a room of palatial splendour, gleaming with mirrors, marbles, chandeliers, gilt and statuary [Pl. 142]. On the east side, under one of the pairs of flanking cupolas, are the apartments of the head of state—a separate entrance with quarters for guards, valets and aides-de-camp. This was among the requirements of the competition and was due to the fact that Napoleon III had only just escaped being assassinated as he was entering the main entrance of the old Opéra. Neither Napoleon nor Eugénie, of course, ever entered the new one.

Pl. 142. Right: the Grand Foyer of the ► Paris Opéra is an unashamed attempt to recreate Versailles, with an added touch of genuine Roman Baroque. Garnier paid handsome tribute to all the craftsmen who made it possible. The gilded statues above the columns represent the different qualities necessary for an artist—Imagination, Hope, Passion, and so on. 'One could indeed fill a book with the allegorical figures in the Opéra,' said Garnier, 'and I confess that by the end I was hard put to think of new ones. I used up everything I could remember out of Ovid, and I will not swear that somewhere there might not be a repetition.'

The auditorium also derives from Louis' Théâtre National [Pl. 141]. Although pulled down in 1820, the interior of this building had been reproduced in the earlier Opéra in the rue le Peletier, built by Debret and much admired by Garnier (it was destroyed in 1873). Four huge arches resting on coupled columns form the basic structure. The columns are Corinthian, and the arches above them are carried on flying angels. In general, however, Garnier tried not to allow the *Salle* to rival the foyer in brilliance, his theory being that the spectators ought to feel themselves in *un milieu artistique et même grandiose*, but should not be distracted by the décor from the actual events on the stage. (One has to remember that all through this period most of the house lights remained on during performances.) The ceiling, from the centre of which hangs the famous chandelier, was painted by Lenepveu with Apollo, Venus, the Muses, the hours of the day and night, beauty, love, song, etc., etc. In 1964 André Malraux was inspired to install a new ceiling by Marc Chagall, whose dreamy innocent figures and scraps of background are agreeable enough but totally inappropriate to their setting. It is painted on canvas—650 square feet of it—and has been fixed in front of the old ceiling so it can, if desired, eventually be taken away again.

The stage half of the building has its own entrance, leading into a gallery that is a minor version of the Grand Vestibule. Each department has its own quarters, including a police station, three concierges and a fire-brigade. The rehearsal room for the ballet, the Foyer de Danse, is nearly as big as the stage, and as richly decorated as any of the public rooms.

The Paris Opéra was naturally imitated in other cities, but it was not the only model. Its rival was the type evolved by Semper at Dresden. The differences between the two were not so much in the stage-auditorium complex as in the grouping of the subsidiary rooms and staircases. The French type favoured a straight front, with the main foyer occupying the first floor, and a central grand staircase behind, leading into the back of the auditorium. The German preferred the curved façade, with its curved vestibule behind, which involved banishing the staircases to the 'transept' position. Many architects followed Gilly in combining a pedimented entrance *à la* Schinkel with curved sides leading back to straight wings. Semper himself used this form in his second Dresden Opera House, built after the first had burnt down in 1869. He also modified the semi-circle of the earlier theatre to a segmental curve, a form we have seen used in certain eighteenth-century theatres, though rarely expressed on the exterior. The Hofburgtheater of Vienna, begun in 1874 by Semper, assisted by the young Karl von Hasenauer, follows the same plan, with the 'transept' staircases here expanded into extremely grand architectural compositions, deliberately challenging Garnier. This plan was criticised because it 'was confessedly based upon plans for opera houses, and consequently the architectural principles involved in carrying it out

Pl. 143. *The Teatro Massimo, Palermo, finished in 1897, surpassed every other opera house in Italy in size, rivalling those of Paris and Vienna. The façade, which lacks vivacity compared with those two, is based primarily on Schinkel, but the dome over the auditorium is purely Italian.*

satisfy operatic rather than dramatic requirements.' It was a criticism that could be levelled at many large theatres of the time, where grandeur had priority over function. Nevertheless, Semper's influence continued well into the twentieth century. Architects were especially fond of the curved vestibule, and often tried to incorporate it into other types of plan, as Barry does, for example, in the stalls bar of Covent Garden.

Both halves of the Dual Monarchy of Austria-Hungary received magnificent new opera houses during this period. That of Vienna formed part of the ambitious programme of public buildings lining the new Ringstrasse. Its architects were August von Siccardsberg and Eduard van der Null, the winners of a competition in 1860. Though too early to be influenced in detail by Garnier, it was a conscious attempt to rival Paris in size (two and a half acres) and richness, and in fact arrived at very similar solutions to the same problems. The stage and auditorium are buried in a vast complex of ceremonial halls and rooms. There were originally two open courtyards, one of which is now roofed and used as a second stage where sets can be assembled. The building has an unhappy history. Van der Null hanged himself in 1863, and a few months later Siccradsberg had a stroke and died. The Budapest Opera House, by Miklós Ybl, completed in 1884, is more French than German in its planning, with a particularly ingenious central staircase. Its stage equipment was the most advanced in Europe, and it was the first theatre east of the Atlantic to use the hydraulic lift.

In Italy, the provision of opera houses was a matter of constant urgency, but the national genius seems to have exhausted itself, and one finds only a series of tame variations on the French and German plans. In 1864, the citizens of Palermo decided to outshine all rivals by holding a competition for a new opera house and invited Schinkel, Van der Null and Semper to be the judges. They were a little disconcerted to learn that the first two were dead, but Semper accepted and with two Italian colleagues chose the design of a local architect, G. B. Basile. Work started in 1875 and was not finished until 1897. The Teatro Massimo is a gargantuan pile, following the Paris Opéra in its combination of dome over the auditorium and gabled roof over the stage, though in this case the dome is raised on a drum and given a wide projecting cornice [Pl. 143]. The flanking rotundas are also Paris-inspired, but the porticoed entrance crowning a flight of steps comes from Schinkel. The auditorium has five tiers, comprising 142 boxes, and holds 2,228 spectators. The original competition also stipulated ten apartments for singers and opera personnel to live in, but even Basile drew the line at that.

Cities which could boast a composer among their sons joyfully named their opera houses after him, like the Teatro Donizetti at Bergamo, or the Teatro Bellini at Catania. The latter, designed by Andrea Scala and Carlo Sada, was completed in 1890 and is a neat example of the combination of Semper's quadrant wings with Garnier's Grand Vestibule. In the auditorium, sixteen chandeliers encircle a huge ceiling-painting of the apotheosis of Bellini. Rome's Teatro dell' Opera (by Achille Sfondrini, 1880, but rebuilt internally in 1926) never attained the predominance that its position in the capital might seem to deserve. Sfondrini's façade, which in fact lies along one flank, is a drab paraphrase of Paris—a long porch of square rusticated piers in the centre, and bays surmounted by segmental pediments at the sides.

This has inevitably been a sparse selection from the dozens of major opera houses erected between 1870 and the first decade of the twentieth century. One could find examples from almost every country in the Western world, for we are speaking of that blessed age when the possession of an opera house was a sort of certificate of civilization. Look east—to that of Odessa, by the Viennese firm of Fellner and Helmer, or the even larger one projected for St. Petersburg by Victor Schroeter (a Russian, in spite of his name). This, had it been built, would have been the apotheosis of Semper—two Semper theatres placed back to back. But, for safety reasons, Schroeter supplied staircases all round the auditorium, thus sacrificing the greatest attraction of the curved façade—the curved vestibule behind it.

Pl. 144.   The old Metropolitan Opera House in New York opened in 1882. It burnt down ten years later and was immediately rebuilt. Its recent destruction and replacement by the new opera house in Lincoln Center leaves New York without any first class setting for opera.

The completely redundant curve at the back was to be used as a theatre library and museum. Or west—to the Metropolitan Opera of New York (recently lamented), opened in 1883 [Pl. 144]; or the Manhattan, its rival, of 1906. The capitals of Latin America, too, made haste to claim their privileges—Mexico City, Santiago, Rio, Lima, all boasted houses of splendour and distinction. Deep in the Amazonian jungle, the opera house of Manaus still bears witness to the rubber boom which eighty years ago made the area one of the most prosperous in Brazil [Pl. 145]. Famous singers from Europe once came here to sing. When the rubber market collapsed Manaus resumed its status as a remote provincial town, its gilt and crimson theatre remaining as a monument to its days of glory.

The ambitions and the values which first produced and then kept these great buildings functioning were not, of course, primarily those of art. Prestige was won, national pride was gratified, but drama and music were increasingly frustrated. Indeed, the more expensive the theatre, the less freedom was the composer given, the more burdensome were the rules and the more absurd the conventions to which he was obliged to adhere. Success or failure was often in the hands of a *claque* who had to be bought or placated. Performances became merely social occasions, with most of the audience arriving late, leaving early and paying attention only to their favourite singers. The lives of Berlioz, Wagner and Verdi are full of their struggles against the whole system. For the sake of true art, it seemed, opera must be saved from the opera house.

XI

THE WAGNERIAN REVOLUTION

Wagner's objection to the operatic régime of his day was two-fold. The conditions of management, rehearsal and performance were incompatible with the full realization of his intentions: he needed time, devotion and absolute authority; he needed a theatre 'entirely free from the influence of the repertory system now in vogue in our permanent theatres', where 'a strictly metropolitan theatre public, with its well-known habits, would not present itself'. But he was also deeply dissatisfied with the prevailing architectural forms. He noted that, as the stage building needed to be 'twice the height required by the auditorium, the result is a conglomerate of two buildings of totally different shape and size. To mask the disproportion of these two buildings as much as possible, most architects of our recent theatres have considerably increased the height of the auditorium, and above that again have added rooms for scene painting and sundry managerial purposes—generally so inconvenient that they are seldom used. Moreover, one can always fall back on the expedient of adding another tier or two of boxes, even allowing the uppermost gallery to lose itself high up above the level of the top of the proscenium—since it is only meant for the poorer classes, upon whom one thinks nothing of inflicting a bird's-eye view of the goings-on below them in the stalls.'

His ideal solution was thus a new theatre designed by himself and Semper in 'one of the smaller German cities, favourably located for the entertainment of distinguished guests'. The story of how King Ludwig II of Bavaria came to his rescue when all seemed hopeless, and made it possible for him to finish *The Ring*, *Tristan*, *The Mastersingers* and *Parsifal*, is too well known to need repetition. At last, it seemed, his theatre could be built. The king was enthusiastic, Semper was summoned to draw up plans, money and workmen were made available. The only drawback in Wagner's eyes was that it would have to be built in Munich, but it had a grandeur which must have exercised a certain compensatory charm. The proposed site was on the far bank of the Isar. It was to be approached over a new bridge and to form the climax of an imposing piece of town planning. Semper's façade allowed for a segmental centre with spreading wings containing staircases. In the internal arrangements, Wagner's ideas were followed implicitly. The auditorium was fan-shaped; there were no boxes or galleries; the orchestra pit was sunk in front of and partly under the stage, out of sight of the audience.

The Festspielhaus an der Isar was never started. The king's relations with his own government came to a crisis, not the least of his troubles being

Wagner's affair with Cosima von Bülow and his arrogant indifference to public opinion. The composer was obliged to leave Munich and live in Switzerland, at Ludwig's expense, where he finished *Siegfried* and *Götterdämmerung*, and considered anew the problem of staging the whole cycle.

By the beginning of 1872 he had settled upon Bayreuth. It was the right size. It was far enough from Munich to be free from the capital's hostility, yet close enough for King Ludwig to visit it. The money was to be raised by subscriptions from local 'Wagner Societies' and other schemes, but they all fell through and it was Ludwig, as usual, who paid two-thirds of the bill.

At first Wagner had intended to adapt Bibiena's old Opera House to his requirements, since it had one of the largest stages in Germany. But he soon realized that it could never answer his purpose—a decision for which we may be profoundly thankful. A new theatre would have to be built. He had Semper's old plans of 1865–7. They were more elaborate than he needed now, but they contained the essence of his idea. To put them into practice he needed an architect who would merely translate them into technical terms and direct the actual construction; he chose Otto Brückwaldt of Leipzig, who is otherwise unknown to fame and whose contribution to the design was practically nil. The foundation stone was laid on Wagner's fifty-ninth birthday, 22 May 1872; after the ceremony, at which it poured with rain, he conducted Beethoven's Ninth Symphony in the old Opera House. Over four years later, on 6 August 1876, the first performance of the complete *Ring* began.

Wagner's intentions at Bayreuth have been explained by himself with admirable clarity, and one can hardly do better than to quote his own words: 'In the proportions and arrangement of the auditorium', he wrote, 'you will find expressed a thought which, once you have grasped it, will place you in a new relation to the drama you are about to witness, a relation quite distinct from that in which you are normally involved when visiting theatres' [Pls. 146–50].

Paramount in his mind was the need to conceal the orchestra [Pls. 149, 150]. The 'constant visibility of the mechanics of music-making is an aggressive nuisance.' In this view Wagner was certainly not original. Goethe, among others, had complained of the distraction of seeing musicians at work, and we have seen how Ledoux and De Marette had proposed to place them wholly or partially under the stage. Nearer to Wagner's time was Count C. di Benevello, who in 1841 published *Azione coreographiche . . . precedute d'alla proposta d'alcune riforme nei moderni teatri*, which is of interest because it puts forward a scheme almost identical to Wagner's, and which Semper at least must have read. Benevello's idea is to adapt the space under the stage for the orchestra, 'giving it an elliptical form and covering it with metal. By this means one would be able to make use of all the space which the orchestra now occupies and, much more important, the curve would direct

Pl. 146. Plan of the Bayreuth Festspiel-haus, 1876. The stage area is provided with extensive wings on either side to facilitate the movement of scenery, and over the years this has been steadily enlarged.

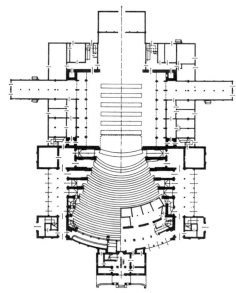

PI. 147.   *This contemporary engraving endows the exterior of the Festspielhaus with rather more charm than it possesses in reality. Wagner's concern was entirely functional. No space was wasted on ceremony or relaxation, though in 1882 a small reception lobby was added to the façade.*

the sound towards the middle of the auditorium, and its volume would be more compact and unified, whereas with the present arrangement one's eardrums are shattered by wind instruments on one side and trumpets on the other.' This prediction about the quality of the sound has come abundantly true at Bayreuth, where the orchestra has a mellow sensuousness, not distracting from the clarity of each instrument, that is unlike any other theatre in the world. Benevello was uncertain what to do with the conductor, whose 'oscillating back view' he wanted to veil from the audience. Wagner solves this problem by his curving hood of wood and leather. The conductor is almost on a level with the stage, while beneath him the orchestra sits on a descending series of steps—first the strings, then the woodwind, and finally, literally under the stage, the brass and percussion.

A considerable gap was, of course, still left between the edge of the stage and the first row of seats. This Wagner welcomed. The auditorium was to

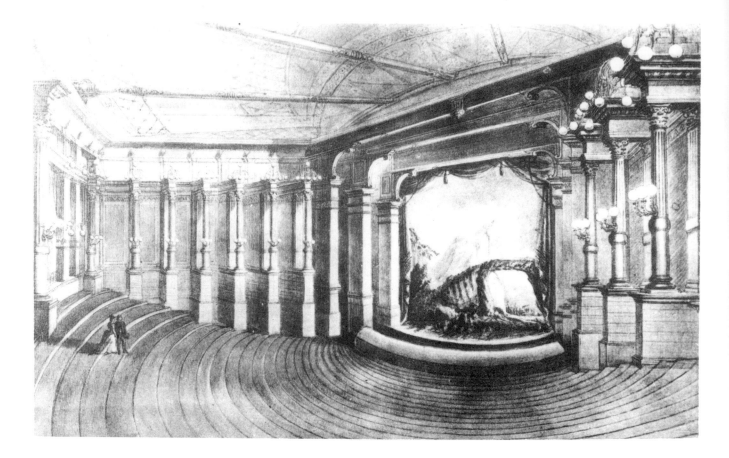

be fan-shaped, without boxes or side seats, focusing upon the stage, which was as usual framed by a proscenium arch. Semper conceived the idea of placing another proscenium in front of the first, the space between the two (where the hidden orchestra lay) being left in darkness. It was the 'mystic gulf', the *mystische Abgrund*, which separated the 'ideal' from the 'real'. It 'makes the spectator imagine the stage is quite far away, though he sees it in all the clearness of its actual proximity; and this in turn gives rise to the illusion that the persons appearing on it are of larger, superhuman stature.'

The form of the auditorium was conditioned by these two factors—the hidden orchestra and the double proscenium [Pl. 148]. Wagner stipulated a single ramp of seats, facing directly towards the stage. The spectator was not there to participate in a social event. He was to find himself in 'a room made ready for no other purpose than *looking* in, and for looking straight in front of him. Between him and the picture to be looked at nothing meets his eyes, only a floating atmosphere of distance, resulting from the architectural adjustment of the two proscenia—whereby the scene is removed, as it were, to the unapproachable world of dreams, while the spectral music sounding from the mystic gulf, like vapour rising from the holy womb of

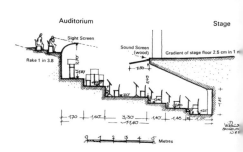

172

Earth beneath the Pythia's tripod, inspires him with that clairvoyance in which the scenic picture melts into the truest likeness of life itself.' He strengthened the hypnotic effect by extinguishing the house lights during the performance, a practice which was not unknown elsewhere (Charles Kean had used it in London) but certainly not very common.

Treatment of the side walls posed a problem. Blank spaces would have been ugly. It was solved by constructing a series of lateral walls or screens ending in Corinthian columns projecting into the auditorium, like, as Wagner says, 'proscenium after proscenium', the width between them becoming wider as one recedes from the stage, 'thus enclosing the entire audience in the vista'. They also provide a very rational series of entrance and exit spaces.

The highest point from which the stage could, and the orchestra could not, be seen determined the position of the last row of seats, which formed the *Furstengallerie* for the use of King Ludwig and other noble guests. The cheapness of the materials (the stalls are cane-seated, the ceiling of sailcloth, the rest nearly all wood) was due merely to economy; Wagner regarded the theatre as temporary and intended to rebuild it if the money was ever forthcoming. The result, however, was one of the most acoustically perfect rooms in the world, and as such it is jealously preserved.

He gave no thought to the appearance of the exterior, though one can still see the skeleton of a Semper plan [Pl. 147]. 'Our very poverty', he wrote, 'compelled us to think of nothing but the sheer objective fitness of our building, the absolute essential for our aim.' There is hardly a foyer, no bar, no restaurant, no grand staircase. It was merely

'the tangible design, so to speak, of what a theatrical structure should outwardly express'.

This single-minded earnestness in the cause of art has probably been Bayreuth's greatest influence on our modern attitude to the drama. The 'religious atmosphere' of which a recent London critic complained must be traced back ultimately to this source. The discarding of superfluous ornament and certain specific features, such as the wedge-shaped auditorium and the dimming of the house lights, are also part of the Wagnerian legacy, but the 'invisible orchestra' remains unacceptable and only a few later theatres were prepared to model themselves structurally on Bayreuth. Its influence comes through more in values than in actual buildings. It is now taken for granted that opera is a composite art in which actors, musicians, producers and designers must work together to create a single effect. 'Festival' conditions are recognized as the ideal. Bayreuth, after nearly a century of triumphs and tribulations (of which Hitler's patronage almost proved the final blow), functions very much as Wagner intended.

In architecture, Wagner's leading disciple was Max Littmann, who designed theatres at Weimar, Hildesheim, Berlin, Stuttgart and Munich.

Pl. 151. Max Littmann's Prinzregententheater, Munich (1902), is an adaptation of Bayreuth to the more monumental style of a city opera house. It has a single ramp of seats, no gallery and no boxes, except at the back, but staircases and foyers are more spacious.

PRINZREGENTEN-THEATER-MUENCHEN.

Pl. 152. *Littmann's Künstlertheater of 1908, also at Munich, again followed Bayreuth in its seating arrangement, absence of boxes, and concealed orchestra. But a straight slope like this was found to provide a less than perfect view of the stage, and later designers increased the height of the back rows, giving the floor a 'dished' shape.*

The Prinzregententheater at Munich (1902) is the best known [Pl. 151]. It was built, ironically enough, very close to the spot where Ludwig's 'dream house' was intended to rise. The exterior is given monumentality in the style of Semper, but the interior is almost a replica of Bayreuth, with plain wooden seats, a single ramp without boxes or galleries, and an invisible orchestra hidden beneath a hood.

Oddly enough, it was a minor subsidiary theory of Wagner's which had more influence on theatre architecture than his actual achievements. Opera he considered 'ideal', drama 'real'; opera was for an *élite*, drama for the people; opera had been evolved by the aristocracy, drama by *das Volk*. It followed that while opera made manifest 'the unapproachable world of dreams' on a mysterious stage remote from the audience, drama was concerned with real life, and should be projected into the centre of an auditorium, as Shakespeare's plays had been. Littmann attempted to put these ideas into practice in some of his theatres, notably the Künstlertheater, Munich, [Pl. 152] whose bare platform stage was later the setting for exciting experiments by avant-garde designers and producers like Max Reinhardt and Georg Fuchs. At the Staatstheater, Stuttgart (1912), he combined both 'opera' and 'drama' in the Wagnerian senses, by building a large and a small theatre linked by administrative buildings; the larger is a simplified Semper plan, with a hidden orchestra but no 'mystic gulf'. Another follower, A. Sturmhoefel, sought to combine the Bayreuth principle of subordinating the auditorium to the needs of the stage with increased audience capacity. His model theatre of 1889, with a steeply raked floor and an even more steeply raked balcony, is curiously prophetic of cinema design in the 1930s.

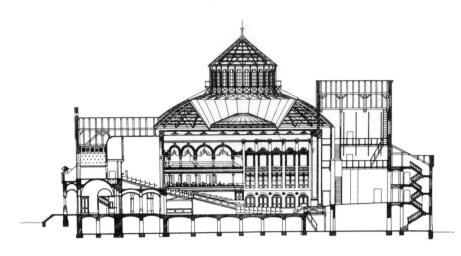

An even more interesting product of this line of thought was the Volkstheater (People's Theatre) of Worms, by Otto March [Pl. 153]. Its origins go back to 1883 when, as part of the local Luther Festival, a play was performed in a large room, since there was no proper theatre available in the city. One of the managers was Friedrich Schoen, a friend of Wagner's, who at once saw the relevance of it, and suggested embodying the same principles in a permanent building. A People's Theatre it really was, since it was paid for by public subscription, and there was nothing quite like it in Europe. March made the main body, the auditorium, circular, following the model of circuses. In section it was like a centralized church, with low 'aisles' surrounding a high clerestoryed 'nave' crowned by a dome. The foyers were at one end, the stage accommodation at the other. The stage itself projected into the audience. Seating was arranged in a fan shape, as at Bayreuth. Boxes were practically dispensed with, and round the upper level ran a gallery, or promenade, opening on to the central space through wide arches—a feature characteristic of variety theatres. There was a large skylight in the dome, so that it could be used by day. Fire-conscious critics were pleased to note that 'in an experimental trial the auditorium was emptied of 1,400 children in forty seconds'. The façade was made Romanesque, presumably to harmonize with the cathedral nearby.

Another reaction against the conventional theatre, which is difficult to fit into the story at any other point, was a project by the young Adolf Loos in 1898 for a 'theatre to hold 4,000'. The auditorium was like an egg lying on its side, the circular stage at one end, and the seats rising in a figure called 'dishing', first used by Davioud and Bourdais in 1875.

Such bold enterprises were rare, though it is in these that the seeds of modern theatre design lie. The majority of theatres, theatres of prestige and commerce ('show' and 'business'), continued along conventional lines until the advent of the cinema almost brought new theatre building to a halt.

XII

SHOW AND BUSINESS

'He was absorbed in what seemed an extravagant worship of Wagner at the time, which I could not share but which I could understand. He would often try to sing the leitmotivs to me and describe the scenes to which they belonged as I sat at my drawing board'—Frank Lloyd Wright speaking of Louis Sullivan, in whose office he went to work in 1887. Among the early architects of the Chicago School, Sullivan was the Romantic poet. Buildings to him were challenges to the imagination, statements of artistic faith. (It may be of interest to connoisseurs of the might-have-been to know that in 1873, when Wagner was trying to arouse support for Bayreuth, the city council of Chicago wrote to him offering to build an opera house with himself in full control. It is a teasing thought that had he accepted, Louis Sullivan might possibly have designed the Festspielhaus.)

Sullivan had settled in Chicago in 1876, after two years at the Paris Beaux-Arts. It was a city of almost unlimited opportunity, a booming commercial and industrial centre, then in the process of massive rebuilding after the catastrophic fire of 1871. Its architects, led by William LeBaron Jenney, Daniel Burnham, John Root and Dankmar Adler, had solved, or were solving, the problems of building tall office blocks on the waterlogged subsoil by spread-footing foundations and iron framing, but aesthetically they were still relying on worn out classicism, Second Empire or neo-Gothic.

In 1880, Sullivan, who was then twenty-nine years old, joined Adler's office, and next year became a full partner. He was the designer, Adler the engineer of the partnership. Adler, who was eleven years older, had already won a brilliant reputation as a technical innovator and (on the strength of his Central Music Hall) as an expert in acoustics. Between 1880 and the building of the Auditorium they designed at least sixty-five buildings. While Adler experimented with concrete and steel, Sullivan searched for a new decorative vocabulary to match the new forms.

The sixty-five buildings included ten theatres. In 1885, they remodelled the McVickers Theater, Chicago, notable for an idea that was to be developed later in the Auditorium. Sullivan records: 'At that time, I believe, was made the first decorative use of the electric lamp. It was a little innovation of my own, that of placing the lamps in a decoration instead of clustering them in fixtures.' In the same year came a much more important commission, the provision of a temporary opera house inside the

Interstate Exposition Building, Grant Park. This was a huge semi-cylinder, like a giant Nissen hut. Inside it, Adler constructed a single wedge-shaped ramp holding about 2,700 people. At the sides near the stage were a series of boxes, and along the rest of the sides and the back was a balcony projecting about twenty-five feet. The whole theatre held over 6,000 people. The semi-circular proscenium arch was forty feet high, the space between it and the roof of the hall being filled with a sloping ceiling which acted as a sounding board. The stage extended twenty feet in front of the curtain in the Anglo-American tradition, and was provided with the usual wings, lofts and fly-galleries for the scenery. The building was lit by gas and heated by steam. Unbelievable as it may be, this whole structure was erected for an opera season of two weeks! Such was Chicago. It was a complete success. Twelve operas were performed, and Adelina Patti made one of her not infrequent farewell appearances.

The Auditorium Building was a direct consequence of this festival, being commissioned by the sponsor, Ferdinand W. Peck. He pursued the sound idea, already tried once in Chicago, of uniting culture with commerce by combining a theatre, a hotel and a block of offices under the same roof. The site is irregular, the hotel and office buildings completely enclosing the theatre which nowhere emerges to the exterior. From the outside, therefore, one sees only cliffs of wall and window ten storeys high. The walls are constructed of load-bearing brick faced with stone (granite for the lower three storeys, Indiana limestone for the rest), though cast-iron supports and beams are extensively used inside. Sullivan articulated the façade by rusticating the bottom three storeys, uniting the next four with a giant semi-classical order, giving the next two a smaller system of arches and crowning the top with an attic and projecting cornice. Over the entrance to the theatre rises a seven-storey tower. This held a water tank for hydraulic machinery, and near the top the new offices of Adler and Sullivan. It had an elevator and, when it was built, was the tallest building in Chicago.

The hotel section is really a shell wrapping round two sides of the theatre and is nowhere more than forty-five feet wide. The entrance lobby, parlours, bars and dining-rooms had therefore to be arranged in a vertical progression (the kitchen was ingeniously fitted in over the stage of the theatre). The auditorium, embedded in the middle, was among the largest ever erected, with a capacity of 4,237 [Pl. 154]. From the entrance at the foot of the tower, a ground-floor foyer leads to the front part of the stalls, while another on the first floor serves the back half. The stalls area is 112 feet long, rising seventeen feet from front to back, a fairly steep rake based by Adler on a principle called the 'isocoustic curve'. A balcony at the back has an even steeper rise of forty feet, while above that—slotted, as it were—into the very roof—are two more smaller galleries, which could be closed off from the body of the auditorium by iron shutters, if the audience

Pl. 154. The interior of the Auditorium Theater, Chicago, (opened in 1889) is a happy marriage of science and art. Adler, the engineer, gave it its basic shape, with steeply rising seats and a ceiling of 'acoustic arches'. Sullivan, the architect, contributed the decoration, the lighting, and the rich theatrical atmosphere. The columns are of cast-iron; cantilevering is still a thing of the future.

was not expected to be large. There were also two tiers of boxes hugging the walls, later carried round the back of the stalls.

The shape of the ceiling was determined almost entirely by acoustic considerations. The high round arches of the front section are not structural, but are suspended from girders above them. Adler's calculations involved absorption, reflection and reverberation, and although acoustic theory was then in its infancy (and in many respects still is) the result was miraculously successful. The arches also, besides carrying Sullivan's decorative electric lights, are used for the ventilation equipment, the air-ducts being disguised as ornaments. The rear part of the seating is covered by a rectangular coved ceiling with a pseudo-skylight of stained glass in the centre. The scale of the lighting fixtures alone was unprecedented— 5,000 house lights, 150 footlights, and scores more to illuminate all parts of the stage. The first night, on 19 December 1889, was *Romeo and Juliet*, with Patti making one more farewell appearance. The whole building is now the property of Roosevelt College, which has turned the hotel into classrooms, libraries and laboratories, but has honourably restored the theatre.

In the remaining years of their partnership, which ended in 1895, Adler and Sullivan designed about forty more buildings, of which ten were theatres, and most of these were combined theatres and offices. The McVickers Theater, which they had remodelled in 1885, was damaged by fire in 1890. In the rebuilding they again used the wide semi-circular proscenium arch decorated with luxuriant Art Nouveau motifs. Sullivan's

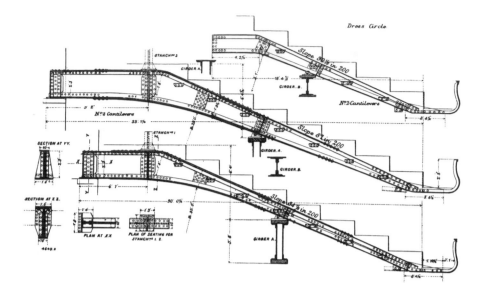

typical squat pillars, which had appeared prominently in the Auditorium Long Bar, were here chamfered into an octagonal section to support the boxes. It was demolished in 1925. More important was the Schiller Building of 1891–2 (later the Garrick Theater). The offices were contained in a tower, the theatre in a projection behind it, the whole ground floor being devoted to the theatre foyer. Here, too, Sullivan contributed outstanding stucco decoration, much of which was saved when the building was demolished, amid public outcry, in 1961.

America was to remain the home of the ingenious and the colossal for many years to come. Steele Mackaye, the man who had introduced the hydraulic lift into the Madison Square Theater [Pl. 156], moved in 1885 to the Lyceum Theater, New York, which he equipped even more lavishly. 'Under the theater', said the *Morning Journal*, 'four steam engines are constantly running. Two furnish the electricity with which the house is lighted throughout; one works the ventilating apparatus which supplies the auditorium with medicated air, charged with ozone; the fourth raises and lowers an elevator car on which the musicians are placed.' In 1893 he embarked on a yet bolder venture, the Spectatorium. This was to be a giant theatre seating 10,000 people, erected as part of the Chicago World's Fair. The plan consisted of two concentric semi-circles, the smaller holding the audience, the larger, enfolding it, the stage, only part of which was visible to the audience through a wide arch. The spectacle to be presented was the voyage of Columbus. The stage area could be flooded; lighting simulated every time of day and every effect of weather, including a rainbow. Dvořák was signed up to write the music. It was all as large as life and twice as expensive. It never happened, but it was in its way the

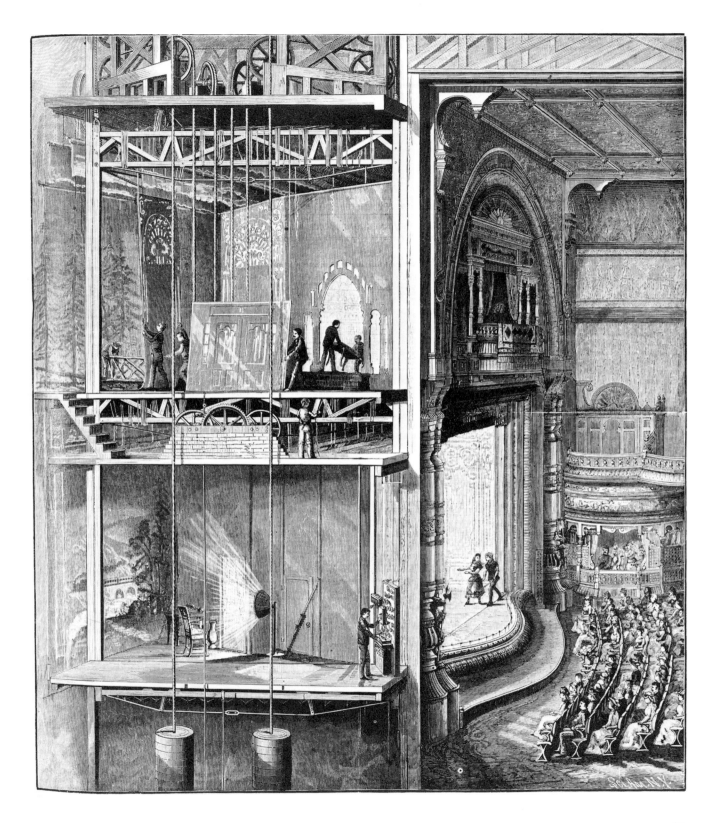

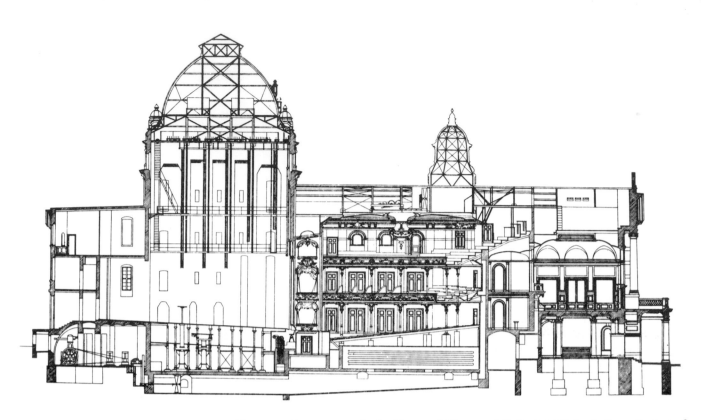

Pl. 157. *Section through the Municipal Theatre of Halle (1886) by Seeling. Typical of its day, it has an imposing entrance, spacious lobby, auditorium with boxes at the side and galleries at the back, and a stage with lifts underneath and a tower above.*

ultimate epitome of the American realistic theatre, which could produce, for instance, *Ben Hur* complete with chariot race, at the Broadway Theater in 1899.

Only a slight sketch can be given of the technical advances, both on the stage and in the auditorium, that helped to change the shape of theatres during these decades. As machinery for lifting scenery was perfected, the fly-tower over the stage grew ever higher. Other pieces of machinery could move whole sets from the wings, or from below the stage, or cause the entire stage to revolve. In the auditorium the most important innovation was steel cantilevering for the balconies, which became general by the 1890s [Pl. 155]. The effect was to make the balconies, or galleries, deeper, a gain in audience capacity but a loss aesthetically. It meant that in many cases people sitting at the back had no sense of being part of an audience, since they could see only a small section of their fellow spectators and usually not the whole height of the stage. In the upper regions yet more people were packed into a 'well' or 'chute' above the level of the ceiling.

Safety in theatres was increasingly a matter of official concern. The nineteenth century's fire record was appalling. America's most serious

Pls. 158, 159. *Façade and section of the Unter den Linden Theatre, Berlin (1892) by Fellner and Helmer—one of the most spectacular works of this highly successful Austrian partnership. It combines features from both Garnier and Semper. The central 'frontispiece' (below, in the section), with its four gesticulating caryatids and crowded pediment, led into a grand staircase hall on the lines of the Paris Opéra. On each side, the smaller gateways admitted carriages into courtyards, and from here one entered a semi-circular foyer modelled on Semper's at Dresden. The auditorium was decorated in a light rococo style, and there were ten private supper rooms behind the circle of boxes. The circle above this, as with all variety theatres, was an open promenade.*

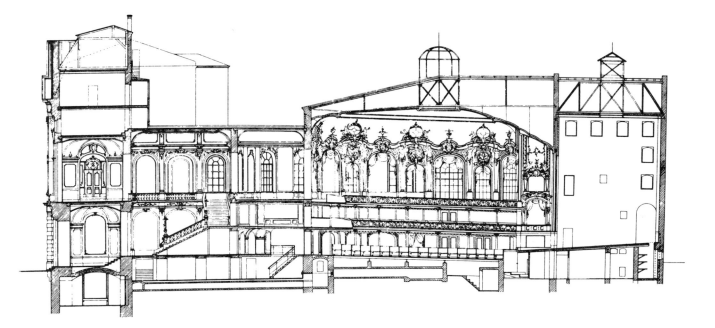

disaster was the fire at Conway's Theater, Brooklyn, in 1876, when 283 people lost their lives. Worst of all was the Ring Theatre fire, Vienna, in 1881, which killed 450. In the same year the municipal theatre at Nice burnt down, killing over 150. Six years later, 170 died at the Opéra Comique in Paris. Catastrophes like these led every country to introduce stringent fire regulations, and inevitably these had a noticeable effect on design. There were three main aspects: first, the use of fire-proof materials, the cladding of iron in masonry, and the reduction of the use of wood; secondly, the provision of an adequate number of exits—architects still preferred to have all, or most, of the audience arrive by a single grand entrance, but they were obliged not to make all the exits funnel into one lobby; and thirdly, the separation of stage and auditorium by a fire-proof safety curtain, which had the effect of preserving the proscenium arch long after many architects and directors wished to discard it. There was also a vogue for building theatres partly underground, the theory being that those in the upper galleries could escape more easily, and those walking upstairs from the stalls were less liable to panic than a similar crowd going downstairs. In addition, many cities, including London and New York, decreed that theatres should not be physically part of buildings used for other purposes. The Auditorium, in other words, could not be repeated. This did not stop theatres, especially in London, from being built in close proximity to hotels (e.g. the Aldwych and Strand as part of the Waldorf Hotel block, or Her Majesty's next to the Carlton Hotel). This legislation has now been repealed, and it is the rule rather than the exception for theatres to be built as part of another building. Façades have disappeared, and modern theatres are often as hard to find as they were in the seventeenth century.

The vast number of commissions in the forty years before World War I meant that firms could specialize in theatres and design virtually no other type of building. Probably the most successful were the Viennese partners Ferdinand Fellner and Hermann Helmer, already mentioned in connection with the Odessa opera house (*see* p. 166). Their firm was responsible for over fifty major theatres all over Europe, in styles that range from Rococo to something very like Expressionism [Pls. 158, 159]. In Germany, the leading theatre architect was Heinrich Seeling, who was also at ease in a variety of styles, and whose work survived in many German cities until 1945 [Pl. 157]. Less admired was the prolific Italian Achille Sfondrini, the designer of the Rome opera house, described in a notice of his Teatro Lirico, Milan, as 'a specialist who travels from town to town erecting theatres and other places of amusement. He is certainly quite an extraordinary character, and one cannot but be struck, on the one hand, by his remarkable ability in directing his men and managing his work, and on the other by his ignorance of the most elementary principles of design.' In England, the busiest man was Frank Matcham, many of whose theatres still exist up and down the

Pl. 160. *Right: Frank Matcham's London Coliseum (1904) represents the next step after the fully developed nineteenth-century opera house (e.g. Pls. 130 and 141). The introduction of cantilevering and the abolition of boxes has made possible three immensely deep galleries, every seat of which faces approximately forward. But this brings with it new problems which Matcham fails to solve entirely satisfactorily. Rather than leave the side walls bare, he adds a few pseudo-boxes, the uppermost perched unhappily on the canopies of those beneath. And the two awkward corners that remain next to the proscenium arch are disguised by the desperate expedient of placing lion-drawn chariots on them. Nevertheless, Matcham possessed the secret of theatrical glamour, which overrules all objections.*

country (e.g. at Buxton and Portsmouth), and whose masterpieces are the London Hippodrome (1900, now the Talk of the Town) and the Coliseum (1904), which in spite of some glaring infelicities has a genuine theatrical panache and, in the split-level foyers, real spatial brilliance [Pl. 160]. C. J. Phipps, with forty theatres, including nine in London, is the runner-up. T. E. Colcutt's amazing François I terracotta front to the Palace Theatre (1891, originally the Royal English Opera House) is an unrepeated *tour de force*. 'It should be specially observed that bathrooms have been provided for the performers, a convenience generally omitted both in this country and abroad.'

By 1870, it was clear that the long dominance of classicism was over. Theatres could be designed in any historical style that seemed either exciting or appropriate. National associations enjoyed a vogue. Amsterdam's Municipal Theatre of 1894 [Pl. 162], by Jan Springer, is in the Flemish Renaissance style, like the Rijksmuseum, the numerous tourelles and gazebos containing emergency exits, if only the audience could find them. In Belgium, the Théâtre Flamand (1883) by Jean Baes is a fantasy of wrought-iron balconies serving the same purpose [Pl. 161]. In England, home of the Gothic Revival, one would expect a theatre in that style, and indeed would give much for a specimen by Burges or Butterfield. But practically the only example was the old Shakespeare Memorial Theatre at Stratford-on-Avon of 1877, by W. F. Unsworth, which was not really Gothic at all but a mixture of everything from Romanesque to Tudor [Pl. 163]. The semi-circular front was a remote echo of Semper, but its mode of entry (via a separate building—the museum—and a bridge) was, to my knowledge, unique. In distant Tiflis, Victor Schroeter (of the St. Petersburg Opera) conscientiously built the municipal theatre in the Caucasian Islamic style, though in many respects (e.g. its fan-shaped auditorium) it was one of the most functional theatres in the world. Islamic was also popular in the West—for example, the Alhambra, London, by Perry and Read, 1883 [Pl. 164], or the short-lived Eden in Paris of the same date, by Klein and Duclos. As one critic remarked, it was 'a style which allows a free treatment without evoking protests from those who take an interest in architecture.'

Art Nouveau, which came into full popularity around the turn of the century, might seem to have offered theatre architects a new style which was at once more genuine and more expressive. But few availed themselves of it. Of the two purest Art Nouveau auditoria, neither was a theatre—that in Horta's Maison du Peuple at Brussels (1896–9) was an assembly hall, and Guimard's Humbert de Romans building in Paris (1902) was intended mainly for concerts. Even so, the latter had a most bizarre and theatrical magic—an elongated octagon with a 'stage' projecting at one end, and the roof supported on eight strange branch-like piers of steel veneered with polished red mahogany, bearing electric lamps like tropical fruit. No real theatre approached Guimard's flair. The nearest is probably August Endell's Buntetheater, Berlin, of 1901, which is conventional enough in structure, but extremely witty in decoration, with painted palm motifs on the walls reaching up to long bell-like chandeliers hanging from the ceiling. The whole of the back elevation is cut into playful Islamic shapes for boxes and galleries. The English vernacular cousin of Art Nouveau, Arts and Crafts, was used with success by at least one theatre architect, Ernest Runz. His theatres at Peckham and Hastings are additionally interesting in that he

Pls. 161, 162. Theatrical historicism: the Flemish Theatre, Brussels and the Municipal Theatre, Amsterdam, both built between 1883 and 1894, look back to the sixteenth-century national styles of their respective countries. At Brussels, the multiplicity of balconies was to provide additional exits in case of fire. The Amsterdam theatre, behind its profusion of ornament, basically follows the model of Vienna, with two grand staircases at the sides.

Pl. 163. The first Shakespeare Memorial Theatre, Stratford-on-Avon, 1877. The block on the left was the library and museum. It also served as the main entrance to the dress circle, reached by means of a bridge, as a fire precaution. Entrance to the stalls was underneath the bridge. The tower served no purpose other than a landmark.

rebelled against the conventional horseshoe and relied on forward-facing seats in the manner of Littmann.

The First World War called a halt to theatre building and the subsequent rise of the cinema effectively prevented it from recovering anything like its old momentum. The interwar years belong to the cinema, an architectural romance in its own right, but one that regretfully cannot be told here. The cinema's own distinctive style was Jazz or Art Deco, and the few notable theatres built during these two decades were inevitably conditioned by it—for instance, the Kroll Opera House, Berlin, by Oskar Kaufmann, of 1924. The Cambridge Theatre, London, (1930), originally decorated with amusing Jazz Age motifs by Serge Chermayeff, is now covered in dull ox-blood paint. In New York, the vast Radio City Music Hall (1932) re-used Adler's 'acoustic' arches springing from ground level to make an auditorium holding over 6,000 [Pl. 165].

The years after World War II saw something like a Renaissance in theatre building. Destroyed national theatres and opera houses were rebuilt and, in Germany especially, a new theatre was a sign of both prosperity and

culture. Many of these buildings are in themselves of distinction, but it would be idle to pretend that they represent the mainstream of theatrical progress. That has shifted to the small-scale experimental theatres, the avant-garde, whose fortunes I shall try to chronicle in the next chapter. After 1945, we are faced with an unusual and in many ways unsatisfactory situation. The theatrical scene is divided. Large, expensive theatres, whether built for prestige or profit, have perforce to follow traditional patterns, since the repertory for which they are designed is traditional. Even if a modern architect is allowed to be 'advanced', he can never be innovatory. The most he can do is to adopt ideas from the avant-garde, modified and attenuated. One solution has been to build theatres in pairs—a large one for traditional productions and a smaller one for experiments. I propose, therefore, at the risk of dislocating chronology, to finish the story of 'show' and 'business' which follows naturally from what has gone before, and then to devote the last chapter to the avant-garde. The logic of this will, I hope, become apparent. We shall be led, in fact, in opposite directions—one towards 'pure' architecture to which the state of drama is largely irrelevant, the other towards a form of drama which is ready to dispense with architecture altogether.

The postwar Renaissance begins before the end of the war, in Sweden: the civic centre of Malmö, opened in 1944 [Pl. 166]. Here already a large and small theatre are combined in a single architectural scheme (the idea

goes back at least as far as Littmann's Stuttgart theatres of 1912). The large theatre has a wide amphitheatre auditorium centering on a classical *orchēstra* which can be raised or lowered to form part of the stage or the audience as required. Germany was quick to adopt the two-theatre scheme, working the changes in a number of ingenious ways. At Münster (1954) something of the old theatrical magic is recaptured in an auditorium that is swathed in black (the seats upholstered in violet) and lit by 1,200 clustered lamps of different shapes hanging like luminous pearls from the ceiling, which can be lowered to balcony level for chamber music concerts. At Gelsenkirchen

Pl. 166. The large auditorium of the Stadsteater of Malmö, Sweden (1944), is adaptable to many different kinds of production. Seating capacity can, by means of false walls, be varied between 1,695 and 553, and the semi-circular apron stage can be lowered to form part of the auditorium.

some years later, the same architects (Ruhnau, Rave and Von Hausen) exploited the traditional staircase with new effect by exposing it completely behind a façade of glass, a particularly attractive picture by night. (Morandi had done the same thing in the Teatro Maestoso at Rome, 1957.) At Wuppertal (1966) that old favourite, the curved foyer, is retained—and expressed on the exterior—in a totally unclassical design by Graupner. Germany, indeed, has been one of the few countries to make the theatre a focus of town planning. Ingolstadt (Hämer, 1966) rises by the Danube, its stark angular forms echoing the old fortifications behind it. Mannheim (Gerhard Weber, 1955) has a Miesian clarity—Mies in fact contributed a design which was not chosen. The theatre of Düsseldorf, by Bernhard Pfau, begun in 1965 and only completed in 1969, wraps its two auditoria in baffling but seductive curves, which, in the words of the architect, 'look like a theatre and nothing but a theatre, but unlike anything that has been built before' [Pl. 168].

The rest of the world has learned much from Germany. Denys Lasdun's new National Theatre in London combines large and small theatres in a similar way [Pl. 167]: in fact these will be three auditoria, like Frankfurt. In America, traditional and experimental theatres are less likely to be found sharing the same roof. Examples of the former, indeed, tend to be disappointingly unadventurous. The New York State Theater, built as part of the Lincoln Center by Philip Johnson in 1964, follows convention faithfully, and the adjacent new Metropolitan Opera, with its flashy and obvious décor, is almost a parody of it. Both façades are vaguely classical,

Pl. 167. The National Theatre, London, by Denys Lasdun. Like most of the modern German theatres, this will combine more than one auditorium under a single roof, but unlike them the main hall (seating 1,165) will have an open stage, the smaller one (seating 895) a proscenium. In addition, there will be a studio theatre for experimental productions.

Pl. 168. The Schauspielhaus, Düsseldorf, by Bernhard Pfau. Beneath the originality of its exterior, the familiar elements of the traditional theatre can still be discerned—the tall fly-tower to the left, and the lower auditorium on the right.

with widely spaced columns framing glass walls. The Charles Center Theater, Baltimore, (1966) by John Johansen, is a good deal bolder. The form of the auditorium is expressed in the exterior and the stage can be adapted to open-stage productions. Further north, in Canada, the Grand Théâtre of Quebec by Victor Prus (1964) follows the European precedent in that it has a luxurious larger auditorium combined with a smaller experimental one. South America, also, is producing some exciting theatres, such as that of Caracas University (1952, Villanueva), a building of aggressive originality, from the ceiling of which hang brightly coloured 'acoustic mobiles' by Alexander Calder.

The triumph and tragedy of large-scale theatre building is nowhere more heroically displayed than in the saga of Jørn Utzon and the Sydney Opera House. I end this chapter, therefore, with a story which, although well known, forms an illuminating parallel with that of Garnier and the Paris Opéra of exactly one hundred years earlier—both examples of conspicuous waste, both buildings in which national vainglory played a larger part than the needs of drama, both architectural masterpieces which can be enjoyed for themselves alone, whatever may or may not take place inside them.

For reasons that are now obscure, the Government of New South Wales decided in November 1954 to commission a new opera house. 'Opera house' was in fact a misnomer from the beginning. The terms of the competition published in September 1955 were for two halls, a large one holding about 3,500 people, and a smaller one holding about 1,200 for plays and recitals; plus a restaurant, rehearsal room, and two public meeting rooms. The site was Bennelong Point, a spur of land jutting into

Sydney Harbour and certainly the most spectacular position ever chosen for an opera house.

There were 233 entries from almost every country in the world, the largest number coming from Australia, Great Britain, West Germany and the United States. The four assessors included Eero Saarinen of Finland and Sir Leslie Martin from London. On 29 January 1957 the name of the winner was announced: a Dane, Jørn Utzon—in his thirties, like Garnier, and, like him, almost completely unknown.

Utzon's design was unprecedented, making an immediate appeal to those who wanted something new and exciting, repelling others by its apparently wilful disregard of practical considerations [Pls. 170–72]. He placed his two halls side by side (most other competitors, in view of the narrow site, had put them end to end). They were raised on a concrete plinth, containing the essential services, with the stages on the landward side and the auditoria, therefore, facing away from the water, the foyers at the back commanding sweeping views over the harbour. What was most captivating about the design, however, was the roofs. Each was to consist of shell-shaped concrete vaults (four per hall) tipped up on end like plates in a rack and rising dramatically in height from auditorium to stage. All opera houses consist of a relatively low auditorium and a fly-tower over the stage. Utzon was retaining this rise in height, but concealing the reason for it. The 'shells', as they soon came to be called, had nothing to do with the ceiling, which was to be suspended inside.

The sources of this strange style (called by Nervi 'the most straightforward anti-functionalism') lie in the Expressionist architecture of thirty years before—in Hermann Finsterlin's Art Centre [Pl. 169], W. and G. Luckhardt's theatre [Pls. 175, 176], and Otto Bartnung's Strahlenkirche. Like them, Utzon was thinking primarily in terms of sculptural form—shape first and function later. In fact, the prize had been won before anyone knew whether it could actually be built. As his structural engineer he chose Ove Arup, and as stage adviser Walter Unruh. Together they began to study the problems. The three most serious were: How were the shells to stand up? How were they to be constructed? And how was the stage to function?

Firstly, imagine the bowl of a spoon (a rather odd ridged spoon with a point at the end) cut in half at right angles to the handle. The piece left over is roughly the shape of one of Utzon's shells. Each hall was to be covered by four of them, one turned towards the land, the other three towards the water. They could, of course, stand up well enough if put down vertically, their bases touching the ground. But in order to fit the auditorium underneath them, they had to be tipped up at an angle, balancing on only two points. How was this to be managed? One scheme was to make all four lean against each other, but there was a danger of them all collapsing like a pack of cards. The solution finally adopted was to make shells 1 and 2 (counting from the land side) lean against each other,

Pl. 169. Was there a precedent for the Sydney Opera House? Not in any theatre actually built, but some wholly imaginative projects of the 1920s, like Hermann Finsterlin's Art Centre (above) or the Luckhardt brothers' People's Theatre (Pls. 175, 176) have been quoted as possible sources. Certainly, like Finsterlin, Utzon conceived his building as a sculptural shape before he worked it out as architecture—an unfashionable way to begin in 1957, the heyday of International Modern.

Pl. 170. Bennelong Point juts out into ▶ Sydney Harbour just to the east of the famous bridge, a site as conspicuous and as significant as that chosen for any opera house in nineteenth-century Europe. In this view (right) we are looking west. The two separate halls can be clearly distinguished: the nearer is the opera theatre, the further the concert hall. Both halls face the land, their backs to the harbour.

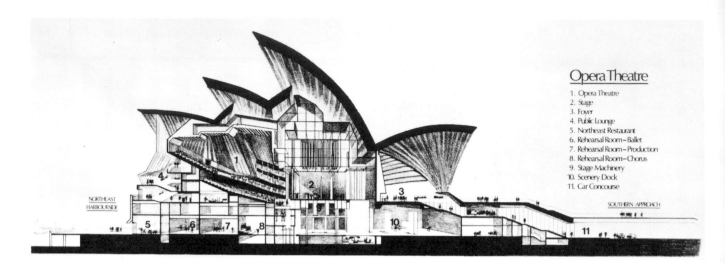

NORTHEAST HARBOURSIDE

SOUTHERN APPROACH

back-to-back. This gave four points of support; two more half-shells were placed at their points of contact, making six 'legs' altogether, a sufficiently stable structure. Shell 3 is similarly supported by a smaller back to back shell concealed inside No. 2, and this pair likewise has an extra pair of legs. Shell 4 is treated in the same way, with a smaller buttressing shell inside No. 3.

Secondly, the form of Utzon's shells as originally designed was that of an elliptical paraboloid, a complicated shape of which the curvature constantly varies. This would have meant that each tiny fabricated section would have to be separately drawn and cast. Utzon himself, at Arup's request, was able to simplify his design so that all the surfaces were sections of a single

NORTHWEST HARBOURSIDE

SOUTHERN APPROACH

sphere, i.e. every section had an identical curvature (of 246 feet in diameter) and could be mass produced in relatively few moulds. In fact, the shells function very much like the bays of a Gothic vault, with ribs carrying the stress to a point of balance and supporting a membrane of white ceramic tiles.

Thirdly, as regards the stage: by placing his two halls side by side Utzon had given himself length but denied himself width. The spacious 'wings' on each side of the normal opera house stage were simply out of the question. To solve this difficulty, he and Unruh devised a complex system of vertical rather than lateral scene-changing. The stage was to be made in nine strips, each worked by a separate elevator. More lifts would lower the orchestra pit for opera and raise it level with the floor for concerts. The proscenium arch was to be made variable in size.

These technical puzzles, however, were straightforward compared to the administrative and political battles that faced Utzon. For political reasons, contracts for the first phases had to be placed before the later ones had been properly planned. This led to modifications and extra expense. The original estimate of seven million dollars grew to ten, then twenty, then thirty. The Opera House became a party issue. Utzon was caught between forces that he could not control. In February 1966 he resigned, to be replaced by an Australian architect under whom the interior is being finished in a drastically reduced fashion. The idea of using the main auditorium for opera has been given up; the stage has been concreted over, Utzon and Unruh's expensive stage machinery scrapped, the proscenium arch not built, the tall 'gridiron' tower over the stage dismantled. Seats are now to be brought forward to a point inside the old stage area. The whole functional excuse for the build up of height on the exterior has gone. And the cost now seems likely to be in the region of ninety-five million dollars.

Utzon himself subsequently designed another theatre at Zurich. It is smaller in scale than Sydney and completely different in approach, for the tall box over the stage rises undisguised from a flat wave-like roof that covers both auditorium and foyers.

If the story of Sydney Opera House teaches anything, it is that the building of a large modern theatre must be a matter of compromise—compromise between the designer and his technical experts, compromise between different theatrical purposes, compromise between functionalism and aesthetic expression, compromise often between theatrical needs and needs other than those of entertainment. Whether these compromises are bad for architecture is an open question; architecture often seems to thrive on compromise. That they have little relation to the health of a living drama can hardly be doubted. To trace the efforts that have been made to avoid just this situation and to bring the theatre back to a proper sense of its own values, we must begin a new chapter and return to the post-Wagnerian stage and the last two decades of the nineteenth century.

Pls. 171, 172. 'Sydney Opera House is the most striking building created by modern man', says the official brochure. It is certainly the most ambitious. Besides five public halls (for concerts, opera, drama, films and exhibitions), it contains two rehearsal rooms, 50 dressing rooms, several restaurants and ample space for promenading—all these fitted into one of the most complicated structures ever erected. The sections above and below left slice through the two series of 'shells'. The concert hall was originally to have been the opera theatre, hence the spaces above and below it which would have accommodated the fly-tower and the stage machinery.

XIII

THE LAST STAGE?

Wagner's Bayreuth had introduced some changes in the planning of the auditorium, but had left the concept of the picture-frame stage intact. Indeed, he had reinforced it, making yet more explicit the separation between illusion ('the ideal') and reality by doubling the proscenium, forcing the audience into hypnotic attention and employing every artifice of stage machinery to produce a world totally distinct from the real world. Nevertheless, it is to Wagner that we have to return in order to trace the beginnings of the modern theatre.

Soon after Wagner's death, Adolphe Appia began to question the assumptions that lay behind the Bayreuth style of production. For him, music was the queen of the arts. Wagner's actual staging, he thought, reflected the narrative and dramatic elements of the operas, but not their music: 'Only when stage pictures take on spatial forms dictated by the rhythms of the music are they not arbitrary, but on the contrary have the quality of being inevitable.' The stage designer, in the interests of a deeper reality, must give up trying to represent the real world. He must convey mood, atmosphere, emotion . . . as music does. The stage picture must not be a flimsy imitation of something else—it must be a genuine work of the imagination. The most important means to such an end is light. Appia's sets in themselves are bare, empty. They need light to give them substance. Light, changes of light, shadows, colours, shifting outlines—these are the visual equivalents of music. In order to realize them, it was necessary to get away not only from the traditional stage realism but from the traditional auditorium too. 'Let us abandon these theatres to their dying past', he wrote, 'and let us erect simple buildings intended merely to cover the space where we work . . . No stage, no amphitheatre, only a bare and empty room at our disposal.'

The whole concept of a 'play' was in the process of changing; instead of being merely the interpretation of a written script, it was becoming something unique in its own right. In the words of Appias' most brilliant follower, Gordon Craig, 'the Art of the Theatre is neither the acting, nor the play, it is not scene nor drama, but it consists of all the elements of which these things are composed: action, which is the very spirit of acting; words, which are the body of the play; line and colour, which are the very heart of the scene; rhythm which is the very essence of dance.' For him the Mystery Plays, masques and pageants of Elizabethan England were 'made for the theatre' in a sense that Hamlet was not. A truly theatrical work is incomplete until it is performed, like the scenario of a ballet or mime.

Not all Appia's ideas are equally powerful in the theatre today. His looming, generalized sets only suit plays and operas whose themes can be universalized. But his theories concerning the dramatic function of light (a function only conceivable after the advent of electricity) are supreme everywhere. Fittingly enough, it is at Bayreuth that he can best be appreciated, in the productions of a talent in equal sympathy with Appia and Wagner—the late Wieland Wagner.

The first practical moves to break down 'the tyranny of the proscenium' came from directors who aimed not at evolving new theatrical forms but at reviving old ones. William Poel in England, Max Kruger in Germany, and Lugné-Poë in France had reconstructed stages from the past, notably of course the Elizabethan (the De Witt drawing of the Swan Theatre was only discovered in 1888). Harvard University built one for *Hamlet* in 1910. At the same time there were several performances of Greek plays in authentic conditions. It was Max Reinhardt who applied some of these historical lessons to the living drama. In 1910 he produced *Oedipus* in an old circus building in Berlin, bringing the stage out into the centre of the auditorium and making the chorus mix with the audience. Later came his production of *The Miracle*, based on a play by Maeterlink. To stage this he transformed the Olympia stadium in London into a cathedral, seating his audience all round the arena and using music, light and spectacle to create his effects [Pl. 173]. The production was taken to Berlin and then to New York, and was extremely influential. Reinhardt enjoyed using buildings other than theatres. He produced *Everyman* on the steps of Salzburg Cathedral, a play by Calderon in the Kollegienkirche there, and *Faust* in the Riding School. There were even plans for *The Miracle* inside Milan Cathedral. But from an architectural point of view his most interesting enterprise was his conversion of the Berlin circus (Zirkus Schumann) into the Grosses Schauspielhaus to the designs of Hans Poelzig [Pl. 174]. Poelzig built a proscenium at one end, but brought out the stage to occupy the whole of the centre. The 5,000 spectators sat in a steeply banked amphitheatre beneath a vault of stalactites, which Poelzig placed there for acoustic reasons, but which made the interior a sort of fantastic Aladdin's cave. His slightly later project for a Salzburg Festival Theatre is a variant of the Grosses Schauspielhaus, but apart from this it had little architectural progeny. W. and H. Luckhardt's model for a People's Theatre (1922) carried the idea further, but could hardly have been actually built, though it was planned logically enough with a tall fly-tower over the stage and a wide amphitheatre auditorium, all concealed under a shell of curving and pointed shapes [Pls. 175, 176]. Other Poelzig-inspired projects were even less practicable—for example, the *plastische Buhne* of Neuzil, Loewitsch and Scherer (which was to have a sort of panoramic proscenium in which miraculous effects were to be achieved) or Ernest de Weerth's yet more unrealizable design for a Tri-Arts Temple in New York.

Reinhardt's assistant when he took *The Miracle* to New York in 1924 was Norman Bel Geddes, a designer already deeply influenced by his work. As early as 1914 he had devised a theatre in which the stage was simply one corner of a large square room. In 1921 he made designs for a Reinhardt-like production of Dante's *Divine Comedy*, in which the audience occupied one side of a sort of crater rising in circular terraces. Other schemes included one with a platform stage running through the audience and, in 1930, a circular playhouse with the audience entirely surrounding the stage. Theatre-in-the-round, in fact, became familiar in American university productions of the thirties, though it did not reach the professional stage until after the War.

Reinhardt's collaboration with Poelzig is an example of a producer finding an equally talented designer who could express his ideas and add to them. The most interesting achievements of the twenties were the result of similar collaborations between producers like Meyerhold, Piscator and Copeau and designers of the calibre of Lissitzky and Gropius.

The subject of Meyerhold and the Russian Revolutionary theatre is one that still receives less attention than it deserves. Meyerhold was recalled from the Red Army and put in charge of the Bolshevik Theatre Department

Pl. 173. Max Reinhardt's most famous production, though probably not his most influential, was his 'wordless spectacle', The Miracle, *at Olympia in London on Christmas Eve, 1911. Reinhardt transformed Olympia into Cologne Cathedral. 'The gold lamps hanging from the roof are each over six feet high,' said* The Times, *'the rose window is fifty feet across—much larger, that is, than the original at Cologne; the cathedral doors are over 120 feet high' . . . and so on. There was a cast of 2,000, an orchestra of 200, and a choir of 500.*

Pl. 174. For Reinhardt, Hans Poelzig in 1919 remodelled a Berlin circus-building into a theatre—the Grosses Schauspielhaus. It was basically an open arena surrounded by the audience on three sides. Poelzig's décor was as eccentric as the form of the theatre was bold.

in 1920. He reacted violently against the naturalism of Stanislavsky, seeing the theatre as a medium for ideological statement and mass involvement. His aim was to take the theatre to the people (sometimes literally—a movable stage on two lorries was designed in 1924 by Babitchev), and he experimented boldly with new techniques for abolishing the barrier between actors and audience. Immense open-air shows were staged with the aid of such designers as Popova and the Vesnin brothers; one of them, re-creating the October Revolution, employed not only crowds, fireworks and searchlights, but even airships! In early Meyerhold productions admission was free, the walls were hung with propaganda placards and the audience showered with leaflets. Conventional theatre buildings had too many reactionary associations. He was prevented from actually demolishing them as he would have wished, but in 1926 he collaborated with El Lissitzky to remodel his Moscow theatre for Tretyakov's play *I Want a Child* [Pl. 177]. Seats were erected on the stage, making it a theatre-in-the-round, and just in front of the old proscenium arch was placed a spiral ramp with access on three levels, leading to a transparent floor in mid air. It was really a Constructivist set that had invaded the auditorium, but, alas, this was never carried out. In 1932, for the production of a play called *A Flying Start*, Schtoffer built a central podium for the actors and a precarious catwalk on poles all round the auditorium. In the same year Barkhin and Vakhtangov drew up plans for a permanent theatre embodying Meyerhold's ideas, but the cold hand of Stalin was already at the controls and nothing came of it. After Meyerhold, the most influential director was Nikolai Okhlopkov. For

Gorky's *Mother* at the Realistic Theatre in 1932 he used a complete arena stage with a raised circular podium for the action. In another production the auditorium was turned into a mountainside, with the audience sitting on rocks and the actors mingling with them.

Large-scale Soviet theatre building under Stalin underwent a strange speeded-up decadence. Looking through Barkhin's *Arkitectura Teatra*, published in 1947, is like seeing the age of Ledoux being replaced by that of Garnier all in the space of one decade. The theatres of the early thirties were clearly influenced by French and German theorists of a century earlier. Barkhin's own project for an opera house at Rostov-on-Don (1930) expanded Semper's curved vestibule into a three-quarter circle, adding the stage building on the segment. The Vesnin brothers' design for a 'Theatre of Massed Musical Action' at Kharkov looks back as far as Durand; while Alabyan and Simbirchev's Theatre of the Red Army in Moscow (1934), the plan of which forms a five-pointed star, is exactly the kind of architectural allegory that would have delighted Ledoux. At Erevan, the large theatre by Tamanyan is a clever adaptation of Schroeter's St. Petersburg opera house to the needs of an open stage, with a double auditorium facing a central arena.

In western Europe the great international exhibitions often produced theatrical ideas destined to bear fruit. At the Berlin Exhibition of 1889, a theatre was built in order to display the workings of the stage and its machinery. The Vienna Music and Theatre Exhibition of 1892 featured a theatre specially designed by Fellner and Helmer as a setting for companies from all over the world to show their varied traditions. It was very plain, with no boxes, a single gallery, and greater ease of access than conventional theatres. In addition, a number of 'model' theatres were proposed by architects or groups mainly interested in fire prevention. Examples are the 'Safety' Theatre devised by Henry Irving in consultation with Alfred Darbyshire, and the Viennese 'Asphaleia' Theatre, promoted by a syndicate whose architect was Franz Roth.

For the Munich Exhibition of 1901, Richard Riemerschmid produced a theatre which was comfortable and stylistically advanced, but not particularly revolutionary. Henry Van de Velde's theatre for the Cologne Werkbund Exhibition of 1914 was more original. Van de Velde knew both Craig and Reinhardt and designed a building which was intended to be adapted to many different styles of production. The stage is divided into three by pillars, but these are not structural; they can be moved on rails. The auditorium is a plain rectangle with no gallery. From the outside the traditional features—foyer, auditorium, stage—are still clearly defined, though expressed in new forms. The Viennese Oskar Strand's *Ringbühne* project of 1923 carried Van de Velde's idea a good deal further. The 'sliding' stage was extended into a complete circle, with the audience in the centre, entering by means of bridges over it. Its critics called it

Pls. 175, 176. Wassili and Hans Luckhardt's project for a People's Theatre (1922) was frankly visionary, though it was no stranger in its organic, almost vegetal, forms than, for instance, Rudolf Steiner's Goetheanum of 1914. As the section shows, it was conceived as a functioning theatre, and after Sydney Opera House who can say that it is impossible to build?

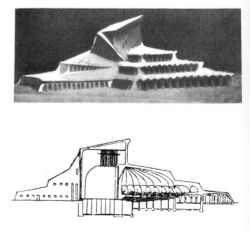

Pl. 177. *The Russian theatre of the 1920s was fertile in ideas affecting the relationship between audience and actors, though only a few bore fruit in terms of theatre building. In 1926 Meyerhold and El Lissitzky collaborated on the remodelling of an existing Moscow theatre for a revolutionary new production. This was never carried out, but a model shows how it would have looked. Seats are erected behind the proscenium arch; the main acting area is in the centre on a series of platforms and sloping ramps accessible from several levels.*

impractical because of the difficulty of gaining access to the auditorium', a serious point, certainly.

The only other notable exhibition theatre is A. and G. Perret's Théâtre de l'Exposition des Arts Décoratifs in Paris, 1925. They had already designed one successful theatre, the Théâtre des Champs Elysées of 1913, which had been remarkable for its decoration (early Jazz) and its use of ferro-concrete; the layout, however, was fairly conventional. In 1925 they attempted something more innovatory. Their chief model was the Vieux Colombier [Pl. 178]. The proscenium was abolished, the stage projecting well into the auditorium and being divided (as at Cologne) by two concrete pillars. Though attractive in illustrations, it failed in practice. The sight-lines were poor, only a small part of the stage being visible to the whole audience at the same time.

The two other producers mentioned a paragraph or two back were Jacques Copeau and Erwin Piscator. Copeau founded his Théâtre du Vieux Colombier as early as 1913, and in 1919 a theatre was built to designs drawn up by Louis Jouvet. There was no proscenium. The audience sat in a bare hall facing a permanent set made of concrete—a series of platforms linked by steps. It had something in common with the Elizabethan stage, but was in no sense a reconstruction, and was intended to be used for all types of play. But the audience soon grew bored, and critics complained of its 'drab puritanism' and 'unbearable monotony'. Copeau took his company to New York in 1917 and adapted the Garrick Theater there in a similar way. The top gallery was abolished and part of the stalls built over, creating 'a free and easy stage which may be entered from a variety of levels'. America and Britain remained on the whole conservative, though Granville-Barker also used the projecting stage, turning the boxes into doors, for a few modern plays.

A far more revolutionary approach was Erwin Piscator's. Committed to the theatre as a medium of political action, he was the first to employ many of the methods later associated with the Berliner Ensemble—anti-naturalism, slogans, slide-projections, etc. For Shaw's *Major Barbara* in Berlin, 1926, he had a huge cannon projecting the whole depth of the auditorium. At about this time, he came into contact with Walter Gropius and the Bauhaus, whose theatrical department was currently employing some of the liveliest talents in Germany. For Piscator, Gropius devised his 'Total Theatre' [Pls. 179, 180]. The starting point, he later recalled, 'was provided by the memory of an unforgettable experience I had had at a Reinhardt production at the Deutschestheater. At a moment of great dramatic tension an actor had suddenly spoken from a box at the back of

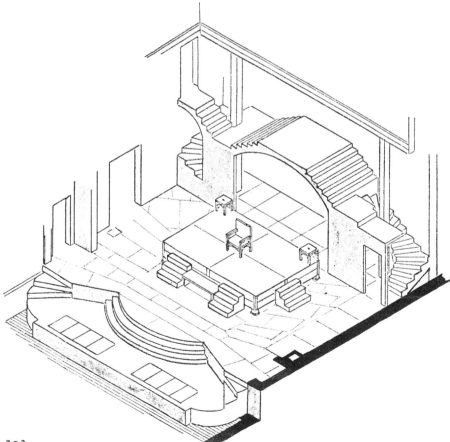

Pl. 178. The stage of Jacques Copeau's Théâtre du Vieux Colombier, Paris, 1919, was an attempt to re-create something like Elizabethan acting conditions. Its concrete steps and doorways formed a permanent set (except for the dais, which was moveable) which could be adapted to almost any type of play by the addition of curtains, painted panels, plants, balustrades, etc.

the stalls. The effect was tremendous. I felt as if I were physically involved in the events being portrayed on the stage. The dividing line between the real and the stage world had suddenly vanished . . . Piscator urged me to create a theatre, the whole of which—including the auditorium—would serve as a place of action. So I produced a plan which included all three classic stage forms—the apron stage, the proscenium stage, and the arena stage—in one theatre.' Gropius's plan is roughly an oval with a circle at one end. The circle itself contains a smaller circle touching the edge. This smaller circle is the stage, the rest seating, but the whole of the large circle can be revolved, bringing the stage area either into the centre of the oval or to one end. There was also to be a raised path all round which could be used by the actors, while film projectors could focus on any part of the walls or ceiling. Detailed plans were drawn up, but the 'Total Theatre' was never built because the Depression intervened. The only theatre that Gropius actually completed in Germany was one at Jena in 1923, which is on a small scale, but typically Bauhaus in its austerity and formal strength [Pl. 181].

Other Bauhaus teachers were even more fascinated by the theatre than Gropius was, but their ideas have had little impact on architecture. Oskar Schlemmer saw the theatre as comprising 'the entire realm between religious cult and naive popular entertainment', but his interest really lay in what we should call ballet. 'We can imagine plays', he wrote, 'whose "plots" consist of nothing more than pure movement of forms, colours and light.' He even conceived a 'curtain play' which would consist of nothing but the curtain rising and falling and 'reveal in an entertaining way the curtain's own secret nature'. Moholy-Nagy experimented with the conventions of the circus and the puppet theatre. He proposed 'suspended bridges and drawbridges running horizontally, diagonally and vertically within the space of the theatre, with platform stages built far into the auditorium, and so on. As well as rotating sections, the stage will have movable space constructions . . . to bring certain action-moments into prominence, as in film close-ups.' Farkas Molnar devised a 'U-stage' with the audience seated on three sides and further stages suspended from the ceiling. He also staged plays out of doors, using actual buildings with their balconies, steps, etc., as the sets. Finally Andreas Weininger designed a completely spherical theatre, in which the spectators would line the inner wall, with the stage at the bottom. 'Because of their all-encompassing view, because of centripetal force, they find themselves in a new psychic, optical and acoustic relationship' (one suspects this to be only a pompous way of expressing the relationship achieved in the traditional opera house).

All these whirling ideas, plus a sure grasp of the real potentialities of drama, came together in the strange, tormented genius of Antonin Artaud. Artaud was prepared to reject practically everything that he saw around him in the theatre of the 1920s and 1930s:

THE STAGE—THE AUDITORIUM: We abolish the stage and the auditorium and replace them by a single site, without partition or barriers of any kind . . . A direct communication will be established between the spectator and the spectacle . . . Thus, abandoning the architecture of present-day theatres, we shall take some hangar or barn . . . The hall will be enclosed by four walls, without any kind of ornament . . . The action will unfold, will extend its trajectory from level to level, point to point; paroxysms will suddenly burst forth, will flare up like fires in different spots . . .

THE SET: There will not be any set . . .

WORKS: We shall not act a written play, but shall make attempts at direct staging around themes, facts or known works . . .

Artaud's ideas are the most important single source of the modern theatre, and are still called 'experimental' whenever any producer is bold enough to try and put them into practice. His arguments still apply. A great gulf, he

Pl. 182. After the Russian experiments of the 1920s, several American universities staged productions using a completely circular stage. The first permanent theatre to be built in this form was the Penthouse Theater of the University of Washington, at Seattle, which opened in 1940. Most of the inspiration came from the producer and theatre historian, Glenn Hughes.

felt, separated the world of the actor from that of the audience; the fiction was that the play was a slice of life which the audience, sitting passively in the dark, accidentally observed. It was controlled by the author, who created his characters (or social message, or poetry) by himself and then presented them, via the actors, to the public. Artaud knew that the theatre could be more than that. In the music-hall, in pantomime, in the circus, in religious ceremonies, in rural folk customs, in pageantry and ritual of any kind, the spectator was himself part of the event. The theatre could be real in a sense undreamed of by the 'realistic' producers. Actors need not be like ventriloquists' dummies, but could be 'like victims burnt at the stake, signalling through the flames'.

Artaud's ideas have something in common with the classical Greek theatre, and probably much more with the pre-classical theatre of which we know so little. What he had in fact seen was the theatre of Indonesia: 'The spectacle of the Balinese theatre, which draws upon dance, song, pantomime—and a little of the theatre as we understand it in the West— restores the theatre, by means of ceremonies of indubitable age and well-tried efficiency, to its original destiny, which it presents as a combination of all these elements fused together in a perspective of hallucination and fear . . . A spectacle like that of the Balinese theatre has nothing to do with entertainment, the notion of useless, artificial amusement, of an evening's pastime, which is characteristic of our theatre. The Balinese productions take shape at the very heart of the matter, life, reality.'

This, for Artaud, was 'pure theatre'—it 'has value, has existence, only in proportion to its degree of objectification *on the stage*'. And its subject matter is not some trivial anecdote but a universal myth of conflict, urgency, agony, 'states of mind', 'the void of fear . . .' 'The magic identification is made: WE KNOW IT IS OURSELVES WHO ARE SPEAKING.'

Independently of Artaud, producers and playwrights of the West were beginning to study Chinese and Japanese theatre with new understanding. What interested them especially was the fact that the stage was accepted simply *as* a stage. Drama relied on convention and symbol, not on the attempt at illusion. There was no scenery, yet the most spectacular actions could be represented: climbing on to a table, for instance, meant scaling a mountain; walking in a circle meant going on a journey; holding up a canvas with a gate painted on it meant entering a city; black flags meant a storm. Devices like these came as a heaven-sent means of escape to the European theatre, which had practically barricaded itself into the drawing-room. After some initial suspicion, the lesson was learnt. Nobody is worried nowadays by seeing a play without scenery, and playgoers find it easy to accept the actor as a man employing certain artificial techniques in order to tell a story, rather than a man pretending to *be* somebody else. Bertolt Brecht compares the actor to a witness giving an account of a street accident; if he re-enacted everything too faithfully we should be embar-

Pl. 183. Tallahassee Civic Center, Florida, when completed, will contain a theatre, library, town hall, youth club, shops and hotel. The theatre was designed by Walter Gropius in such a way that it could be used for a wide variety of purposes, including baseball games. The whole roof is suspended from the central arch, completely eliminating the need for interior supports.

rassed and probably fail to get the point. He must place a 'distance' between himself and the character he represents—the 'alienation effect'.

Once the pretence that the stage represented (or rather *was*) a place other than a platform in front of an audience had been given up, there was no reason to preserve the proscenium, and the open stage, in one form or another, became accepted everywhere. The experiments that had been made in American colleges before the Second World War led to more elaborate theatres in the forties and fifties, the first being the Penthouse Theater on the University of Washington Campus at Seattle by Carl F. Gould (1940) [Pl. 182]. But the completely open, arena stage, with the audience on all four sides, proved difficult in practice, and the usual compromise was to reserve one side for the actors. Since it was normally desired to put on plays of all types, the ideal was one of flexibility. Many modern experimental theatres are masterpieces of ingenuity in this respect, though they sometimes pay the price of being somewhat characterless as architecture. An interesting forerunner was Richard Neutra's project of 1937 for the Theater Art Center, Wheaten College, Mass., which was to be adaptable to all kinds of performance, including those in the open air.

The number of so-called 'studio' theatres in the U.S.A. is now very large, and the examples quoted here are necessarily selective. Among the pioneers was Little and Manley's theatre for Miami University (1940), which has essentially a circular stage, but is equipped with machinery to turn it back into a conventional theatre. At Sarah Lawrence College, Bronxville (1952), Marcel Breuer successfully solved the problem of a building that could be adapted as a stage for teaching theatre techniques, as a classroom, and even as a night club (every other row of seats can be taken out and replaced by tables). Neutra and Alexander, for the Orange Coast College, Costa Mesa, provided one of the most unorthodox plans—a rectangle joined to a kind of bubble. Acting area and auditorium can be either in one part or the other according to the kind of production required; it can be divided into compartments for separate simultaneous rehearsals, and there are even arrangements for it to open out at the back to face an audience sitting in an open-air grass amphitheatre. By contrast, one of the simplest solutions is Caudill, Rowlett and Scott's theatre for the A. and M. Consolidated High School, Texas—a perfect circle with the stage, another circle, placed off-centre (this whole design owes a great deal to Charles Rennie Mackintosh's unexecuted project for a concert hall). At Dallas, also in Texas, Frank Lloyd Wright built his Kalita Humphreys

Pl. 184. The Shakespeare Festival Theatre at Stratford, Ontario, grew out of Tyrone Guthrie's experiments in open staging. It is the Elizabethan theatre reduced to its essentials, though the use of amphitheatre planning instead of galleries produces a quite different space.

Pl. 185. Powell and Moya's Festival Theatre at Chichester is virtually nothing but an exposed auditorium. Its seating area is larger than its ground plan, since the upper parts are cantilevered out and the foyer occupies only part of the space beneath. It is a hexagon of six concrete ribs braced by steel cables. Inside, these serve to carry the roof and the lighting equipment.

Theater (1960), the outcome of thoughts going back to his days with Sullivan; it is so lavishly supplied with machinery that it can hardly be called a 'studio', but so cleverly planned—most of the works being hidden underground—that the impression is still deceptively one of simplicity.

Gropius's 'Total Theatre' seems destined to bear fruit at last in the Tallahassee Civic Center Theater, Florida [Pl. 183]. Here Gropius proposed a theatre shaped like a double fan, each splay consisting of seven tunnel-vaults narrowing until they could be contained beneath a wide concrete parabola. Acting and viewing spaces can be transformed into an almost infinite number of shapes, becoming by turns a skating rink, a basket-ball court, a boxing ring and a meeting-hall. At its maximum it can hold over 4,500 people.

All this activity has led again to a situation when a firm of architects can afford to specialize in theatres. One of the more interesting American teams is Hardy, Holzman and Pfeiffer, responsible for twelve theatres in the last few years. They see their work as a series of experiments in involving an audience without incurring the charge of architectural formlessness. In such theatres as the Playhouse in the Park, Cincinnati, the Center for the Performing Arts, Toledo, or the New Lafayette, New York, they have fragmented the seating areas, so that the audience does not have a single fixed focus, and the actors are encouraged to use the whole space [Pl. 187].

The productions of the Irish director Tyrone Guthrie in the Assembly Hall at Edinburgh led to his building (in 1957) a theatre at Stratford, Ontario, intended to rival that at Stratford-on-Avon in England. It has a deep apron stage with the audience closely surrounding it on three sides [Pl. 184]. This theatre in turn influenced the Chichester Festival Theatre, England, by Powell and Moya, which is one of the few avant-garde theatres to attain architectural distinction in its own right [Pl. 185]. The shell of the auditorium is completely exposed, with the foyers and offices packed economically (some say too economically) underneath the rise of seats.

There is no space here to mention all the variants of the open stage produced in Europe during the last twenty years. In Italy, the Teatro S. Erasmo, Milan, by Carminati and De Carli, broke new ground with its octagonal stage. In Germany, many of the small theatres attached to the large ones have shown sensitive awareness of new theatrical techniques, for instance Weber's small theatre at Mannheim [Pl. 186], the stage of which can be transformed in numerous ways, including a ramp through the centre of the audience. Littmann's small theatre at Stuttgart was destroyed in the war and replaced by an elegant structure by Volkart, Pläcking and Perlia. In England, a host of 'intimate' theatres have sprung up and lead a lively if precarious life. Among the most successful architecturally are the Questors Theatre, Ealing, by Hattrell and Partners, and the Northcott Theatre, Exeter, by William Holford.

Pl. 186. The new Nationaltheater at Mannheim (1955–57) consists of two auditoria: a large one planned traditionally and a small one for experimental productions. This is the small one, arranged with a narrow strip of stage in the middle, with audience on both sides. The actors reach it by the suspended paths on the walls. The architect was Gerhard Weber.

There is, however, a paradox at the heart of avant-garde theatre building. Many directors have sympathized with Artaud in his exhortation to abandon the whole idea of a 'theatre' and 'take some hangar or barn', free from the shackling associations of tradition. Warehouses, factories, a disused engine-shed, a maltings . . . any structure will serve, in Appia's words, 'to cover the space where we work'. Directors, actors and audiences have been stimulated by these new surroundings to a theatrical experience which in some ways looks towards the future envisaged by Artaud, in others back to the Middle Ages. In Europe, Jean-Louis Barrault's *Rabelais*, Luca Ronconi's *Orlando Farioso* and Ariane Mnouchkine's *1789* [Pl. 188], and in America groups such as Peter Schumann's 'Bread and Puppet Theater' have had a revolutionary effect on our ideas of what the theatre can do. On temporary and multiple stages actors address the spectators at close quarters, mingle with them, surround them with action on all sides. In these conditions, architects are understandably at sea. Their dilemma is well illustrated by the case of the Young Vic Theatre, London, built by W. G. Howell, of Howell, Killick, Partridge and Amis, under the supervision of an Old Vic director, Frank Dunlop. Dunlop originally wanted a building which he could convert, and only reluctantly agreed to a new theatre. As it is, the foyer and offices are in an old butcher's shop, and the auditorium is given an air of improvisation, with the fewest possible architectural features. Even the benches on which the spectators sit have a makeshift appearance, on the theory (probably correct) that a crowded, slightly uncomfortable audience is more responsive than a pampered one, and that people are more likely to tolerate such conditions cheerfully in a nondescript hall than in an obviously purpose-built auditorium. In this case, Dunlop had the full and unselfish co-operation of his architect. Other partnerships have not been so happy.

211

Pl. 188. *Some modern producers reject the whole apparatus of the post-Renaissance theatre and go back to a bare hall with platforms surrounded by spectators. In 1789, Ariane Mnouchkine stages the French Revolution as a series of crude, circus-like acts, accepting the audience for what it is—a crowd of people watching whatever happens to be going on. (Compare the medieval* Castle of Perservance, *Pls.* 29, 30). *Drama now seems to have reached a point, as it did in the Middle Ages, when it has no further need of architecture.*

It would be facile to see these developments as unqualified advances. Their value, and even their meaning, have yet to be made clear. Many directors and critics use words like Gropius's and talk of 'the dividing line between the real and the stage world' having suddenly vanished, a fallacy that was exposed long ago when Dr. Johnson said: 'The truth is, that the spectators are always in their senses and know, from the first act to the last, that the stage is only a stage and that the players are only players.' Indeed, the new theatre is based on a recognition of just that fact. Its opportunities are boundless, but whether it can ever aspire to the condition of ritual that the theatre enjoyed in ancient Greece or the European Middle Ages (and which, it can be maintained, is enjoyed in the modern world by a great spectator sport like football) may fairly be doubted. There are many barriers, the most crucial being that very urge to experiment, to innovate, to reflect new ideas, in which the modern theatre places its justification. The audience of an Indian, Chinese, Japanese, Greek or medieval play knew exactly what to expect and identified itself with it through a shared code of beliefs. The audience at an avant-garde evening in the West does not know what to expect; that is part of its appeal. It hopes to be astonished. Are we, then, really participating in a uniquely dramatic event, as the producers wish us to think, or are we like the spectators of the seventeenth-century theatre of magic, looking for things to take our breath away (psychologically, intellectually, morally, rather than visually)—gripped, in Wordsworth's phrase, by 'the degrading thirst for outrageous stimulation'?

BIBLIOGRAPHY

The following bibliography is not only a list for recommended further reading, but also a grateful acknowledgement of some of the books I have found most useful and upon which I have leant most heavily. For original sources, whether by architects who have published their own work (e.g. Schinkel, Ledoux, Garnier) or by theorists (Sabbatini, Patte, Saunders, etc.,) I have assumed that the references given in the text are sufficient.

GENERAL

Altman, G. *Theater Pictorial*, University of California Press, Berkeley and Los Angeles 1953.
Cheney, S. *The Theater*, Longmans, Green & Co., New York 1952.
Enciclopedia dello Spettacolo, Rome 1954–66.
Gascoigne, A. B. *World Theatre*, Ebury Press, London 1968.
Glasstone, V. 'Architecture', in *The Oxford Companion to the Theatre*, 1967.
Leacroft, H. and R. *The Theatre*, Methuen, London 1958.
Lukomsky, G. K. *Les Théâtres anciens et modernes*, Paris 1935.
Mullin, D. C. *The Development of the Playhouse*, University of California Press, Berkeley and Los Angeles 1970.
Nicoll, A. *The Development of the Theatre*, George G. Harrap, London 1958.

GREEK AND ROMAN

Beare, W. *The Roman Stage*, Methuen, London 1950.
Bieber, M. *History of the Greek and Roman Theater*, Princeton University Press, Princeton 1939.

MEDIEVAL

Evans, M. B. *The Passion Play of Lucerne*, New York 1943.
Southern, R. *The Medieval Theatre in the Round*, Faber & Faber, London 1957.

RENAISSANCE

Lawrenson, T. E. *The French Stage*, Manchester University Press, Manchester 1957.
Leclerc, H. *Les Origines italiennes de l'architecture théâtrale moderne*, Paris 1946.
Nagler, A. M. *Shakespeare's Stage*, Yale University Press, New Haven 1959.

EIGHTEENTH CENTURY

Baur-Heinhold, M. *Baroque Theatre*, Thames & Hudson, London 1967.
Southern, R. *The Georgian Playhouse*, Pleiades Books, London 1948.

NINETEENTH CENTURY

Biermann, F. B. *Die Plane für Reform des Theaterbaus*, Berlin 1928.

Hughes, P. C. *Great Opera House*, Weidenfeld & Nicolson, London 1956.

Sachs, E. O. and Woodrow, E. A. F. *Modern Opera Houses and Theatres*, Batsford, London 1896–98.

Survey of London, 1900– , especially Vol. 35 (Drury Lane and Covent Garden Theatres).

MODERN

Aloi, R. *Architettura per lo spettacolo*, Milan 1958.

Fuerst, W. R. and Hume, S. J. *Twentieth-Century Stage Decoration*, Dover Publications, New York 1967.

Yeomans, J. *The Other Taj Mahal* (on Sydney Opera House), Longmans, London 1968.

Zucker, P. *Theater und Lichtspielhäuser*, Berlin 1926.

AMERICAN THEATRES

Coad, O. S. and Mims, E. *The American Stage*, Yale University Press, New Haven 1929.

Hewitt, B. *Theater U.S.A.*, McGraw Hill, New York 1959.

Hughes, G. *A History of the American Theater*, Samuel French, New York 1951.

MacNamara, B. *The American Playhouse in the Eighteenth Century*, Harvard University Press, Cambridge, Mass. 1969.

Morrison, H. *Louis Sullivan*, New York 1935.

LIST OF ILLUSTRATIONS

The author and publishers are grateful to the many official bodies, institutions, and individuals who kindly supplied illustrative material.

1 Fragment of a crater from Taranto showing a costumed actor holding a mask, late fourth century BC. Photo: by courtesy of the Martin von Wagner-Museum der Universität Würzburg.

2 Fragment of a crater from Taranto showing stage scenery and figures, mid-fourth century BC. Photo: by courtesy of the Martin von Wagner-Museum der Universität Würzburg.

3 Plan of the theatre at Epidauros, c. 350 BC. Drawn by Lucinda Laurie.

4 General view of the theatre at Epidauros, c. 350 BC. Photo: by courtesy of Bildarchiv Foto Marburg.

5 One of the restored gateways of the theatre at Epidauros, c. 350 BC. By courtesy of the Courtauld Institute of Art, London. Photo: Professor A. W. Lawrence.

6 The theatre of Dionysus at Athens, with the walls of the Acropolis in the background. Photo: Alinari.

7 A general view of the theatre at Syracuse. Photo: by courtesy of Hirmer Fotoarchiv, Munich.

8 Dancers dressed as birds: a scene from a black-figure vase, c. 500 BC. Photo: by courtesy of the Trustees of the British Museum.

9 Comic scene from a fresco in the House of Casca, Pompeii. Photo: Alinari.

10 The theatre at Priene, Asia Minor, late second century BC. Photo: by courtesy of Hirmer Fotoarchiv, Munich.

11 Reconstruction of the theatre at Priene in its Hellenistic state. After A. von Gerkan.

12 Reconstruction by H. Wirsing of the theatre at Segesta. From Bulle, *Untersuchungen an Griechischen Theatern*, Vol. XXXIII, Munich 1928.

13 The theatre at Pergamon, seen from the north. Photo: by courtesy of Hirmer Fotoarchiv, Munich.

14 The theatre and the Temple of Apollo at Delphi. Photo: by courtesy of Hirmer Fotoarchiv, Munich.

15 Junction of the auditorium and the stage of the theatre at Sabratha, Libya. Photo: J. Powell.

16 The *orchēstra*, stage and *scaenae frons* of the theatre at Sabratha. Photo: J. Powell.

17 The theatre at Lepcis Magna, Libya. Photo: J. Powell.

18 Exterior of the theatre at Aspendos, Asia Minor. Photo: by courtesy of Professor Dr. Jale Inan.

19 One of the reconstructions by G. Niemann of the *scaenae frons* of the theatre at Ephesus. Photo: by courtesy of the Osterreichisches Archäologisches Institut, Vienna.

20 Miniature from a copy of a late Roman manuscript of Terence (Codex Vaticanus 3868) showing Scene II. 4. of *Adelphi*. Photo: by courtesy of the Biblioteca Apostolica Vaticana, Rome.

21 Tragic scene, from a wall-painting in the Columbarium in the Villa Doria-Pamphili, Rome. Photo: by courtesy of the Soprintendenza alle Antichità, Rome.

22, 23 Section and reconstruction of the Odeum of Agrippa on the Agora of Athens. Photos: by courtesy of the American School of Classical Studies at Athens.

24 Reconstruction of the theatre, stadium and forum at Orange, in France. From Caristie, *Monuments antiques à Orange*, Paris 1856.

25 Roman theatre at Kom el Dik, Alexandria, 1st century AD. Photo: by courtesy of John G. Ross.

26 Miniature from the *Quem Quaeritis* trope, c. 1100, showing the three Maries at the Sepulchre. By courtesy of the Biblioteca Capitolare, Piacenza. Photo: Manzotti.

27 Plan from *Ordinale de Origine Mundi*. From T. C. Peter, *The Old Cornish Drama*, London 1906.

28 Scene showing Noah and the Ark, from the Cornish Ordinalia performed by the Bristol University Drama Department in 1969 at the Piran Round. Photo: by courtesy of Roger Gilmour.

29 Reconstruction by Dr. Richard Southern of a theatre of the hill-and-ditch variety for *The Castle of Perseverance*. By courtesy of Dr. Richard Southern. Photo: Theatre Collection, University of Bristol.

30 Manuscript plan, c. 1440–75, of the theatre for *The Castle of Perse-*

by courtesy of the Phototèque du Centre Régional de Documentation Pédagogique, Bordeaux.

97 Staircase of the Grand Théâtre at Bordeaux. Photo: by courtesy of the Phototèque du Centre Regional de Documentation Pédagogique, Bordeaux.

98 Section, showing the stage, of the theatre at Imola, 1779, by Cosimo Morelli. From G. Saunders, *A Treatise on Theatres*, London 1790. Photo: by courtesy of the Trustees of the British Museum.

99 Auditorium of the theatre in the Hermitage, Leningrad, by G. Quarenghi. Photo: by courtesy of the State Hermitage Museum, Leningrad.

100 Auditorium of the theatre in Gripsholm Castle, near Stockholm, 1781. Photo: by courtesy of the Nationalmuseum, Stockholm.

101 View of the auditorium and plans of the ground floor and first floor of the Théâtre Faydeau, Paris, 1788–91. From A. Donnet, *Architectonographie des Théâtres*, Atlas Vol, Plates, Paris 1937–40. Photo: A. C. Cooper.

102 Friedrich Gilly's project for a National Theatre in Berlin, 1798. Photo: by courtesy of Dr. Franz Stoedtner.

103 Unexecuted design by Sir John Soane for an opera house in Leicester Square, London, 1789. By courtesy of the Trustees of Sir John Soane's Museum, London. Photo: A. C. Cooper.

104, 105 Façade and auditorium of the Theatre Royal, Bristol. By courtesy of the Theatre Royal, Bristol. Photos: Derek Balmer.

106 Interior of the Drury Lane Theatre, after its reconstruction by Robert Adam, 1775. From Robert & James Adam, *The Works in Architecture of Robert and James Adam*, Vol. II, No. 5, London 1779. Photo: by courtesy of the Trustees of the British Museum.

107 Plan at pit level of the rebuilt Drury Lane Theatre by Henry Holland, 1794. Redrawn by G. March, by courtesy of Mr. Robert Eddison.

108 Plan at pit level of the Drury Lane Theatre by Benjamin Wyatt, 1812. From Benjamin Wyatt, *Observations on the design for the Theatre Royal, Drury Lane*, London 1813. Photo: by courtesy of the Trustees of the British Museum.

109 Section through the domed rotunda and principal staircases of Wyatt's Drury Lane Theatre. From Benjamin Wyatt, *Observations on the design for the Theatre Royal, Drury Lane*, London 1813. Photo: by courtesy of the Trustees of the British Museum.

110 Engraving by G. Hawkins of the North East view of Covent Garden Opera House, 1809, by Robert Smirke. From the King's Topographical Collection, Vol. XXV, British Museum. By courtesy of the Trustees of the British Museum. Photo: A. C. Cooper.

111 Plan of Covent Garden Opera House by Smirke. From J. Britton and A. Pugin, *Illustrations of the Public Buildings of London*, Vol. I, London 1825. Photo: by courtesy of the Trustees of the British Museum.

112, 113 Elevation and plan of Robert Adam's unexecuted design for an opera house in the Haymarket, London. By courtesy of the Trustees of Sir John Soane's Museum, London. Photos: A. C. Cooper.

114 Auditorium of the Georgian Theatre at Richmond, Yorkshire, built in 1788 and restored in 1962. Photo: by courtesy of the Georgian Theatre (Richmond) Trust Ltd.

115 Façade, added in 1804 by Benjamin Latrobe, of the Chestnut Street Theater, Philadelphia. Aquatint by Gilbert Fox after the 1804 engraving by William Birch. Photo:

by courtesy of the Harvard Theatre Collection.

116 Interior of the Chestnut Street Theater, Philadelphia, 1794. Engraving by Ralph after a drawing by S. Lewis. From *The New York Magazine*, V, No. 4, 1794. Photo: by courtesy of the Harvard Theatre Collection.

117, 118 Benjamin Latrobe's design of the front boxes and plan of the first floor of his proposed theatre at Richmond, Virginia, 1798. Photos: by courtesy of the Library of Congress, Washington, D.C.

119 Watercolour by John C. Hind (1809) of the façade of the Park Theater, New York, 1798. Photo: by courtesy of the Harvard Theatre Collection.

120 Watercolour drawing by John Searles (1822) of the interior of the new Park Theater, New York, 1821, by William Strickland. Photo: by courtesy of the New York Historical Society, New York City.

121 A cut-open drawing of the Theatre Royal, Plymouth, 1811, reconstructed from John Foulston's designs. From Richard Leacroft, *The Development of the English Playhouse*, Eyre Methuen Ltd., London 1973. Photo: A. C. Cooper.

122 Engraving of the façade of the Theatre Royal, Plymouth, 1811, by John Foulston. Photo: by courtesy of the City of Plymouth Public Library.

123 Auditorium of the Theatre Royal, Bury St. Edmunds, 1819, by William Wilkins. Photo: O. G. Jarman.

124 Engraving by R. Wilkinson (1823) of the interior of the Haymarket Theatre, 1821, by Nash. By courtesy of the Greater London Council Print Collection. Photo: R. B. Fleming & Co. Ltd.

125 Auditorium of La Scala, Milan. Photo: by courtesy of the Teatro alla Scala, Milan.

126 Auditorium of the Fenice Theatre, Venice. Photo: by courtesy of the Fenice Theatre, Venice.

127 Façade of the San Carlo Opera House, Naples, by Antonio Niccolini. By courtesy of the San Carlo Opera House, Naples. Photo: Troncone.

128 Auditorium of the Teatro Regio, Parma, 1828. Photo: by courtesy of the Ente Provinciale per il Turismo, Parma.

129 Engraving (1849) of the auditorium of the Royal Opera House, Covent Garden, as reconstructed by Benedetto Albano in 1846–47. By courtesy of *The Illustrated London News*. Photo: L.E.A.

130 Fish-eye view of the present Royal Opera House, Covent Garden, 1858, by E. M. Barry. Photo: by courtesy of The Times Newspapers Ltd.

131 Lithograph by H. A. Thomas (1825) of the interior of the Chatham Garden Theater, New York, 1824. Photo: by courtesy of the New York Historical Society, New York City.

132 Engraving after a drawing by A. J. Davis of the first Bowery Theater, 1826. Photo: by courtesy of the New York Historical Society, New York City.

133 Engraving by Richardson after a drawing by A. C. Warren of the second Bowery Theater, 1828. Photo: by courtesy of the New York Historical Society, New York City.

134 Lithograph of the second St. Charles Theater, New Orleans, 1843. Photo: by courtesy of the Leonard V. Huber Collection, New Orleans, Louisiana.

135 Façade of the Bolshoi Theatre, Moscow. Photo: by courtesy of the Bolshoi Theatre, Moscow.

136 Engraving of the façade of the Neues Schauspielhaus, Berlin. From C. F. Schinkel, *Sammlung architektonisches Entwürfe*, 1873.

Photo: by courtesy of the Theatermuseum, Munich.

137 Engraving of the façade of the Dresden Opera House, 1838–41, by Gottfried Semper. Dresden Gallery (Old Masters). Photo: by courtesy of the Deutsche Fotothek Dresden.

138 Grand Staircase of the Paris Opéra. Photo: N. D. Roger-Viollet.

139 Plan of the ground floor of the Paris Opéra. From C. Garnier, *Le Nouvel Opéra de Paris*, Vol. I, Paris 1880. Photo: A. C. Cooper.

140 Façade of the Paris Opéra. By courtesy of Le Théâtre National de l'Opéra. Photo: Chevojon Frères. © by S.P.A.D.E.M. Paris 1973.

141 Auditorium of the Paris Opéra. By courtesy of Le Théâtre National de l'Opéra. Photo: Chevojon Frères. © by S.P.A.D.E.M. Paris 1973.

142 The Grand Foyer of the Paris Opéra. By courtesy of Le Théâtre National de l'Opéra. Photo: Chevojon Frères. © by S.P.A.D.E.M. Paris 1973.

143 Façade of the Teatro Massimo, Palermo, 1897. Photo: by courtesy of the Italian State Tourist Office, London.

144 Auditorium of the old Metropolitan Opera House, New York, 1882. By courtesy of the Lincoln Center for the Performing Arts, Inc. Photo: Louis Mélançon.

145 Façade of the Opera House at Manaus, Brazil. Photo: by courtesy of O.A.S. Photos.

146 Plan of the Festspielhaus, Bayreuth, 1876. By courtesy of the Bildarchiv Bayreuther Festspiele.

147 Engraving of the exterior of the Festspielhaus, Bayreuth. Photo: by courtesy of the Theatermuseum, Munich.

148 Engraving of the auditorium of the Festspielhaus, Bayreuth. Photo: by courtesy of the Bildarchiv Bayreuther Festspiele.

149 Section of the orchestra pit in the Festspielhaus, Bayreuth. By courtesy of the Bildarchiv Bayreuther Festspiele.

150 An old photograph of Wagner's son, Siegfried, preparing to conduct the orchestra at the Festspielhaus, Bayreuth. Photo: by courtesy of the Richard Wagner-Gedänkstätte der Stadt Bayreuth.

151 Opened view of the Prinzregententheater, Munich. From Max Littmann, *Das Prinzregententheater in München*, 1901. Photo: A. C. Cooper.

152 Interior of the Künstlertheater, Munich, 1908, by Max Littmann. Photo: Jaeger & Goergen.

153 Longitudinal section of the People's Theatre, Worms. From E. O. Sachs and L. A. E. Woodrow, *Modern Opera Houses and Theatres*, Vol. I, London 1896. Photo: A. C. Cooper.

154 Interior of the Auditorium Theater, Chicago, 1889. By courtesy of the Pioneer Press Inc. Photo: Jerrold Howard.

155 Drawings of the cantilevered galleries used at the Royal English Opera House, London. From E. O. Sachs and L. A. E. Woodrow, *Modern Opera Houses and Theatres*, Vol. III, London 1896. Photo: A. C. Cooper.

156 Diagram of the Madison Square Theater, New York, showing stage and machinery. From *The Scientific American*, Vol. L, No. 14, 5th April 1884. Photo: by courtesy of the Trustees of the British Museum.

157 Longitudinal section of the Municipal Theatre, Halle, 1886, by Heinrich Seeling. From E. O. Sachs and L. A. E. Woodrow, *Modern Opera Houses and Theatres*, Vol. I, London 1896.

158 Façade of the Unter den Linden Theatre, Berlin, 1892, by Fellner and Helmer. Photo: by courtesy of the Märkisches Museum, Berlin.

INDEX

Numbers in *italic* refer to plates and their captions.